ROUTLEDGE LIBRARY EDITIONS:
SOVIET SOCIETY

Volume 23

SOVIET SCIENCE

SOVIET SCIENCE

J. G. CROWTHER

Routledge
Taylor & Francis Group

LONDON AND NEW YORK

First published in 1936 by Kegan Paul, Trench, Trubner & Co., Ltd.

This edition first published in 2025
by Routledge
4 Park Square, Milton Park, Abingdon, Oxon OX14 4RN

and by Routledge
605 Third Avenue, New York, NY 10158

Routledge is an imprint of the Taylor & Francis Group, an informa business

© 1936

British Library Cataloguing in Publication Data
A catalogue record for this book is available from the British Library

ISBN: 978-1-032-86028-2 (Set)
ISBN: 978-1-032-88107-2 (Volume 23) (hbk)
ISBN: 978-1-032-88111-9 (Volume 23) (pbk)
ISBN: 978-1-003-53622-2 (Volume 23) (ebk)

DOI: 10.4324/9781003536222

Publisher's Note
The publisher has gone to great lengths to ensure the quality of this reprint but points out that some imperfections in the original copies may be apparent.

Disclaimer
The publisher has made every effort to trace copyright holders and would welcome correspondence from those they have been unable to trace.

PLATE 1

Photo. Planet News Ltd.

The Academy of Science's new Headquarters in Moscow
(See page 27)

[front.

SOVIET SCIENCE

BY

J. G. CROWTHER

LONDON
KEGAN PAUL, TRENCH, TRUBNER & CO., LTD.
BROADWAY HOUSE, CARTER LANE, E.C.
1936

Printed in Great Britain by Butler & Tanner Ltd., Frome and London

CONTENTS

v

CONTENTS

PART IV: APPLIED SCIENCE

PART V: BIOLOGY

PART VI: THE HISTORY OF SCIENCE

PLATES

PREFACE

A GENERAL impression of Soviet science has been acquired through seven visits to the Soviet Union in the last seven years. The material described in this book has been collected mainly on a lengthy visit in the winter of 1934–5, when I had the privilege of being the guest of institutes belonging to the department of M. Armand, the Director of NIS, the Scientific Research Sector of the Department of Heavy Industry; and of VOKS, the Society for Cultural Relations with Foreign Countries. The main object of my last visit was to study the research institutes attached to NIS. The intention of writing the book was accelerated by B. D. Budnitsky, the former administrative director of the Physico-Technical Institute at Leningrad, who was anxious that some fairly readable account of the institute should be available in English.

I have visited all of the institutes I have described at least once and, in many cases, several times during intervals of years.

The aim of this book is mainly to give information about the sort and conditions of research in Soviet scientific institutes. It contains little discussion on the relation of political freedom to scientific research and discovery. Before this problem may be discussed profitably, it is necessary to see what can be done under the conditions of a working-class and communist dictatorship.

I am very glad to be able to thank here M. Armand and M. Kulyabko and their colleagues for the hospitality and assistance given to me on behalf of NIS and VOKS. I am also particularly obliged to Professor A. Frumkin, for assisting me with my programme in Moscow, and to Miss A. Wilm for assistance in Leningrad.

Professor N. I. Vavilov was, as always, kind, helpful and stimulating; and I was happy to be able to continue discussions once again with Professors B. Hessen, Levin, Levit, and Tamm.

Professor A. Leipunsky has helped to remove some of the errors from the book, and I am deeply obliged in particular to Professors Baumgart, Davidovitch, Eltenton, Finkelstein, Hey, Joffe, Kurdumov, Linnik, Ruhemann, Semenov, Sinelnikov, Talmud, Terenin, Vassiliev, S. I. Vavilov, and many others, whom I thank collectively for all their kindness and assistance to me.

J. G. CROWTHER.

LONDON
January 1936

SOVIET SCIENCE

PART I

THEORY AND ORGANIZATION

CHAPTER 1

DIALECTICAL MATERIALISM

LITTLE insight into the most original characteristics of the present developments of science in the Soviet Union can be acquired without some knowledge of the dialectical materialist philosophy. The literature of this philosophy is vast, and the best parts of it are complicated and profound. The truth of the various theses and principles of dialectical materialism will not be discussed here, but a simple statement of some of them is necessary, for the reader cannot see the information given later in this book in a correct perspective, without having these ideas in mind.

The main ideas of dialectical materialism were propounded by Karl Marx. He did not give any complete short statement of them, but expressed them as they arose at appropriate points in his voluminous writings. They were extended and applied also by his friend Friedrich Engels, and by Lenin, especially in the sphere of practical politics. As a philosopher, Marx had a genius of a higher order than that of Engels and Lenin, who excelled most in application and practice. This is not meant to suggest that Lenin did not know much about science. His writings on the philosophy of physics in his book

Materialism and Empirio-Criticism, which were composed when the theory of relativity was only about three years old, are perhaps the most remarkable essays on science ever written by a statesman of the highest order of genius. But the numerous short passages where Marx expresses particular or general aspects of his views are still the most illuminating sources of instruction on the principles of his philosophy.

The dialectical materialists regard the world, or cosmos, as a unity.   They are therefore a particular sort of monist.

The world is in process of change.   It cannot be understood without considering it from a historical point of view.   Further, the developing world cannot be understood without a knowledge of the mechanism of change or development.

This mechanism of the development of the world is the dialectical process.   Dialectic is a Greek word meaning disputation.   The Greek philosophers used to dispute about the nature of things, and out of their opposing arguments new truths emerged.   One philosopher supported a thesis, and another opposed it.   A new view, or synthesis, arose out of the struggle between the supporter and opposer of the thesis.

Hegel supposed that this was the mechanism of the development of the world, the inside works, as it were, of history.   He supposed that the whole world resembled Greek philosophers, and was engaged in arriving by the process of thesis, antithesis, and synthesis, at absolute truth as end.

Through Greek influence Hegel supposed that the ideas used to describe the various events and processes that could be seen in history were the basic reality, and the material world was a product of their development by the dialectical process of birth or proposal, contradiction or opposition, leading to new truth or fact.

It will be noted that Hegel's theory of the development of the world is evolutionary.   As a profound student of history he was impelled towards an evolutionary theory.

Marx adopted Hegel's view that universal history had

an evolutionary character. Through this adoption, Marx acquired an evolutionary conception of universal history long before Darwin had finally established the fact of evolution in that part of universal history concerned with the history of plants and animals.

The philosophers who took their conception of evolution from Darwin not only took the general idea of evolution, but also the particular process or mechanics of evolution that Darwin had adopted. Darwin's conception of the mechanics of evolution was of a gradual process of change. This idea of gradual change had been partly, and more or less unconsciously, acquired from the Newtonian conception of change in mechanics. Newton conceived change as a continuous process. He invented the differential calculus, which is a mathematical method specially suited to the description of continuous change. He was predominantly interested in continuous change because the motions of the celestial bodies are continuous. The motions of large bodies such as the moon and planets are not jumpy, so a mechanics devised to describe them is apt to assume continuity in natural phenomena as an axiom.

The Darwinian theory of evolution assumed a continuous mechanism of change, whereas the Hegelian, and hence the Marxian, theory assumed a discontinuous mechanism of change.

The conflict or contradiction of opposites is an essential part of the Hegel-Marx mechanics of development. This makes the notion of discontinuous change entirely conformable with, and natural in, Marxist philosophy. As the existence of contradictions and their struggle for resolution in a higher synthesis is a basic property of the world, and an essential part in the mechanism of its development, discontinuous concepts of natural phenomena and their motion are entirely acceptable to dialectical materialists. They find contradictory concepts such as the modern wave-particle conception of the electron entirely natural, and are unable to see any reason for believing that the recent discoveries in theoretical physics raise any fundamental philosophical difficulties in the conception of natural processes. Indeed, they welcome them as being more reasonable than the continuous theories in vogue since Newton's time. It follows that they are unable to see any philosophical point in the writings of scientists such as A. S. Eddington and J. H. Jeans, who suppose that recent discoveries in theoretical physics, due especially to the development of the quantum theory, have new philosophical implications, and strengthen the evidence for subjective idealism. The dialectical materialists regard the disturbed philosophical condition of those astronomers and their many followers as the natural result of the neglect of earlier philosophical thinking. In their youth they accepted Newtonian mechanics without noticing its philosophical limitations in the description of reality, and when its limitations have become very clear through the progress of the quantum theory, they are involved in intellectual confusion.

The dialectical materialists regard all theories of change which derive their conception of the mechanism of change, like Darwinism, from the continuous Newtonian mechanics, as "mechanistic". In this sense, then, they are anti-mechanistic. Dialectical materialists laugh when they are accused of being mechanists, and supposed to believe in a Laplacian theory of the world, which asserts that if the configuration of the world is given at any instant, then its condition at any other instant could be calculated according to the laws of Newtonian mechanics, by a mathematician of sufficient power. They do not feel the dilemma of Newton and his followers, who required a First Cause to set the whole machinery in motion.

The difference between Hegel and Marx lies in their conception of the substance in which the dialectical process of thesis, antithesis and synthesis works. Hegel supposed that this substance was ideas. Marx said that the true substance in which they operated was the material out of which the world is made. Thus the process of world development was the dialectical evolution of material; dialectical materialism.

The application of the idea of the dialectical process of

development to the interpretation of universal history provides an inexhaustible series of suggestions.

The origin of man is found in the pre-human animal world, which is the thesis. The beginning of the human type arises as the antithesis out of the thesis. In the struggle between the animal world, the thesis, and the newly arising human type, the antithesis, the definitely human type is produced, the synthesis.

With the appearance of the synthesis, the human being, human society comes into existence, and simultaneously with the appearance of human society, various contradictory movements begin in it, forming a number of theses and antitheses leading to new syntheses.

The conception of the development of human society as motivated by struggles between classes fits directly into the dialectical materialist philosophy.

The fundamental characteristics of human society at any epoch are determined by the nature of the contemporary class struggles. Without class struggles there would have been no history, for the syntheses which have motivated the development of human society have arisen through struggles between theses and antitheses in the shape of social classes.

Development in some other spheres, such as those of science and philosophy, depends on struggles between theory and practice. A theory arises, and forms the thesis, new facts are discovered, and form the antithesis, the struggle to harmonize them produces a new synthesis, represented by a new theory and practice.

In dialectical materialism theory and practice are inseparable, and neither has scientific meaning without the other. This leads to what is named the unity of theory and practice, and provides dialectical materialism with the strong without the weak features of pragmatism. It gives dialectical materialists a proper appreciation of the importance of experiment in natural science. This is a particularly interesting feature. The majority of philosophers tend to believe that theory is more important than experiment, that mathematics is more powerful than observation. This tendency is noticeable in idealist and subjectivist philosophers.

Marx says that views which exalt theory over practice contain illusions, and has explained why. They arise from members of leisured classes, who live without having to do manual work. This situation creates the illusion that knowledge of nature can be learned through theory and thinking alone, and without performing manual experiments. This divorce between theory and practice inevitably leads to error.

The struggle between theory and practice raises the problem of the struggle between the material world, and the world of ideas. Marx regards the external world as prior. The universe and the earth existed before man. Out of the struggles of the animal world man arose. After he had been able to snatch sufficient food to keep him alive, he began to have the opportunity to think. Thus the first concern of man is production, the production of food. The achievement of production provides the opportunity for thought, thus the mode of production of the goods to satisfy human needs comes to condition human thought.

Marx therefore said that the general character of the thought of any historical period, the nature of its art, science and laws, is a reflection of the mode of production that exists at that epoch.

The application of this principle helps to explain the characteristics of science during the modern period, starting from the time of Galileo and Torricelli.

These scientists were leaders in the introduction of isolated experiments for the investigation of phenomena. The medieval philosophers desired only to give a comprehensive account of phenomena. Galileo discarded this view, and decided to isolate relatively simple phenomena, and obtain accurate notions of them, without considering their complete relations with the rest of the universe. According to the Marxists, this intellectual attitude was a reflection of the increasing subdivision of labour in the contemporary mode of production. The results of its introduction were similar. It stimulated an enormous increase in knowledge of fact, as the subdivision of labour had in the production of goods.

But the neglect of comprehensive synthesis by which all the facts could be ordered led to intellectual chaos, just as the blind drive to increase production of goods, without working out any comprehensive system of distribution, led to chaos in social life.

In fact, the chaos of contemporary scientific thought is a reflection of the chaos of contemporary society. Profound thinkers have always been aware of the necessity for synthesis. For instance, Descartes synthesized algebra and geometry, as part of a scheme for a synthetic philosophy of mechanics, optics, physiology and psychology. Newton gave a synthetic account of the behaviour of the solar system, and Joule and Mayer, Darwin, and Mendeleev, gave synthetic accounts of energy, living organisms and chemistry, respectively. In our own day Einstein has improved on Newton's system with the general theory of relativity.

The dialectical materialists point out that all these tremendous achievements of the best minds were contemporaneous with the production of vast quantities of puerile theories. At the present time, the growth of the theory of relativity and of the quantum theory has been parallel, in the land of their origin, with the growth of reactionary philosophies, and a decline to the beliefs of barbarism. It is evident that some fundamental ordering principle is lacking. The increasing specialization of scientists, following the growth of the subdivision of labour, has left them as individuals more and more restricted in experience and general knowledge, and easier and easier prey to all sorts of nonsense outside their special domain. Thus the paradox arises, that as scientists achieve more and more extraordinary triumphs in their own branches, they seem as a class to become more and more stupid.

The undirected extension of specialization in science, and subdivision of labour in industry, leads to brilliance and stupidity in both domains. Marvellous discoveries about the nature of things are made by men whose general know-

B

ledge of politics, business, art, and even of science, is in-
fantile. The human and intellectual limitations of the
great Faraday provide an illustration of this phenomenon.

Today young persons make marvellous motor-cars and
radio-sets by mass-production methods which establish in
them the most trivial habits of thought and skill.

The dialectical materialists say that this contradiction
between increasing discovery and increasing chaos in science
and philosophy is a reflection of the similar contradiction
and chaos in social life. It arises from this social contradiction and can be resolved only when the prior social
contradiction has been resolved. The chaos in social life
arises from the character of the capitalist system of production, in which an owning class struggles to obtain the
maximum profit for itself, with little regard for the non-
owning class.

This struggle for private profit precipitates the struggle
of the working class against exploitation. The progress
of this struggle produces the social chaos, which is reflected
in the scientific and philosophical chaos. The chaos may
only be resolved by the triumph of one class, and in the
end, this must be the working class, because the owning
class is prevented by its belief in the necessity for the private
ownership of the means of production from making the
organizational changes in the distribution of property
required to end the chaos.

The dialectical materialists point out that in the Soviet
Union the working-class has succeeded already in seizing
power. Not having any false ideas about private ownership
of the means of production, they are in a position to start
the reorganization required in order to make proper social
use of modern knowledge in manufacturing technique and
science. They have therefore created the State Planning
Commission. The task of this institution is to work out
the details of the rational organization of social life, so that
modern knowledge is employed with maximum efficiency.
As the State Planning Commission extends its work, and
covers more and more of the economic organization of the
social life with rational system, it provides a framework for

the rational organization of scientific research and philosophical thought. The scientific specialist is given the maximum scope in his own field, and on subjects in which he is not expert he must defer to those who are. In this way a social and intellectual structure is erected, in which every scientist knows his place, and the degree of his dependence on others. He is unable to give harmful expression to illusory ideas of absolute freedom, or behave with social irresponsibility, or to use his authority as a specialist in one branch of science to urge the adoption of his views on other aspects of human activity.

The dialectical materialists believe the resolution of the class-struggle in human society by the victory of the working class will provide the conditions for the beginning of the creation of a complete and comprehensive philosophy of the world. The intellectual dilemmas of the scientists and philosophers will persist, and become worse and worse, until society has been reconstructed from its foundations. When that has been done, and world socialism has been established, the next stage in the dialectical development will be the struggle for the further mastery of nature. The earth will be utterly subdued, and then, perhaps, the solar system, and more and more of the cosmos. Parallel with this, man will resolve the contradictions of his own nature, and, in Gordon Childe's phrase, continue the making of himself.

The organization of society on a socialist scheme will provide enormously extended opportunity for scientific research. The State Planning Commission in the Soviet Union is already focusing attention on numerous scientific problems whose solution is required for the extension of socialist construction. An example of these is the strength of materials, which must be known in order to construct the super-high-power and high-pressure steam-turbines which can be afforded, and used with confidence, more easily in the productive system of a socialist than in any other form of state.

Another example is the problem of super-high-tension insulation for an electrical grid-system for Siberia. The size of such a system enables engineers to think in working voltages of half a million or a million volts.   Such researches point at once to further investigations into the structure and properties of matter.   As they are supported by the full interest and resources of the state, fundamental researches of the latter character are splendidly endowed.

Further, as these researches are not conducted in the interest of any firm expected to produce immediate profits for shareholders, they can be pursued without any need to show immediate results.   The desire quickly to produce some tangible result, which has such a paralysing effect on most research done for private firms, is removed, and the investigator can ultimately expect help with material and resources far beyond those within the means of any private firm.

The first and most obvious result of the organization of science by dialectical materialists is an increase in the size of endowments for research.   The proportion of the national wealth devoted to science is far greater in the Soviet Union than in any other country.   The second result is the increase in planning and organization.   This consideration of the interrelation of science with industry and life promotes an increased interest in problems of classification in science.   It is to be expected that Soviet scientists will tend to see unexpected relationships between phenomena already known.

It is possible, too, that the ideas of dialectical materialism will prove directly applicable in the pursuit of research in the laboratory and in the study.   In 1930 considerable claims were being made for direct applications, in the theory of genetics, for example.   Less stress is being laid on such claims now.

More may be learned of dialectical materialism from the books recommended at the end of this chapter.   But it is hoped that these few preliminary words will have given some impression of the intellectual vitality of the Soviet thinkers, and a suggestion of why they pursue such gigantic scientific plans.   The activities to be described in this book could not have been conceived, and brought to the present state of development in eighteen years, without the inspiration of some remarkable doctrine.

REFERENCES

1. *Marxism and Modern Thought.* N. I. Bukharin, and others.
2. *Scientific Construction in the U.S.S.R.*   Vol. V of Voks publications. 1933.
3. *Science at the Cross Roads.* N. I. Bukharin and others.
4. *Materialism and Empirio-Criticism.* V. I. Lenin.
5. The Works of K. Marx and F. Engels.

CHAPTER 2

THE ORGANIZATION OF
PHYSICAL RESEARCH

THE most prominent feature of scientific research in the Soviet Union is its organization. The differences between scientific research in the Soviet Union and in Western Europe are in its relation to social life, rather than in peculiarity of technical methods. There are no obvious differences between the technique of physical, chemical or biological research in Soviet laboratories and in laboratories in other countries. The methods of using microscopes, galvanometers and chemical reagents in Soviet and in other laboratories are similar in principle. If this were not so, the results of research by Soviet scientists would either be of little international interest, or they would create new regions of investigation, in fact, new branches of science different in type from those previously known. The Soviet scientists have not created a special sort of Soviet physics, or Soviet chemistry or Soviet biology, but have pursued these sciences along lines consonant with the various strands and tendencies of the development of social life in the Soviet Union. From the aspect of physical, chemical and biological technique there are no primary differences between these sciences in the Soviet Union and in other countries. But there is a fundamental difference in Soviet social philosophy and that of Western countries in the conception of the rôle of science in the organization of society. In Western countries science is not conceived as a necessary part of the social organization. Politicians and state administrators are not supposed to require any training in science. For example, in Britain this attitude is seen clearly in the system of education used at Oxford for training future politicians and administrators. The majority of these students study ancient and modern history and literature, and latterly, economics. This training provides an acquaintance with the methods of managing affairs employed by politicians and administrators in the past. The student learns of the vast importance of gaining a place in a group of persons who hold power, and of the arts which will enable him to influence this group. He learns how to conduct conversation in a manner that will give him power in committees. At the same time he learns the different technique of public speaking. Much can be learnt from Greek authors of the art of discomfiting opponents in private and public discussions.

The past success of the verbal method of education in producing effective politicians is a proof that it contains some sound principles. In the past the art of managing persons has been the chief part of politics. The changes in the structure of the social organization were too slow to demand any special knowledge of their nature in the politicians who were influencing their direction. This has led to the possibility of imagining a pure politics in which persons are governed by adroit management. It follows from this conception that a person could be fully qualified for the arts of government without having any knowledge of several of the most important factors in social change. This notion of pure politics, of verbal methods of government, is still very influential in Western theories of politics as exemplified by the Oxford school. It persists in spite of the enormous growth and influence of technology and science. The modern Western conception of government by pure politicians who retain expert advisers without political power has evolved out of the ancient notion of verbal government. This explains the origin of one of the extraordinary features of contemporary Western European civilization. The most prominent characteristic of this civilization is the development of technology and science. The growth of this characteristic has modified but made no fundamental change in Western European conceptions of the technique of government.   The influence of Greek ideas evolved in a pre-technological era remains greater than that of post-Galilean scientific ideas.

The governors of Western Europe do not in theory consider technology and science a necessary part of the social organism.   They could, in theory, have no difficulty in imagining a satisfactory civilization without it.   Their practice shows they in fact consider technology and science are a necessary part of the social organization, as they organize state departments for scientific research.   Technology and science appear to the contemporary Western politician as just two more factors which enter into the material of his manipulations, and not as sources of power that transform the nature of political problems, and vastly increase the importance in the art of government of planning as compared with verbal argument.   The modes of thought which have produced the great development of technology and science are not effectively more than four hundred years old.   They have already had secondary effects on the contemporary conceptions of the art of government, but have not yet permeated them.   Until the permeation is deeper, it is unreasonable to suppose that politicians will find any solution to that group of immense social problems raised by the modern developments of technology and science.   The importance of H. G. Wells as a sociologist is due to his vigorous exposition of aspects of this problem.

The social philosophy of Western Europe has roots deep in a pretechnological era.   The social philosophy of Soviet Russia, dialectical materialism, is founded on modern physical and biological investigation.   Natural science is an organic part of Marx's philosophy.   Consequently, a social system established according to the principles of his philosophy must be founded on technology and science, and the scientific mode of thought must permeate the intellectual activity of its governors.

The profound difference between Western European civilization and that of the Soviet Union is that the governors of the former would not be embarrassed if they could ignore technological and scientific problems, while the latter would consider the notion of ignoring such problems fundamentally absurd.

The results of this theoretical difference concerning the rôle of science and technology in the social structure are immediately recognizable in the features of the organization of science which exists in the Soviet Union. The relation of laboratories and institutes to factories and universities are thought out carefully, and they are directly designed for the purposes for which they are to be used.

The principles by which the need for, and size of, an institute are calculated, may be sketched very simply. They are the same for all social planning. The planners start from the calculation of the needs of the population. There are about one hundred and sixty million persons in the U.S.S.R. It is estimated that the population will grow to three hundred millions during the next forty years. How much food, clothing and housing will be necessary to provide the whole of this expanding population with an adequate standard of living? The amount of bread, meat, fruits, suits, boots, houses, bathrooms, water-closets, radio, gramophones, motor-cars, etc., necessary to provide the approved standard for everyone is estimated. The figures are immense, and vastly greater than the population of the Soviet Union is receiving at present. But the figures may be planned for, and the State Planning Commission addresses itself to this problem. It is a very large organization, with special universities for training candidates for its staff. It attracts many of the ablest members of the population. For instance, it enjoys more prestige than the Soviet Foreign Office. It is possible to meet Soviet diplomats who are seeking positions in the State Planning Commission, and able young persons often have service in the Planning Commission as the aim of ambition.

This is not difficult to understand, as the State Planning Commission is the most original product of the Bolshevik Revolution. As a structure it is more original than the Communist Party, whose organization resembles that of various parties with different philosophical principles that have existed in history.

The Russian Bolsheviks are not perfect examples of Marxian Communists, though they can justly claim that they are far better examples than any other persons. They cannot escape the influence of Russian traditions. The tradition of verbal government and the management of persons is still strong in the Communist Party, but it is to be expected that it will become weaker as the social organism created by the State Planning Commission becomes stronger and more efficient. There are theoretical besides practical reasons for supposing that the verbal tradition will decline in the Soviet Union, but there are no theoretical reasons, though there are practical ones, for supposing that it will decline in Western Europe.

When the planners have calculated the quantity of food, and goods, necessary for an adequate standard of living, they can calculate the size of agriculture and industry to produce those quantities, and the size of the transport system to distribute them. The agricultural output will require the supply of so many machines, farm buildings, and seeds. The manufacture of the machines will put certain demands on the metal industry, and the construction of railways, ships and buildings will also put certain demands on that industry.

The motive power for the metal and other industries will require the provision of a certain quantity of heat and electrical energy. The construction of power stations will provide a further demand for metal work, and a demand for electrical machinery and equipment.

The development of agriculture to the desired degree of productivity and variety will require the improvement of the breeds of domestic plants and animals.

When the planners have derived estimates of the size of the various departments of industry and agriculture they can calculate what is necessary for the successful operation of each department. For instance, consider the needs of an electrical industry which has to produce and distribute a definite and very large quantity of electrical energy. So many generating stations with a total output equal to this quantity will have to be built and operated. Thousands of miles of transmission lines and cables, much operating at a very high tension, will have to be constructed. Thousands of transformers will have to be made for transforming the current to tensions suitable for local consumption.

All of these works will require thousands of trained engineers to supervise their construction and operation.

The review of the population's needs prompts the investigation of the country's resources. These are material and human. Hydroelectric power plants are erected in places where vast quantities of water power are available, and appropriate factories are built in districts with rich mineral resources. Following the same argument of common sense, the planners provide special research institutes for men of proved genius. The chemist who is a genius is a natural resource, as a vast deposit of phosphate rock is a natural resource, and suitable institutions are provided for the utilization of their respective values. This attitude helps to explain the existence of many almost personal research institutes directed by exceptional men, within the structure of a planned research system. Visitors to the U.S.S.R. are often puzzled by this apparent contradiction, because they assume planned research must neglect the particular abilities of individual scientists. According to the Soviet view, the organization of a system of research without giving weight to the talents of the available research workers would be an example of faulty planning.

A large electrical industry offers many problems of construction and operation. The conditions in all countries are different, owing to social, geographic and climatic differences. The Soviet Union is a very large country. This is a condition for very large-scale power plants and operations. There is plenty of room. This combination provides a tendency to make exceptionally big machines, and not to strive too much for economy of size in proportion to power. If a power station is to be erected in a place where land values are very high, there will be a tendency

to design compact machinery.   For instance, the stations and
rolling stock of the London Underground Railway are on
a small scale, though the underground system is very large.
The Moscow Underground has much larger stations.
Similar features are noticed in the railways.   The locomotives and rolling stock are much larger and higher than
those in Britain, and the gauge of the track is wider.
This is due to the availability of land, and the rarity of hills
and mountains.   It is well-known that part of the early
railways in Britain were built with a broad gauge.   In
time the standardization of the gauge became necessary,
and a choice between broad and narrow gauge had to be
made.   The narrow gauge was chosen because most of the
railways had been constructed with it, and also because the
adoption of a broad gauge would have required the widening
of tracks, embankments, bridges and tunnels; which would
have involved enormous expenditure.   Again, the difference in track conditions between Britain and the U.S.S.R.
is great.   In Britain many tracks carry a very frequent
service of trains.   The permanent way has to be very
strongly built in order to carry the frequent loads.   In
U.S.S.R. that class of strains connected with metallurgical
fatigue may in certain parts of railway engineering practice
be less than those met in the corresponding British practice.
In contrast with this, the momentary strains owing to the
movement of loads may be much larger in Soviet than in
British practice, owing to the greater size of trains.

These differences make the tendencies of Soviet research
in the strength of materials different from those of British
practice.   The vast distances in the U.S.S.R. stimulate
a special interest in the problems of the long-distance
transmission of electrical energy.   By operating at very
high tensions, the quantity of material in transmission lines
can be reduced, and the cost of construction reduced.   But
the highest tension that can be used efficiently in the open
air is about 500,000 volts, as the waste through the leakage
of electricity from the wire into the air is already equal to
the saving of materials in construction.   The practical
limits of high tension in different countries are affected by

various factors, such as climate. Humidity and the presence of impurities affect the insulating quality of the air. The frequency of rain and snow, and of very low winter temperatures, all influence the design of transmission lines and insulators, and may make differences in practice necessary in countries such as America and U.S.S.R., whose engineering problems resemble each other in scale.

For such reasons, the U.S.S.R. could not depend entirely on engineering practice in other countries, even if she wanted to. Special problems are presented by their own conditions, which are not of immediate interest to engineers and scientists in other countries. Engineers in Britain or Germany may be invited to attack some of these problems, but they cannot avoid approaching them with a slightly artificial interest, because their solutions may not have direct value for British or German practice. The peculiar problems arising in the U.S.S.R. stimulate the interest and attention of Soviet investigators more naturally than those of other investigators. In any research familiarity with the environment of the problem is of great importance. Thorough acquaintance with the locality provides an unconscious insight that often cannot be replaced by intelligence, and experience in another region. A famous pure mathematician once said that twenty years' study of mathematics was necessary to develop the mathematical insight, the power to choose fruitful lines of research, and a judgment of the value of mathematical ideas whose truth could not yet be established.

The Soviet authorities will tend to employ less and less foreign technical assistance because it is expensive, because they desire on principle to be independent of it, and because by certain problems they will be forced back on to themselves. That will happen in the case of those problems which arise out of peculiarities of the conditions in U.S.S.R., and which are necessarily known and understood better by Soviet than by other investigators.

The construction of a vast electrical industry cannot be done without a certain amount of research. Further, even if the equipment for such an industry is designed and made in other countries, and erected by foreign engineers in the U.S.S.R., its operation must be conducted by Soviet engineers. From time to time the equipment will break down. Turbines will fail, and transmission lines will be struck down by lightning. The Soviet authorities cannot afford the money or the time to send to America or Western Europe for a spare part each time a machine breaks down. They must therefore possess institutes where the usual and the unusual causes of breakdowns in the operations of machinery may be investigated. The problems of operation, besides those of construction, require institutes where they may be studied.

In this way, the State Planning Commission arrives at some general notion of the requirement by each industry of a certain equipment of research institutes for solving the routine and the new problems of construction and operation. This line of thought shows the need for research institutes for the solution of problems and the provision of things. Research institutes are needed for other reasons, also. The construction and operation of a machine industry requires many thousands of engineers. These must be educated in technical high schools. They must be taught by professors with first-class qualifications. The professors can obtain a thorough insight into the principles of science only through research. The proof of complete mastery of a subject consists in extending it. The man who is able to discover new knowledge must know what the old knowledge is, and where it ends. Persons cannot be first-class teachers of advanced science without engaging in research. If they do not attempt to advance the frontiers of knowledge, the frontiers rapidly leave them behind. Their methods of exposition become stereotyped, and their teaching of the old fundamental facts of their subject loses its inspiration. The first-class teacher must discover how to modify the presentation of old facts in the perspective of new knowledge, besides learning the new knowledge.

The connection between the construction and operation of a machine industry and scientific research explains why many of the best physical research institutes in the U.S.S.R.

PLATE 2

The House of Industry, Kharkov.   The relations between the planning of industry and of scientific research in the U.S.S.R. are organic.   The planning and management of industry in the Ukraine are conducted from these buildings

[face p. 21

are attached to the Commissariat of Heavy Industry. This Department has the charge of the construction and operation of the power, metallurgical and electrical industries. The research laboratories maintained by the Department are organized in a division named the Scientific Research Sector of the People's Commissariat of Heavy Industry, usually known as NIS. This organization, which is directed by M. Armand, is the nearest Soviet parallel to the British Department of Scientific and Industrial Research. It finances many of the best-known laboratories in the U.S.S.R., such as the Physico-Technical Institute of Leningrad directed by Professor Joffe, the Institute of Chemical Physics of Leningrad directed by Professor Semenov, the Optical Institute of Leningrad directed by Professor S. I. Vavilov, the Karpov Institute of Physical Chemistry directed by Professor Bach, and the Physico-Technical Institute of Kharkov directed by Professor Davidovitch.

The laboratories organized by NIS are concerned with research into the fundamental principles of the physical sciences which underlie the technique of industrial processes. Until recently NIS also included under its control many laboratories concerned with the direct application of physical science to the problems of industrial processes and the solution of particular problems arising in the process of manufacture. These factory laboratories have now been placed under the direct control of the industries with which they are connected, though their programmes of research are co-ordinated through NIS.

The co-ordination of programmes of research is accomplished through a series of about a dozen committees. These contain about ten to fifteen members, and have two or more meetings in the year. Each committee constructs a general plan for research for its subject for each year, and lays down the general line of research in each of the laboratories represented on it.

The committees may have much difficulty in apportioning research between different laboratories. For instance, much discussion was necessary in order to make a satisfactory division of research on high-tension direct current transmission between the Experimental Electro-Technical Institute in Moscow, the Electro-Physical Institute in Leningrad, the Physico-Technical Institute at Kharkov, the Laboratory of the Electrosila Factory in Leningrad and the Laboratory of the Electrical Machine Factory in Kharkov.

The committees of NIS have other duties besides the determination of the general lines of research. They have to decide the size of allowances for books, literature, and monographs, and to arrange conferences on problems of research and organization.

The most important of the bi-yearly meetings of the committees is that which is held at the end of the year. Reports on the previous year's work in the various institutes are read, and the general lines of plans for the forthcoming year are published. These have been prepared during the past year. Most of the committee's work is done by correspondence, and most of the members are directors of institutes. It is estimated that about two weeks of the working year of each member are devoted to the committee's business.

The planning of research within institutes is illustrated most easily by some accounts of the work and organization of particular institutes.

At present about three-quarters of the first-class research in the Soviet Union is done in Moscow, Leningrad and Kharkov. The development of large new institutes at Dniepropetrovsk, Sverdlovsk, Novosibirsk, Tashkent, and other places, and the growth of the research laboratories in the large factories will gradually extend the decentralization from the capital cities.

The prominence given to collaborators in the publication of results is a feature of scientific research in the Soviet Union. There is a large amount of collective research by groups of three or four persons.

The part of communist scientists is at present more prominent in applied than in pure science.

CHAPTER 3

THE ACADEMY OF SCIENCES

I

THE headquarters of the Academy of Sciences have been transferred from Leningrad to Moscow, and the first meeting under the new arrangement was held in Moscow in December, 1934. This is the most recent of the great changes in the organization of the Academy since the revolution.

The Russian Academy of Sciences was founded by Peter the Great about 1724-5, under the influence of French models. It was established in the new capital city that he had built, and during two centuries had acquired a number of large museums and institutes in addition to the fine building erected for it in the centre of the city, on a bank of the River Neva. The full membership of the Academy was restricted to about forty persons, according to the French tradition. In virtue of their membership they received salaries. Thus the Academy has never been a private society like the Royal Society of London.

Not all of its members were distinguished scientists. As it was controlled by the Tsarist State, many of its chairs were awarded as sinecures to favourites.

The best explanation of the character of the Tsarist academy is offered by Thorstein Veblen's theory of ostentation and conspicuous consumption by a leisure class. The Academy was created by Peter mainly because he considered his state was incomplete without such an ornament, and demonstration of wealth and intellectual superiority. He also had personal interest in science and technique, and believed his state would be strengthened by the cultivation of science. But the Academy was chiefly conceived as an elaborate decoration.

After the revolution the Academy was adopted by the new government, and retained many of the characteristics of the old organization. There was no thorough change in the working organization of the Academy during the first ten years after the Revolution. The inauguration of the First Five Years' Plan made such a change necessary. The construction of a socialist state, with the imperative demand for scientific and technical advice, made the Government look to the Academy as an adviser and partner in the creation of the new form of social life. The Academy was expected to advise on the solution of those problems set by socialist construction which demanded deep scientific and technical knowledge.

The situation created by the First Five Years' Plan destroyed the remnants of the ornamental tradition in the Academy. It could no longer continue in any degree as an emblem of power, and an ostentatious demonstration of the wealth which gave clever men the leisure to perform impressive feats of intellectual skill. It was earnestly expected to be a leading partner in the creation of the new society.

These circumstances have produced a series of fundamental changes in the organization of the Academy during the last six years.

According to the new statutes, the first duty of the Academy is to plan and direct the study and application of science towards the fulfilment of socialist construction, and the further growth of the socialist order.

The Academy formerly included no technicians among its members, and, of course, no Marxist philosophers. In order to remove these anomalies, and provide a membership in closer contact with the social forces developing the state, the membership has been doubled.

There are now about ninety academicians. Four of these are physicists, eight engineers, eighteen chemists, ten geologists, eight biologists, thirteen historians, six economists, ten philologists, eight orientalists and two philosophers.

There are about seventy honorary members, and three hundred corresponding members.

The studies are divided into three departments, natural science, sociology, and technology, and are pursued in twenty institutes. In addition there are large museums for zoology, mineralogy, social science, anthropology, biology and the history of religion. It possesses also a fine botanical garden. The Academy's library contains 3,500,000 volumes.

About four thousand scientists are engaged in the work of these and smaller institutions belonging to the Academy.

The president of the Academy is the venerable geologist, A. P. Karpinsky. He was born in 1846, was elected a member in 1886, and president in 1916. During the difficult years of his presidency he has superintended the Academy's affairs with extraordinary vitality, charm and tact.

The vice-president is G. M. Krzhizhanovsky, who is the chief author of the Five Years' Plans. Lenin was much influenced by him in promulgating the schemes for the electrification of the U.S.S.R., which led to the formulation of the plans. Other eminent leaders of the Academy are I. P. Pavlov, N. I. Bukharin, A. E. Fersman, I. M. Vinogradov, A. E. Joffe, and the brothers N. I. and S. I. Vavilov. They are the first example of two brothers being simultaneously full members.

The Academy's Second Five Years' Plan of research for the years 1932–7 includes the study of the scientific principles underlying following groups of problems:

(1) the structure of matter, and its bearing on astronomy, physics, chemical physics and chemistry,
(2) the survey and utilization of the natural resources of the U.S.S.R.,
(3) the survey and planning of the power resources of the U.S.S.R.,
(4) problems of distribution, building materials, hygiene, etc., arising out of construction.

(5) the general introduction of chemistry in industry and agriculture,

(6) the study of biological evolution, and the bearing of its results on agriculture and materials for light industry,

(7) the provision of the historical and social theory for combating the ideas of capitalism, and dissolving the prejudices which survive in the minds of the people, and have been transmitted from earlier forms of society.

The Academy has been very active in organizing expeditions. In 1932 140 were sent out, making investigations in 30 different branches of sciences, and staffed by 600 persons.

The Government has reported that the expeditionary work of the Academy in connection with geological prospecting for ores, coal and petroleum has profoundly transformed the conceptions of the resources of the country. This in turn has transformed the ideas for the development of the country.

The organization of expeditions and the study of the country's productive forces is directed by a council of academicians under the chairmanship of I. M. Gubkin. Other members of the council include Bukharin, N. I. Vavilov, Joffe and Fersman.

The reorganizations of 1930–2 have been followed by equally great changes in 1934, with the transference of the Academy to Moscow. The magnitude of this upheaval may easily be imagined. Institutes and a certain scientific atmosphere had grown in Leningrad for two centuries. The accumulation of buildings was great. Many of the older scientists were dismayed by the prospect of the change. But several strong reasons prompted the decision to move it. Leningrad is no longer the capital city of the Soviet Union. As the Academy has acquired a very important position in the direction of the country's development, the advice of its members is continually required by the Government. The existence of so many experts at a considerable distance from the seat of government was a serious inconvenience.

The Government also desired to have the intellectual centre of the country in Moscow.

Again, it was felt that the intellectual atmosphere in Leningrad was not even yet assimilated to that of the new communist society. It was considered that if the intellectual centre was also at the headquarters of the Government, and nearer to the spiritual sources of the new ideology, the defects in its intellectual atmosphere would be removed by the closer contact.

Further, Leningrad is on one of the most vulnerable frontiers of the Soviet Union. It was desirable that the chief intellectual resources of the country should be in some less vulnerable place.

The transfer to Moscow has occurred at this particular time because special provision has been made in the second half of the Second Five Years' Plan for cultural construction. The First Five Years' Plan was designed to supply the country with a foundation of industrial culture, and has succeeded in this object. It is now necessary to build a large scientific and cultural superstructure on this foundation.

Plans and drawings for a vast group of new institutes have been prepared, unfortunately in the neo-classical styles which have recently returned to fashion. It is proposed to construct an academic suburb in Moscow, near the Park of Culture and Rest, rather like a larger Berlin-Dahlem.

The new buildings will not be ready for some years. While they are being erected the Academy's administrative offices and meeting-halls have been established in a small palace on the site of the new suburb. The scientific institutes are being temporarily housed in neighbouring institutes whose former occupants have been transferred to buildings in other districts. The upheaval has interfered with the continuity of research, but has caused less disorganization than expected. The shortage of flats at a convenient distance from the new academic centre presents

one of the most serious immediate difficulties.   Staffs that
have been transferred as a whole from Leningrad to Moscow,
have sometimes had to camp in their new laboratories before
they could find rooms.

II

The Academy's new Biological Institute is directed by
N. I. Vavilov, and is established in the former building of
the Textile Institute.   The genetics department is directed
by the famous American geneticist H. J. Muller, who first
demonstrated the possibility of producing heritable changes
in living organisms by modifying the germ plasm by X-rays.

He has twenty research colleagues and is pursuing
brilliant and fruitful investigations.   Among his latest
researches are results which seem to show that the X-ray
mutations arise from the splitting and transposition of
parts of genes, and not to the conversion of genes from one
sort to another, as originally supposed.   In collaboration
with the ultra-microscopists of the Leningrad Optical
Institute he has observed units in chromosomes, which seem
either to be individual genes, or small groups of genes.
His colleagues include C. A. Offerman of Argentina, D.
Kostov of Bulgaria, and D. Raffel of America.

The former building of the Institute of Human Biology
and Medicine is being reconstructed for the Academy's
Institute of Technology and Energetics.

The former Institute of Biophysics, which was opened
in 1915 and was directed by the Academician Lasarev, has
been converted into the Physical Institute of the Academy.
A short account of its state and activities will give some
indication of the conditions in the new temporary institutes
of the Academy that have been established in Moscow.

The director of the institute is S. I. Vavilov.   He is also
the director of the large Optical Institute in Leningrad,
besides being a member of many important committees.
Enormous labours devolve on him, and he is unable to
spend more than two or three days of the week at the
institute.   Like many eminent Soviet scientists, he spends
a considerable part of his life travelling in trains between

Moscow and Leningrad, which, like London and Edinburgh, are exactly four hundred miles apart.

It is expected that this extreme pressure on the leading scientists of mature age will be relieved within a few years, when the best of the young post-revolutionary scientists have acquired the necessary experience for the senior directive posts.

Many of the directors of the departments of the institute are also part-time workers. The university professors Hessen, Mandelstamm and Tamm direct research in the institute, and the laboratory of chemical physics is directed by P. Rehbinder, who also works in at least two other institutes in Moscow. B. Wul has a laboratory for the study of insulators and dielectrics, and Levshin has been pursuing extensive researches on fluorescence and luminescence. S. I. Vavilov is interested in the optical properties of feeble rays of light, the sensitivity of the eye, and allied questions. The general line of the researches of Vavilov, and of Wul, are described in another chapter.

P. Rehbinder has published many papers on the physics and chemistry of surfaces. He is a young and enthusiastic scientist with many ideas, and much more is to be expected from him in the future.

Rehbinder has interesting views on the relation of science to industry. He does not consider the primary function of applied science is to solve the problems of industrial production, but to create new industries. The applied scientist should by research and imagination discover what can be done with the materials of nature and then indicate in which direction the creation of new industries and the improvement of old ones is possible. He believes the old conception of the industrial scientist as a consultant who will merely solve difficulties that arise during manufacture is false and uneconomic. The scientist will be most economically valuable when he is leading the direction of economic development, for his power of discovering the possibility of new industries is vastly more valuable than his capacity for making trifling improvements in conventional manufacturing processes. In conducting his own

researches on surface chemistry, Rehbinder seeks continually for indications of the possibility of new industries
in the new phenomena being apprehended.   The erection
of this attitude to the status of a philosophic principle,
rather than a practical, opportunist habit, is original.
Applied scientists in other countries are trying to see
the industrial possibilities in new scientific discoveries,
but they approach the problem as the servants and not the
masters of industry, and can give no close philosophical
statement of the reasons for their action.   In the Soviet
Union, the ideas of scientists can be put into practice
through the understanding and controlling power of the
Communist Party.

About ten or fifteen years ago, the best imaginative
writers on science were biologists.   The most brilliant
British example was J. B. S. Haldane.   The initiative in the
imaginative exploration of the possibilities of science seems
today to have passed to the students of the structure of
material.   The same sort of imaginative insight is found
simultaneously in different parts of the world.   In the
Soviet Union, Rehbinder exhibits this quality, and in
England, J. D. Bernal.   This phenomenon shows the deep
significance of the studies of atomic and molecular structure
for contemporary scientific culture, and immediate industrial
developments.

Rehbinder's work on the theory of hardness is particularly interesting.   The hardness of minerals, crystals, and
other solids can be studied by measuring the amount of
pressure needed to crush them.   But there is another
method.   The hardness may be deduced from measurements of the strength of the molecular field at the surface
of the solid.   This will provide information without
crushing or spoiling the specimen.   Solid bodies may be
arranged in a series according to the strength of the
molecular field at their surface, which may be measured
by their angles of wetability.   If the specimen is put in
benzol, and a drop of water is laid on its surface, the angle
between the specimen and the surface of the drop at the
point where they meet is the angle of wetability.   It is a

measure of the strength of the molecular field at the surface of the solid, because the angle of inclination between the surfaces of the drop and the specimen is a function of the attractive forces between the atoms in the respective surfaces. The cosine of this angle will have some value between -1 and $+1$. Thus the molecular field of any solid may be represented by a point on the line between -1 and $+1$. If the point lies between zero and $+1$, the specimen is water-attractive, or hydrophilic; if between zero and -1, it is water-repulsive, or hydrophobic.

It is found that all water-attractive substances, such as quartz, calcite and glass, are hard; while water-repulsive substances, such as graphite, are soft. All materials that feel oily, such as graphite and talcum (soapstone—the basis of toilet powders, magnesium silicate) are soft, and water-repulsive.

The silicates may be arranged in a series of hardness from talc to quartz. This corresponds with their order on the wetability graph.

Mineralogists have devised an empirical rule for determining hardness by scratching. An order of hardness is arranged according to the ability of a mineral to scratch others lower in the order.

Accurate methods of measuring hardness show that the mineralogists have unconsciously used the Weber-Fechner intuitive logarithmic scale, as they determined the degree of scratchability by their sensations when they rubbed one mineral on another.

The knowledge of the molecular field is of direct value in the technique of mineral separation by flotation. If the measure of wetability of a mineral is negative, then particles of the mineral will collect on the surface of bubbles blown through a mixture of the particles with water. Thus gold, platinum, dust, etc., which are negatively wetable, may be removed by this method.

If talc is not to be taken from the mixture, how can it be made to sink? By covering it with an adsorbed layer of molecules whose own surface has contrary properties of wetability.

In a similar way quartz can be made to float by coating it with a layer of adsorbed molecules whose own surface will have the contrary properties.

Rehbinder and his colleagues have constructed graphs showing the change in wetability of various minerals on the addition of increasing quantities of adsorbable substances.

When the surface of a mineral has a strong molecular field it must be covered with a layer of fatty substances, and when the field is weak a layer of water will be necessary.

The surface properties of carbon-black, zinc oxide, etc., explain how rubber is strengthened by their inclusion. Chalk cannot be directly incorporated in rubber, but if its surface is covered with a suitable adsorbed layer, this will act as a bridge. In this way chalk may, as it were, be used as a white carbon-black.

The effect of adsorption of molecular layers on the faces of stone and metal being bored or drilled is of technical importance. A correct choice of material for forming such layers will reduce the surface hardness, and hence the wear and consumption of energy in operations, such as boring, grinding, polishing, filing, sawing, etc.

Solutions of polar substances, such as camphor and colophony are effective lubricants for glass-cutting, and solutions of soap for steel-cutting. Their efficacy probably depends on the fall in the hardness of the surface caused by the adsorption of substances from these solutions.

W. L. Levshin has made extensive studies of fluorescence. He has shown that the curves of fluorescence and absorption spectra for various dyestuffs between 20° and 70° C. are mirror images. This is true for the benzene curves.

With W. W. Antonov-Romanovsky he has shown that the decay of phosphorescence of zinc sulphide follows an exponential law through the observable period of decay, and the law was found to apply to Lenard phosphors also.

With the additional collaboration of L. A. Tumerman he has studied the quenching of phosphorescence by infra-red rays. They found that the total amount of light emitted, and the character of the law of decay were unchanged. The quenching of the phosphorescent light produces a decrease in the blackening of an exposed photographic plate. This decrease obeys the ordinary laws of photographic blackening, and suggests a possibility of quantitative as well as qualitative infra-red photography.

B. Wul is extending the researches on electrical insulation described in another chapter, especially in connection with the use of high pressure gases.

A laboratory for cosmic ray research is being equipped, and a Wilson chamber is being erected.

III

The first session of the Academy held in Moscow since its transference occurred in December, 1934. The scientific meetings were held in the small palace which is now the administrative building, and was formerly one of the Tsar's summer pleasure palaces. It was built in the eighteenth century, and is a restrained and elegant example of the neoclassical style.

During the period of the session the weather was extremely cold, about $-20°$ to $-30°$ C. The warmth of the building seemed to make its comfort even more attractive.

A small restaurant for the academicians and members of the sessions had been established at a short distance from the headquarters, and buffets for light refreshments had been opened in the building.

The catering in this restaurant was extremely good, and the cost of the meals was nominal. Better food and cooking could not have been found in Europe.

Open semi-popular meetings were held in a large building in the city, which is the Academy's club. A. E. Fersman, N. I. Vavilov, and others gave semi-popular lectures on the objects of the Academy's work and on their own researches. A special meeting was held in honour of I. P. Pavlov's eighty-fifth birthday, and a series of semi-popular accounts of recent advances in physiology were read.

About forty papers were read at the scientific meetings in the palace. Many of them dealt with researches that have been mentioned in this book.

At the physics meetings Joffe described his researches on the photo-electricity of copper oxide, S. I. Vavilov spoke on apparent luminescence, and Sokolov read an interesting paper on a new method of studying metals by radiation.   The hall was not too large and the audience usually contained about one hundred scientists.   The change in the appearance of scientific audiences during recent years was noticeable.   Many of the speakers were well and even smartly dressed, and had a new air of cheerful prosperity.   The conduct of the session conveyed the impression that the occasion was considered by the authorities to be important, and the arrangements had been made with much energy.

The air of strain and struggle noticeable at earlier scientific meetings in the Soviet Union was absent from this.

An idea of the scope of the session will be conveyed by a list of the authors and titles of the papers read:

1. Fersman: "Geo-energetic problems in geo-chemistry."
2. Richter: "Physiological problems in collecting the harvest and overcoming climatic conditions."
3. Arkadiev: "Photography of Herzian waves."
4. Joffe: "Photo-electric properties of cuprite."
5. Sokolov: "New Methods of irradiating and investigating metals."
6. Vinogradov: "Existence in the earth's crust."
7. A. Shubnikov: "On the achievements of the crystallographic sector in the sphere of technique."
8. Ratchkovsky: "Main features of North Mongolia: Tuva."
9. Nadson: "The problem of biological action of metals over a distance.   Their sphere of influence."
10. H. J. Muller: "The continuity and discontinuity of inherited characters."
11. A. A. Sapegin: "X-ray mutations in wheat."
12. Schaksel: "Regeneration processes."
13. Lasarev: "Action of light on the feeling apparatus of the human body."
14. Polinov: "The soil of humid sub-tropics."
15. Prasolov: "Work on the new soil map of the U.S.S.R."
16. Grekov: "Engels and the problem of the tribal system in Western Slavs."

17. Bikovsky: "Engels and the origin of cattle breeding."
18. Vinnikov: "Ethnographical sources used by Engels in his revision of his book on the Family."
19. Oksman: "The technique of the historical novel, as written by Pushkin."
20. Piksanov: "Griboyedov and Alexander Bestuzhev. (The ideological atmosphere in the Decembrist milieu.)"
21. Balukhaty: "Maxim Gorky's Lower Depths. (A chapter from the book: *M. Gorky and the Theatre*.)"
22. S. I. Vavilov and Tchornyakov: "Apparent luminescence of certain fluids under gamma radiation."
23. Arkadiev: "Present state of the problem of magnetic spectra."
24. Gerassimovitch: "Dark nebula and the transparency of space."
25. Wul and Goldman: "The electric stability of compressed gases."
26. Dneprovsky: "Fundamental problems of stellar measurements."
27. Kirpitcheva: "Treatment of thermal processes by the theory of similarity."
28. Zaitsev: "The study of abrasion."
29. Semenov: "The catalytic action on gas reactions of traces of oxygen."
30. Levinson-Lessing: "On two correlations between atomic numbers and weights of chemical elements."
31. Petrov and Antsus: "On the catalytic hydrolisation and the polymerization of acetylene under pressure."
32. Stepanov: "Isothermic reactions."
33. Nikolaiev: "Salt richness of the Kalmik region."
34. Zvyagintsev: "Geochemistry of platinum."
35. Klebansky: "Synthetic rubber and soprenine."
36. Belyankin: "The petrography of clay-earth clinker."
37. Lebedev: "Complexes of alkaline and iron ore deposits."
38. Belyankin: "Minerals of clays."
39. Kupletsky: "The quantitative mineralogical classification of mining deposits."
40. Ginsberg: "Raw material from Tulansk for the artificial stone industry."
41. Shtsherbina: "The negative parogenesis of minerals."
42. D. Kostov: "The genetics of tobacco."
43. Konrad: "The distributive system in Japan in the eighth century."
44. Alexeiev: "The Chinese language as a general factor of the philological and linguistic preparation of officials. Language as a system of officials mnemonics."
45. Alexeiev: "The builder of society, according to the theory of one of the epigones of Confucianism. Su-Sun. (1009–66.)"

46. Obnorsky: "Russian law as a record of Russian literary language."
47. Bikhovskaya: "The construction of Verba Sentiendi."
48. Frank-Kaminetsky: "Divorce as a metaphor of death in myth and poetry.   Analysis of folklore episodes in Mahab-Harata."

CHAPTER 4

THE SCIENTISTS' HOUSE, LENINGRAD

IN Moscow, Leningrad, Kharkov, and other cities there are large clubs for scientists. The Leningrad Scientists' House may be described from personal experience. It is a palace on a bank of the Neva, adjacent to the former Winter Palace, and was occupied before the revolution by the Grand Duke Vladimir Alexander, an uncle of the Tsar. The ducal reception rooms are decorated in an imperially elaborate style. One is furnished in crimson plush and gold, and another in a Mohammedan style. These rooms, on the first floor, have a magnificent view over the Neva. They are closed during the morning, and in the afternoon and evening some are used for small meetings of mathematical and other societies. Many members play chess, or read, or talk in the rooms. There is a library, and upstairs there are billiard-rooms, and an office for arranging holidays in the country. The crimson and gilt room has an enormous open-fire grate in a style resembling the Tudor. Open fires in large houses are unusual in the Soviet Union.

The huge banqueting hall, which is covered with complicated wood carving, has been converted into a restaurant. This is open, except for a short interval, from the middle of the afternoon until midnight. The catering is excellent and the prices are reasonable. Many scientists dine there almost every evening. There is a buffet in a room next to the restaurant. This appears to have been the former ducal bar. It has most elaborately carved dark-wood cupboards filled with wineglasses and other table glass. When the restaurant is closed, tea and cakes may be obtained at the buffet. They have a sort of short-bread covered with a layer of jam and a network of honey icing which is very attractive.

The dancing hall is used for meetings, lectures and cinema shows. Several films are shown every week. Within a few days one saw the Chelyuskin picture, an interesting film on the social habits of the aristocracy, and instructional films on engineering. Scientific and technical exhibitions are also arranged, for example, on the most recent sorts of insulating materials, and designs of insulators.

The chief meeting during the same period was in memory of Kirov, the Secretary of the Executive Committee of the Communist Party in the Leningrad province, who had been assassinated in the preceding days. All of the most distinguished scientists in the province spoke on that occasion.

On one evening during the same days, a casual visit to the lecture hall revealed familiar views of London being thrown on the screen. These proved to be illustrations of a lecture by Yagin on his experiences during his visit to England for the Cambridge meeting of the International Congress of Applied Mechanics. It was entertaining to hear him speaking on London, after having seen him there a few months before.

The rooms for accommodating scientists from the provinces who are visiting Leningrad show the class-distinctions of Tsarist society. There are suites of rooms that apparently belonged to butlers, and that grade of servant. The rank of the occupants and the proprietary dignity of the owner led to a nice balancing of plainness and decoration in the style. Then there were other quarters of the lower ranks. The fantastic difference between the styles of the highest and the lowest apartments impairs the usefulness of these old palaces. They are not at all convenient for a communist society, and apart from illustrations of the former social system, are not worth preserving.

Most of the heating is done by stoves built in the walls. These burn wood, and demand an immense amount of labour for carrying and chopping.

In spite of the strict management, the rooms are not

entirely free from vermin. This gets in the cracks of the wall-plaster near the stoves.

The arrangements of the former society are unpleasantly noticeable in the provision of wash-basins and water-closets. There are only two closets for males in the residential part of the club. These are quite insufficient, with the obvious uncomfortable consequences.

The adoption of old imperial palaces as clubs for working scientists is a magnificent social gesture. After a decade or two the justifiable pride of triumph in this usage will doubtless have been completely satisfied, and entirely new and convenient buildings will be erected for the scientists' clubs. This has already happened, to a considerable extent, in Moscow. A club for the scientists at the group of institutes at Lesnoe in Leningrad is being erected.

The membership of the club is restricted to scientists engaged in research and factory laboratories. The majority of the members who frequent the club belong to the middle intellectual rank of the scientific profession.

PART II

PHYSICS

CHAPTER 5

THE PHYSICO-TECHNICAL
INSTITUTE, LENINGRAD

THIS famous institute was organized by Professor A. E. Joffe. He has given the following verbal account of its origin.

In the earlier stages of the social upheavals in Russia connected with the Great War the nature of their probable outcome was not obvious to the non-political observer, but during the summer of 1918 it became clear that the revolution would succeed. As the socialist type of organization would certainly be introduced, and as this is based on a high degree of industrial technique, the preparation of the scientists and technicians necessary for the creation and operation of such an economy had to be started immediately.

Joffe was professor of physics in the Polytechnical Institute at that time. This was a high school for engineers. The preparation for the corps of technicians for the new highly technical socialist society could not be completed in the high school, as there were not sufficient opportunities for fundamental research. If scientists with creative technical power were to be produced, they would have to be trained in institutes devoted to fundamental research, in which teaching had a secondary place.

In September, 1918, Joffe was able to start the Physico-Technical Institute. At first it was assigned a few rooms in the Polytechnical Institute. In 1923 it was housed in a building the erection of which had been begun by the Russian nobility in 1914 as a home for retired engineers. During the war this building had been used as a mental hospital. It has been greatly extended, but the nature of its origin explains the eighteenth-century appearance of the architecture of the entrance to the best-known physical institute in the Soviet Union.

For the first five years the institute was devoted to the training of a group of good physicists. At the same time technical physicists, such as Tchernitchev, were invited to join the staff.

The original staff consisted of eight persons, including Joffe, Semenov, Tchernitchev, Dorfmann, Lukirsky and Frenkel. The first researches were on X-rays and atomic theory.

In 1927–8 large new buildings were added to the institute, and by 1929–30 it had grown to an unwieldy size. Most of the ablest students from all parts of the U.S.S.R. had been sent to study there. It had a staff of about 2000 of every grade, 700 physicists and 1300 assistants. The policy of centralization had achieved the aim of creating a nucleus of physicists for the Soviet Union, where previously there had been almost none. But decentralization now became necessary. New institutes were split off, and established in various parts of the country to act as nuclei for still further extension. The institutes at Kharkov, Dniepropetrovsk, Tomsk and Samarkand were founded. The department of chemical physics was established as an independent institute under the direction of Semenov, and the department of electro-physics as the Electro-Physical Institute under the direction of Tchernitchev. Two other independent institutes were formed.

With the development of the land collectivization movement there was an increased demand for agricultural physicists. In 1931–2 rooms in the Physico-Technical Institute were set apart for an institute of agricultural physics. The Röntgen Institute directed by Nemenov started in 1918 as part of Joffe's institute.

PLATE 3

Prof. A. Joffe and Prof. Niels Bohr in the grounds of the
Physico-technical Institute, Leningrad

An open-air cinema in the Hope Kolhoz near Kharkov (see page 121)

[face p. 42

B. Budnitzky, the former administrative manager of the organization of the Physico-Technical Institute, has provided some details. It now has a staff of about 136, of which 65 are research physicists. The Institute of Chemical Physics has a staff of 180, with 70 chemical physicists, and the Electro-Physical Institute has a staff of 450, with 200 physicists.

The directors of these institutes form a general committee of which Joffe is the chairman. The yearly plans of work for all of these institutes are co-ordinated by this committee, and the various problems are distributed among them.

The Soviet Association of Physicists has a committee which considers what physical problems should be of interest to industry. Fifteen physicists consider respectively fifteen industries in order to form an idea of the scope of physics in each of these industries, and in what directions new applications might reasonably be sought. Their function is partly that of what H. G. Wells would name a Committee of Foresight. The Soviet authorities do not consider the relations between physics and industry are yet entirely satisfactory.

The plans for research in the Joffe institute are arranged in the following way. The chief scientists in the institute meet together. Each prepares a plan for his own work for the coming year. As far as possible, the continuity of each scientist's special line of work is preserved. In the Soviet system of planning the special talents of individual workers are not overlooked ; one of the objects of planning is to enable gifted persons to persevere, and develop to the utmost their ideas and skill. Planning is not conceived as merely an efficient system of issuing orders to a corps of scientists. Plans of research are useless if they do not attract and incorporate the enthusiasm of the research worker, and convince him that they will make the achievement of his aims easier.

The plans for research suggested by the chief scientists and the staffs of their departments are discussed by the institute's general committee, or soviet.

After they have been amended and approved, they are discussed by the committee of all the local institutes, and co-ordinated. This is important, as particular researches may be conducted partly in each of these institutes, and research workers may be engaged on different problems in different institutes. For instance, Kondratiev works on isotopes in the Physico-Technical Institute, and on the dynamics of chemical reactions in the Institute of Chemical Physics across the road.

The plans of the Electro-Physical Institute are worked out in close collaboration with industry, owing to the direct industrial importance of much of its work.

The Association of Physicists has sub-committees on the different subjects, such as magnetism and radio-communication. These sub-committees co-ordinate researches in laboratories throughout the U.S.S.R. in their respective subjects, and prevent overlapping. No physicist in the Soviet Union unwittingly pursues the same line of research as another physicist : if both are working on the same problem, they know of it. In Western countries the research worker is conceived as a pure individualist who is theoretically free to choose any subject for research, without the obligation to inform anyone except his immediate superiors. In practice this rarely happens, but nevertheless the ordinary research worker supposes he has theoretical freedom of choice of problem. The Soviet plan is to encourage individual initiative, but to lend it as much co-operative support as possible. The mere possibility of choice is not greatly esteemed. In Western countries, freedom to choose the subject of research is considered to have enormous value, irrespective of whether the freedom is supported by adequate means and technical assistance. Mere freedom is not of much value to the physicist if he is not also given the necessary equipment, assistants, and workshop facilities.

When the plans for research have been approved by the committees of the institutes, and groups of institutes, they are placed before M. Armand, the secretary of the Scientific Research Sector of the Department of Heavy Industry.

The research institutes of the Academy of Sciences and of the universities are more academic in type.

The plans for research are prepared at the end of October and are ready by the end of December. The object of the plans is to relate research to social needs, and at the same time to refrain as much as possible from interfering with the individuality of the workers.

The preparation of the plans does not absorb very much time. There are two official meetings in the year. The details of the plans are discussed in free time. The discussions on the planning help workers to learn what others are doing.

In the Leningrad Physico-Technical Institute there are about fifteen Communists in a total staff of 136. About ten of the fifteen are research workers, and there are seven young Communists under the age of twenty-five. It will be noted that the number of Communists is small. It is considered to be far too small, and efforts are strenuously made to increase it. In the scientific research institutes the Communists have come in late, and the percentage is much smaller than in the industrial organizations. In the future, when the new generation of communist students has completed its training, the percentage of Communists among research workers will greatly increase.

In the Physico-Technical Institute the Communist lead has been given by Vassiliev, and until recently by Budnitzky. The Communists agitate to improve and deepen the collective work of the institute, and strengthen the team spirit. Simultaneously, they support individual workers whose work and suggestions have not received as much encouragement as they have deserved. The Communist group is expected to be alert, and to be the first to discover the necessity for any changes and improvements, and to prevent the wastage of equipment and personnel.

The group of party members in the institute is responsible to the party for the satisfactory adherence by the institute to the general lines of policy decided by the Central Executive Committee of the party. It is expected to see that the practical interpretation of the instructions are correct.   It has to explain the meaning of these instructions and see that no mistakes are made in carrying them out. The party group is not concerned with administration, but is expected to encourage and stimulate the staff.

With the exception of the secretary of the institute's party committee, the members are not allowed to do party work during the working hours.   They have to give about six free hours to party work in a week of five days.

It is interesting to compare these details of organization with those given in Chapter 6 on the Physico-Technical Institute at Kharkov.

Joffe has made some interesting experiments on the introduction of workers to scientific research without the usual preliminary training.   It is reasonable to suppose that in any large population there exists a large quantity of undiscovered scientific ability.   Perhaps persons of such ability might be able to start scientific research with an abbreviated form of scientific training.

Acting on this supposition, about twenty factory workers who had shown definite talent for inventing details in machinery and processes were selected, and set to work in the physical research laboratories.   They were given a special course of instruction to acquaint them with the general ideas and objects of the researches to which they were set.   The experiment did not succeed.   Though everyone was a successful inventor, it appeared that none had any special aptitude for scientific research.   Joffe said that the men proved to be inventors of machines, and not inventors of ideas, and that the two processes appear to be distinct.   Progress in scientific research apparently depends on the invention of scientific ideas, and not directly on the invention of ingenious apparatuses.

Another interpretation of the result of this experiment is that a mature man cannot be trained to do something else within two years.

The chief lines of research in the Physico-Technical Institute are on Electrical Semi-Conductors, which is Joffe's own subject of research at present; Nuclear Physics, which includes Skobeltzyn's work on Cosmic Rays,

Kurtchatov's work on artificial disintegration, Alikhanov's work on the Positron, Kondratiev on the Mass Spectrograph, Dukelsky's on Radiation Expeditions and Artzimonitch's on High Voltage; Electron Theory, which includes Lukirsky's experimental work on Electron Diffraction, Laskariev's on the same subject, Alikhanian's on Electrons, Dukelsky's on X-ray's, and Prilaejaiev's on Photoelectricity.

Davidenkov works on the Solid State, and Pressures in the Earth, and Dam Structures.

Kobeko works on the Amorphous State, and its electrical and mechanical properties, and the invention of new insulating materials.

Fredericks works on Anisotropic Crystals, and Nasledov on Semi-Conductors.

The Theoretical Department is directed by Frenkel.

Professor Joffe and his wife Anne Joffe have been investigating recently the photoelectromotive forces in crystals of the semi-conductor copper oxide, cuprite. Professor Joffe first investigated semi-conductors in 1901–2, and he still continues his interest in their properties.

In 1919 W. Coblenz observed that if an area of a photoconducting single crystal is illuminated, a difference of potential between the illuminated and the dark parts arises, and may be as high as 0·2 volts. In 1931 Dember observed this phenomenon again, and since then a number of workers have studied it. Dember suggested that the light pressure pushed the photo electrons along the light ray from the illuminated area through to the point where the light ray emerged from the crystal, and also that the electric field counterbalances the diffusion of electrons, from the illuminated area where the concentration of electrons is higher, to the dark area where the concentration is lower.

The first of these suggestions cannot be correct because the observed electromotive force is about a million times stronger than would be theoretically expected.

If the second suggestion were correct, the electromotive force should increase with increase in the intensity of illumination.

Dember and others have found that the sign of the

electromotive force may change with change in the intensity
or frequency of the light.   They made their experiments
with crystals in contact with opaque electrodes, and this
prevented the area of the crystal in contact with the electrodes from being illuminated.   The Joffes have repeated
the experiments with transparent gold electrodes and found
that the charge on the illuminated electrode was positive
and independent of the intensity or wave-length of the light.
The reversal in electromotive force proved to be due to the
absorption of certain wave-lengths of the light in the crystal.
Further investigations have led to the conclusion that the
photoelectromotive forces in crystals are due to a difference
in the concentration of electrons at the electrodes, which
produces a flow of electrons from the illuminated area.

The ratio of the concentrations of electrons at the electrodes may be estimated by the ratio of the conductivities
of the layers near the electrodes.   The electromotive force
rises at low and falls at high temperatures, and is in agreement with theory.   All of the known facts satisfy the
picture of a continuous circulation of electrons in the
illuminated crystal.   This produces different concentrations
in various regions, and a stationary maintained difference of
potential between these regions, which is manifested as a
photoelectromotive force.

In semi-conductors there are two sorts of effect.   One
occurs inside, and the other on the surface.   Differences
in wave-length of the illuminating light do not produce
parallel differences in the two effects.   The phenomenon
can be investigated by illuminating a thin wedge of cuprous
oxide far from the edge, and near to the edge.   As the ray
is moved nearer the edge the effect changes from an inside
to a surface effect.   Jouse has laid very thin sheets on semi-
conductors by evaporation in a vacuum, and found that
they gave a three-hundredfold increase in rectification and
for the photoelectric effect.

Semi-conductors are important because they are the
typical substances.   Metals and insulators are abnormal
substances in which electrons are respectively free and fixed.
The study of semi-conductors should provide insight into

the nature of the breakdown in insulators, because their electrons are not entirely free or fixed, and the experimenter should be able to determine how the movement of electrons which forms the breakdown, or beginning of conductivity in an insulator, starts and develops. This cannot easily be studied in a metal because the breakdown, or beginning of the flow of current, starts too easily, and it cannot easily be studied in an insulator because the breakdown is too sudden.

The researches on the nature of the solid state are among the most original in the Leningrad Physico-Technical Institute. They have grown out of Joffe's interest in and study of the crystalline and amorphous states. Joffe's discussions of the cause of the low value of mechanical strength in solids, and of the mechanism of the rupture of brittle substances, are admirable examples of the work of the Leningrad school. Solid bodies are known to consist of tightly packed collections of atoms. X-ray analysis has shown that the majority of solids are crystalline, and has given exact information about the distances between the individual atoms and between the ordered rows of atoms, in very many crystalline substances. The knowledge of the inner structure of solids, combined with the general knowledge of the physical properties of atoms, provides a method of estimating the mechanical strength of a solid, as the mechanical strength of a brick wall might be calculated from a knowledge of the strength of the bricks and the mortar binding them together.

When the strength of a solid is calculated from the arrangement of its constituent molecules and atoms, and the mutual forces between them, a remarkable result is obtained. It is found that solids should be many thousand times stronger than the strengths found in practice by simple mechanical tests. Besides offering an extraordinary contradiction between theory and practice, this fact is of great suggestive significance. If the tensile strength of solids is several thousand times less than is theoretically possible, the explanation of the cause of the weakness may lead to methods of removing it. Technical physicists

would then be able to supply humanity with materials
thousands of times stronger than those in use. The
effect of this on industry, architecture, and all of the
material accessories of human life would be revolutionary,
and the appearance of the world of human construction
would be transformed.

Joffe considers that this disagreement is easily explained
by an examination of the mechanism of rupture. The stress
at the place where rupture occurs is always many times
greater than the mean value of the stress of the whole of the
cross-section. He says the best evidence for this is provided by the brilliant experiments of A. Griffith on the
influence of discontinuities on the tensile strength of glass.

Recent researches on the solid state are showing that the
researches made by Griffith on the strength of materials are
of even greater importance than had been generally supposed. His insight seems to have been touched with
genius.

The calculated strength of a crystal of rock salt is about
200 kilograms per square millimetre, while the observed
strength is 0·4 kg. per sq. mm.

Another indication that the strength of molecular cohesion is much greater than the average stress producing
rupture is given by the observation that the rupture often
starts in places where the material is still elastic. If the
rupture were directly due to the breakdown of the forces
between the molecules of the material, it would not be
expected to occur while the material was still obeying
Hooke's law, but it would be expected that the stress
producing rupture would be reached when the elasticity
had disappeared, and the material had become plastic.
In practice, the rupture often occurs when the material
ought to be able to recover, if its strength is directly due to
molecular cohesion.

Joffe, Levitskaya, and others have demonstrated the
remarkable fact that the strength of rock salt is increased
twenty times when immersed in hot water. Griffith showed
that the strength of glass increases ten times if the crevices
in its surface are suitably treated. Orowan has shown that

if mica is stretched so that the edges receive no stress, its strength increases by ten times from 30 to 300 kg. per sq. mm. There are two sorts of rupture, plastic and brittle. The first is usually accompanied by an appreciable change in form of the material under stress, while the second is not. Both sorts may be produced in the same material by changing the rate of loading.

Kirpitchova, Levitskaya and Joffe made the first measurement of the elastic limit of a crystal of rock salt by X-ray methods, and obtained the low value of 920 gm. per sq. mm., or about half a ton to the square inch. Later measurements by a mechanical method gave 200 gm. per sq. mm. Obreimov devised an ingenious method of measuring the elastic limit by the appearance of optical double refraction along the planes where the gliding of the crystal layers began. This gave the value 70 gm. per sq. mm. Classen-Nekludova applied the method to carefully annealed pure artificial and natural crystals, and obtained the value of about 10 gm. per sq. mm.

Podashevsky has obtained the same value by measuring the change in photoelectric current produced in the crystal by plastic deformation. The elastic limit of single crystals of metals is also equally low, and increases rapidly as plastic deformation increases up to the point of continuous flow.

The opinion that a solid body is distinguished from a liquid by the possession of a high elastic limit for shearing stresses, is founded on the study of glasses and crystalline materials that have previously been plastically deformed. The mechanical properties of a crystal are changed by plastic deformation.

Kirpitchova and Joffe showed in 1918 that the plastic deformation of a rock salt crystal distorts the crystal lattice, and breaks the crystal into a number of pieces along the planes of slip. Obreimov and Shubnikov in 1927 showed by double-refraction methods that tensile and compressive stresses of 10 kg. per sq. mm. occur at the boundaries of the pieces. The phenomenon of deformation first observed by P. Ehrenfest and Joffe was carefully studied by Classen-Nekludova, who found that it consisted of multiples of unit shearing motions. Orowan has recently given a theory of this mechanism.

In 1932 Stepanov made the important suggestion that when the layers in a crystal began to slip under strain, the energy developed between the adjacent layers should produce a temporary rise of temperature. His suggestion appears to be confirmed by the observation that the electrical conductivity along slip planes in rock salt increases during plastic deformation, and may be due to a temporary melting of the adjacent material. There is evidence from annealing and recrystallization effects that large changes of temperature occur at the planes of slip in other crystals when they are bent or deformed, though the temporary rises may not be sufficient to produce melting.

During the short period of slipping the cohesion in the boundary layer may fall even to that of the liquid state. The sliding produces crevices, inside the crystal and on its surface, which reduce its strength. Layers adjacent to the slip region are left in a state of stress.

It is generally supposed, contrary to Stepanov's theory, that plastic deformation increases the tensile strength, but the effect is secondary. It increases the elastic limit mainly by distorting the crystal lattice. This has the effect of preventing sliding up to a new higher limit, so rupture does not occur.

When the amount of slip between the crystal planes is increased the stresses at the discontinuities increases until at some point, probably on the surface, the theoretical limit of strength is reached, and the rupture begins. The elastic limit and mechanical strength of non-crystalline substances such as glass, resin and varnish, are not influenced by plastic flow.

If the elastic limit of a crystal is made, by suitable treatment, equal to the practical tensile strength, the material becomes brittle. Rupture occurs without plastic deformation, but the observed strength is much less than the calculated strength. Smekal and Zwicky have suggested this is due to internal faults, and Griffith and Joffe that it is due to surface cracks. Joffe remarks that while internal irregularities may produce weaknesses along, for example, the sharp edge of an included crystal, the mosaic formation should make the slip planes uneven and prevent sliding, and so increase the strength.

The importance of surface conditions was shown by two experiments made by Joffe and Levitskaya. A crystal of rock salt was loaded, and the surface dissolved away by hot water during the experiment. The strength of the crystal increased by more than twenty times. The result was widely criticised. Polanyi suggested the elastic limit had been lowered by the water. When, however, the elastic limit was measured, it was found to be unchanged. Smekal suggested the water had penetrated the crystal and made sliding between the planes easier, which produced an increase in strength.

Joffe and Levitskaya showed, also, that a saturated solution of salt had no strengthening effect, so its water was unable to penetrate the crystal, in contradiction to Smekal's suggestion.

Classen-Nekludova then smeared a thin strip of vaseline on a crystal, leaving the rest of the surface uncovered. When this crystal was loaded and treated with hot water, it showed no increase of strength over that of a dry crystal. This one small dry area on the surface was sufficient to prevent the crystal from being strengthened. Though nearly the whole of the surface of the crystal was exposed to the hot water, there was no increase in strength due to penetration of water through the exposed surface, as there should have been, if Smekal's suggestion had been correct.

Joffe and Levitskaya plunged a sphere of rock crystal, that had been thoroughly cooled in liquid air, into a bath of hot water or liquid tin. Calculations show that after one or two seconds the core of the crystal should be stretched by the expanded outer layers by a tension of 70 kg. per sq. mm. But the sphere was not ruptured in spite of the stress being far beyond that of the practical strength. As already mentioned, E. Orowan of Budapest has shown that the tensile strength of mica is increased ten times when the stress is applied without involving the edges.

Orowan showed also that sheets of mica without crevices on the edges emitted a clear sound, when struck, and had high strength, while the same sheets with crevices on the edges emitted a dull clang and had low strength.

Davidenkov and Wittmann found that the rupture of polycrystalline steel under a blow from a pendulum changes from the brittle to the plastic sort at a temperature of — 120° Centigrade. This transition point is decreased by 20° C. if the surface of the steel is etched and polished, and implies that the tensile strength is increased by the removal of discontinuities from the surface of the steel.

Joffe concludes that these various experiments indicate that the practical weakness of materials is principally due to cracks or sharp discontinuities on the surface, and not to small internal faults. The internal faults of a crystalline substance may, however, be of practical importance as they increase the elastic limit, and hence alter the distribution of stresses producing rupture at low temperature.

Various phenomena suggest that the strength of substances such as glass and quartz depends on the condition of the surface. Excellent experiments bearing on this theory have been made by Yurkov and Alexandrov. The tensile strength of the material in a glass rod increases with decrease in diameter : the glass in a fibre is much stronger than the glass in a rod, though both may have been taken from the same specimen of glass. Griffith suggested that the extra strength of the fibres was due to a layer of orientated molecules on the surface, which had much greater strength than normal glass. His suggestion was disproved by dissolving the surface from a glass rod, about 1 square millimetre in cross-section, with fluoric acid. The tensile strength of the glass in the thin filament left after the removal of the supposedly extra strong surface layer was not less than that of the glass in the normal rod, but was three to five times greater. The strength of filaments prepared by dissolving the surface proved to be the same as that of filaments prepared by softening in a gas flame, and stretching.

The influence of the condition of the surface has been

demonstrated by condensing vapours on the surfaces of filaments. The strength of glass and quartz filaments that have been thoroughly dried in a good vacuum is about five times that of filaments on which water-vapour has been condensed. Alcohol and benzol reduce the strength to one-third and one-half, respectively. It has been shown that the effective layers must be more than one molecule thick.

These experiments indicated that the normal weakness of glass and quartz is due to sharp irregularities on the surface, and the experimenters then inquired whether these irregularities persisted throughout the material. The tensile strengths were measured during the process of solution. If the sharp faults were distributed evenly throughout the material, some of them would be uncovered from time to time by the dissolving fluid. The smoothing of such faults occurs slowly, while the elastic stresses produced at a sharp end of a fault spread with the velocity of sound, so the uncovering of the faults ought to lead to rupture, as in a rod whose surface had not been dissolved away. Experiment confirmed that there was no difference in strength between an ordinary filament loaded in air, and a dissolved filament loaded in fluoric acid solution. A filament that had been strengthened by etching in fluoric acid regained its initial weakness when replaced in the same fluoric acid solution.

These experiments showed that the faults responsible for rupture occur throughout the material but are dangerous only when they reach the surface.

Grebenshtchikov showed that the surface of glass is usually covered by a colloidal sheet that expands by absorption when exposed to water. He was able to detect a measurable stress produced in crevices by the swelling of the colloidal silica. Every surface crevice is distended in this way, and under a small additional load the crevice extends.

The theory of the dependence of the tensile strength of bodies on cracks in the surface would suggest, at the first sight, that there should be large variations in the strengths of materials, according to the accidental existence of an excessively large or small number of surface cracks. This is in conflict with the fact that glasses have fairly definite strengths. The contradiction is explained by the large number of small faults spread through a body. The statistical effect of the large number and distribution is to confer fairly definite normal strengths. The existence of the statistical effect is confirmed by experiments on the variation of strength in thin filaments. As the filaments become thinner the variation becomes larger, owing to the relative increase in the irregularity of the distribution of faults. The strengths of a hundred samples of filaments of pyrex glass varied from 12 to 43 kg. per sq. mm., about a mean of about 25, in a roughly Gaussian distribution. The fluctuations in glasses of complicated composition were much greater.

These observations are easily explained by supposing that the strength of the glass depends on faults on the surface. The strength of a glass rod is determined by the size of the largest crevice or fault on its surface. As a big rod would have a large surface the chance of a large fault appearing on it would be greater, and the practical tensile strength of its glass ought to be relatively small. As the rod becomes thinner, the chance of a big fault being on its surface decreases, and the difference in size between the various faults becomes less. This explains the better agreement between observed and theoretical strength for filaments. The tensile strength of the very thin filament must be greater than that of rods because the big faults would be larger than the thickness of the filament. The filament could not have been made if the existence of the big faults had persisted, for at some stage in the thinning process the thickness of the filament would suddenly have become zero when the whole cross-section of the filament was occupied by the big fault.

According to the same principles, a long should be weaker than a short filament, because the chance of a big fault occurring in its surface should be greater. The Leningrad experimenters find the strength of a 5 cm. filament was 42 kg. per sq. mm., while a 9-cm. filament was 32.

It follows from this theory of the strength of glass and quartz fibres that the practical tensile strength of the thinnest filaments, or of rods whose surface faults have been rendered innocuous, should approach the theoretical value deduced from molecular cohesion.

Joffe and his colleagues found the strength of rock salt to increase from 0·4 kg. per sq. mm. in air to 10 or 30, and even as much as 160 kg. per sq. mm., in hot water. Piatty observed values of the same order. The theoretical tensile strength of rock crystal is 200 kg. per sq. mm.

Walter has shown that the tensile strength of thin sheets of mica may rise to 500 kg. per sq. mm., compared with the normal figure of 10. Yurkov has shown that the strength of thin quartz fibres was about 2000 kg. per sq. mm., compared with the normal 100 ; and thin glass filaments was 400 kg. per sq. mm., compared with the normal 10. Joffe concludes that the theoretical strengths of these materials deduced from the cohesion of their molecules may be correct. The Griffith crack theory explains the weakness of these materials in practice, and is confirmed by the statistical variation in the strengths of specimens that have been tested.

The strong interest of the Leningrad school in the problems of the solid state is seen in the researches of P. P. Kobeko, I. J. Nelidov, and others on the nature of amorphous bodies and its relation to the property of electrical insulation. As Kobeko has remarked, an examination of electrical engineering practice shows that amorphous bodies are usually employed for electrical insulation. The usual insulating materials include natural and artificial resins, vulcanized rubber compounds and films of dry oils, all of which are amorphous. Crystalline films of cellulose ethers are used, but in a state in which they resemble colloidal systems. Paper is converted into an insulator by impregnating it with a suitable oil or substance with uniform structure.

This employment of amorphous bodies as insulators is not unexpected, as their electrical homogeneity is enormously greater than that of crystalline aggregates, and there is the possibility of transition into a plastic state simply by the change of the coefficient of viscosity of the material.

The explanation of the insulating properties of amorphous bodies must depend also on an understanding of their structure, and of the phenomenon of under-cooling in which a substance remains non-crystalline far below the normal temperature of crystallization, and of the phenomena of condensation, polymerization, and vulcanization, by which substances are converted into the amorphous state.

The influence of structure on the electrical properties of substances is illustrated by the electrical conductivity of micro-crystalline aggregates. These usually contain interstices filled with air. Their surfaces are usually damp and the electric current passes through the damp surfaces and not through the body of the material. The properties of the aggregate depend on those of its pores. For instance, the electrical resistance of calcium carbonate in the forms of a crystalline aggregate is one million times less than that of a pure single crystal of calcium carbonate.

Tamman and others have shown that a liquid substance is strictly amorphous only below a definite characteristic temperature. At this temperature its physical properties change suddenly. The change of the specific heat and the dielectric constant are related to the rotation of the molecules, and are connected with a sharp change in the viscosity. The critical temperature is different for different substances. For glass it is about $400°$ C., for colophane it is $29°$ C., and for ethylalcohol it is $-190°$ C. In the neighbourhood of, and below, the critical temperature the amorphous body is brittle and friable.

This critical temperature is of great importance in connection with the electrical and mechanical properties of amorphous insulators. The shape and properties of the molecules of the constituent materials is also of great importance. This is shown by their relation to the dielectric constant. If the molecules are polar, or lop-sided, they will require more energy than homopolar, or symmetrical molecules, for orientation by electrical forces. It follows that dielectric losses in insulators made of symmetrical molecules will tend to be small.

As the temperature rises to the critical point, and the insulator becomes plastic, the molecules can rotate and absorb energy and produce dielectric losses.

Kobeko has shown that the dielectric losses of insulators used at a particular temperature can be calculated from the melting-point of the material. It is possible to deduce from a simple law some of the properties of an insulator made of a mixture of two amorphous bodies each of whose melting-points is known. For instance, the melting-points of alcohol and of sugar are known. The temperature of solidification of the mixture, which lies between those temperatures, determines the variation of the electrical properties of the mixture with temperature.

This discovery is of industrial importance as it indicates that insulators made of amorphous materials whose critical temperatures are known will break down under conditions that might not have been foreseen in factory tests. The knowledge of adhesive substances is also advanced by these studies of amorphous bodies. The sticking power of guns is influenced by the critical temperature. Under this temperature they are brittle, and at some distance above, they become lubricants.

The best adhesives are made out of polymerized substances. Polymerization is that process of making the molecules of substances cling together in chains. Molecules individually simple sometimes are able to cling together in chains containing hundreds of members. These chains coil up and become mixed together. Artificial rubber is an example of a material produced out of relatively simple individual molecules by polymerization. Such materials tend to become amorphous as the long chains become involved and intricated. They cannot crystallize, because they cannot order themselves. As J. D. Bernal has put it, molecules with arms and legs cannot be fitted together. When the molecules of a substance are small, they tend to arrange themselves in crystals. The difference in behaviour of small and large molecules of the same

substance is illustrated by sterol. If it is cooled, it crystal-
lizes, but if it is heated its molecules assemble in chains
and it becomes amorphous.

These studies of the amorphous state suggest the directions in which technologists will search in future for new
insulating, adhesive and elastic materials. They will not
be satisfied with empirical experiment as in the past, but
will begin with a statement of the desired properties in a
material and then attempt to synthesize it according to
the fundamental laws of the properties of materials, being
gradually discovered by researches in which the Leningrad
school has a distinguished part.

Nasledov and Charavsky have been investigating the
properties of semi-conductors. They have been measuring
the conductivity produced in selenium by the photoelectric
effect. It is measured when the selenium is not illuminated,
and then when it is illuminated with a 1000-watt lamp.
After the lamp is switched off, the conductivity remains
greater than before illumination, it does not fall to its
original value. They attempt to find how the growth of
conductivity can be explained in terms of the number of
quanta of light energy needed to produce the result. There
is a close connection between them.

They are also investigating the behaviour of semi-
conductors at high pressures. According to the theory
of Fröhlich, the conductivity should increase by 50 per
cent at high pressures. The pressures are applied through
a liquid and are homogeneous. Experiment shows that
under a pressure of 6000 kg. per sq. cm. the conductivity
rises, but not as much as predicted by Fröhlich; the rise
is 8 per cent only.

The dependence of the photoelectric effect on the surface
layer has been studied by investigating the behaviour of a
layer of cuprous oxide, separated from a copper plate by a
layer of silica.

Several interesting researches have been conducted by
Dukelsky. He was a member of the meteorological
expedition to Mount Alaguez in the Caucasus. This
expedition collected valuable observations on solar radiation,

cosmic rays and other phenomena. Dukelsky is much interested in mountain-climbing. He said that Alaguez is not interesting to mountaineers, and was chosen because heavy apparatus can be carried up easily. Mount Elbrus is also very tedious to a mountaineer.

The expedition was absent from Leningrad for about two and a half months. Observations were made at a station on the top of Alaguez by three men for six weeks. For cosmic-ray observations they used chambers of the type designed by Johnson of the Bartel Foundation, with direct-current feeding. They discovered that the cosmic rays had an aximuthal asymmetry, i.e. the strength of the rays coming from the east is different from those coming from the west, of 9 per cent at a height of 3300 metres.

The observations were made daily for a period of sixteen to eighteen hours. When the temperature was not too low, they worked all night. The temperature varied from $+ 10$ to $- 8°$ C. They had no stove.

The apparatus worked well. They had a petrol engine to drive a dynamo for charging the accumulators. Sometimes they ran out of gasolene.

Dukelsky found that Geiger counters gave trouble. They do not seem to work well in summer, owing, perhaps, to spurious electric charges on the surfaces. The theory and properties of the counter require further study.

The expedition to Mount Elbrus had a Wilson camera. Many cosmic ray photographs were obtained at a height of 4 kilometres, but a large number of these were spoilt during the developing. It was found that the number of cosmic-ray showers increases rapidly with height.

At this point a short account of observations made by A. B. Verigo of the Leningrad Geophysical Institute may be conveniently introduced. He measured the intensity of the rays at heights of 3300, 4200 and 5400 metres. The measures of the latter height were made continuously during thirty hours. No significant change of intensity was observed, and no evidence of a connection with sun-rays or star-rays was obtained. His results agreed with those found by Millikan at analogous heights in America,

but were considerably less than those obtained by Kolhörster.   At 5400 metres the intensities were three times
less than those reported by Kolhörster.   Verigo carried the
electrometer on his back to the top of the mountain, and
sat there during the periods of observation.

Verigo measured the absorption of cosmic rays in water
by taking a Kolhörster electrometer in a submarine during
a journey under the surface of the water in the Gulf of
Finland.   This method of measuring the absorption of
cosmic rays by water has the advantage of avoiding the
exposure of the electrometer to changes of temperature and
pressure, which occurs when it is sunk by itself.

Verigo placed an electrometer in a big gun on a battle-
ship.   The electrometer was protected by the steel of the
gun-barrel and the armoured turret, and was used to
measure the absorption of the cosmic rays by known thicknesses of steel.   The electrometer was placed in three
positions; outside on the top of the gun-turret, within the
turret on the barrel of a gun, and in the breech of the gun
within the turret.

The increase of the absorption coefficient after the rays
pass through a thick layer of steel was observed, and the
absolute value of the mass coefficient of absorption of the
steel was found to be the same, within the limits of experiment, as that of water.

Dukelsky's laboratory researches include studies of
X-ray phenomena.   He has worked for a long period on
the energy distribution of the continuous X-ray spectrum.
It is difficult to do this satisfactorily as the target must be
very thin, in order to ensure that the cathode rays exciting
the X-rays do not produce more than one excitation.   But
the X-rays from the thin cathode are very feeble, as the
thin foil melts if bombarded intensely, and the measurement
of their energy distribution with a crystal spectrometer is
very difficult.   Dukelsky found that the energy distribution
in a continuous spectrum from aluminium foil could be
investigated with an ionization chamber equipped with a
Geiger-Müller counter.   For thin targets the energy is
found to be independent of the frequency, and at the

high-frequency limit there is a sharp discontinuity. This
result is in accord with Sommerfeld's theory of the continuous X-ray spectrum. With thick targets the energy
distribution is represented by Kulenkampff's well-known
formula.

The X-ray department is superintended by Lukirsky.
He says that the development of science since the revolution has greatly increased his opportunities for research.
His experimental work shows high manipulative skill. He
works on electron diffraction, and uses apparatuses that are
masterpieces of the glassblower's art. He has investigated
the index of refraction for fast and slow electrons. The
index for the slow electrons was determined with single
crystals of graphite. All of the measurements were made
in vacuum. The variation of the angle of reflection with
speed, and of refraction with temperature, have been
measured. The accomplishment of these varied measurements in vacuum demands very complicated vacuum apparatus. The apparatus made by Lukirsky and the Institute's
glass-blowers bears comparison with the best, and surpasses
most, of the similar apparatuses made in physics laboratories in other parts of the world.

In this department, Usiskin, who was killed in one of
the stratosphere ascents, determined the position of the
hydrogen atom in ammonium chloride, or sal ammoniac, by
X-rays. This was the first determination of the position
of a hydrogen ion in a lattice.

The Simon point for ammonium chloride is — 70° C.
They believe it is connected with a change in the position
of the hydrogen ion.

They have investigated the depth of surface which gives
the maximum refraction for an electron wave. The thickness of a layer of silver on a cellophane sheet was determined
by making a layer of equal thickness on a tungsten wire.
The thickness of the layer was determined through the
evaporation of the silver by sending a powerful current
through the wire. It was found that the thickness that
can be penetrated by the wave of a fast electron is very
small.

Reyanov is investigating photoelectric phenomena, particularly the effect of layers of hydrogen atoms on pieces of potassium.   A layer of hydrogen atoms one atom thick greatly increases the effect, but a second layer decreases it. They suggest the first layer of hydrogen atoms goes under the surface of the potassium, while the second layer lies above the surface.   The atoms of the first layer are strongly attached to the potassium atoms, and provide an example of a new type of adsorption.

When potassium with a double layer of adsorbed hydrogen atoms is heated the upper hydrogen layer evaporates, and the photoelectric effect increases.

In another experiment a piece of potassium was cooled to the temperature of liquid air, and its surface was covered with a single layer of hydrogen atoms by adsorption.   This produced a decrease in the strength of the photoelectric effect.   It appears that at the temperature of liquid air the first type of internal adsorption is not possible.   When the liquid air is removed, the temperature rises, the sort of adsorption changes, and the strength of the photoelectric effect increases.

Prilezear is investigating the velocity distribution of photoelectrons.   It is influenced by the thickness of the metals, and varies with the work-function.   The spectral distribution is a function of the optical properties of the surface.   When the intensity of light under the surface of a metal is examined, it is found to vary selectively with different polarizations.   This provides the explanation of the selective photoelectric effect.

Reyanov is attempting to find a wave-mechanical theory of the hydrogen adsorption influence on the photoelectric effect.

Machalov is studying the total reflection of X-rays in unimolecular layers.   A single layer of molecules of a fatty acid may produce interference effects, because the distance between the two surfaces may be relatively large.   He has been experimenting with a compound of stearin amide with one atom of iodine.   The intensities of the reflected and direct beams are measured simultaneously.

The researches of the Leningrad school on cosmic rays have been distinguished. D. Skobeltzyn's discovery of very swift particles connected with cosmic rays is one of the chief discoveries in recent experimental physics, and perhaps the most important single physical experiment that has been made in the Soviet Union. In 1923 he started a systematic study of the wave-radiations from radioactive substances. In 1926 he extended his study to the velocity of electrons struck by wave-radiations from radioactive sources. The electrons were released by the wave-radiations in the chamber of a Wilson apparatus. In order to determine their velocities, the chamber was enclosed in a magnetic field. The degree of the curvature of the electron tracks by the field indicated the speeds of the electrons.

Skobeltzyn found that nearly all the tracks of the electrons were severely bent, and some formed complete circles. But a few tracks were almost perfectly straight. The difference between the two sorts of track was most pronounced. The straight tracks were due to particles too swift to be noticeably deflected by a field of 1,500 gauss. Skobeltzyn thought at first that these very swift particles might be due to " runaway " electrons generated by thunderstorms, according to the suggestion of Wilson, as they seemed to start from outside the chamber. It was clear that these electrons were far more energetic than any emitted from radioactive substances. By 1929 Skobeltzyn had collected thirty-two examples of straight tracks in 631 photographs. He found conization was produced by them at a rate about equal to the rate at which air is ionized by cosmic rays. The measurement of the curvature of the tracks showed that some of the electrons had an energy of at least 15 million volts. Some of the tracks occurred in pairs, and one was a triplet. The independent appearance of pairs and triplets is exceedingly improbable, so they probably came from one centre. Rutherford had suggested the cosmic rays might disintegrate atoms: these multiple tracks appeared at first to be examples of such disintegrations. Later research has shown this is not so, and that the multiple tracks are probably due to radiations started by the cosmic rays through another mechanism.

Skobeltzyn's methods were followed by C. D. Anderson at the California Institute of Technology. He used more powerful fields. In 1932 he found a track that appeared to be due to an electron, but was bent the wrong way. The electron had behaved as if it had a positive instead of a negative charge. This was followed by the confirmatory observations of Blackett and Occhialini, and the existence of the positive electron became clear.

The discovery of the positive electron revealed the exact meaning of the extraordinary implications of the wave-equation, pointed out by Dirac. He had explained that the equation contains two series of roots, and that both presumably had a physical significance. He interpreted the negative values as referring to protons, and conceived the proton as an image of the electron. This was not quite correct, as the proton is very much heavier than the electron. Anderson's discovery proved that Dirac had deduced the existence of the positron by theoretical arguments, but had not been bold enough to assert the existence of a new unit of nature on purely mathematical evidence. Dirac illustrated his theory of the positron by the idea of a hole in an electron-packed universe. Such a hole would have some of the properties of a positively charged particle. When an electron dropped into the hole, it would combine with the positron. The particles would be annihilated, and be converted into two units of wave-energy, or radiation.

This theory suggested at once that high-energy radiation might have the power of being converted back into pairs of negative and positive electrons. Blackett and the Curie-Joliots soon observed examples of the phenomenon, and Skobeltzyn found examples among his old photographs.

At present Skobeltzyn is studying this phenomenon of materialization, as it has been named by the Curie-Joliots, with his customary originality and independence. In collaboration with E. Stepanova he has collected evidence that positrons may be produced during the collision of electrons. They have detected one positron for every twenty-five or thirty electrons with energies of more than one million volts emitted under ordinary conditions from a common radium preparation.

The positrons are mostly slow, of about 100,000 volts energy. They have calculated the mean effective cross-section of primary particles of energies of 1 to 3 million volts from their data. They find the cross-section of an atom of lead is of the order 10^{-22} square centimetres, and the effective area per atom appears to be proportional to the atomic number. This value of the effective area is about one hundred times greater than that given by the photoelectric emission of positrons by photons of the same energy. Skobeltzyn points out that this appears wholly incompatible with theoretical results. He considers that the Wilson cloud chamber provides a reliable means of establishing the emission of secondary positrons by electrons, and for studying the phenomenon, but that it seems impossible to reconcile experimental results with theoretical predictions. He is inclined to believe there are other types of positrons, besides those foreseen by Dirac, and that a simple law of emission exists.

Skobeltzyn's bold confidence in experimental results, and acceptance of their implications, though they may conflict most uncomfortably with current theoretical views, is characteristic. He is a scientist of the finest quality.

The Physico-Technical Institute has some rooms in the old Polytechnical Institute, now named the Industrial Institute. Skobeltzyn's laboratory is in one of these rooms. His apparatus, though complicated, is made of the simplest materials, and various oddments have been incorporated in it. The timing is done by an old Atwood's machine. Who would have expected such an ancient familiar of the class-room to have had a part in the discovery of the particulate nature of cosmic rays? The illumination of the chamber is done with a 20-ampere lamp which is subjected to an overcurrent of 100 amperes for one second. In the ingenious use of simple apparatus, and independence of judgment, Skobeltzyn resembles C. T. R. Wilson. He has four scientific colleagues and one laboratory assistant.

The Soviet researches on cosmic rays are not restricted to the discovery of the swift particles. In 1926 Myssovsky and Tuvim first observed the relation between the barometric pressure and the intensity of the rays. Observations by the River Neva showed the intensity is generally weaker when the barometer is high than when it is low. This is explained by the greater mass of air in the atmosphere above the apparatus when the barometer is high, and the consequent greater absorption of the rays during the penetration of the atmosphere.

They also investigated the direction of the rays through the watertower at Leningrad, and concluded that they arrived uniformly from all points on the celestial globe. The preference to the vertical at sea-level was due to absorption of rays inclined to the vertical, and hence having had a longer path through the air. Myssovsky now works at the Radium Institute and is engaged on plans for a Wilson chamber that will operate in a magnetic field of 80,000 gauss.

Soviet physicists have also assisted in the stratosphere ascents, and have collected data of the intensity of the cosmic rays at great altitudes.

Excellent experimental work on radioactivity and nuclear physics is being done by A. I. Alikhanov. He has devised an ingenious combination of Geiger-Müller counters with a magnetic field, so that the charged particles in the beam from a radioactive source can be separated from the wave-radiations. He obtained the first curve of the decay of radio-nitrogen, and showed that different methods of preparation gave substances with the same radioactive properties. He found that the disintegration of radio-aluminium prepared by bombarding magnesium with helium nuclei gave negative electrons.

In a paper with M. S. Kosodaev he has given a description of the distribution of the velocities of positive electrons produced by bombarding lead with wave-radiations from a radium preparation, and also of positive electrons emitted directly from a radioactive source.

If the positive electrons emitted directly from a radio-

active source are due to a change in the nuclei of the radioactive atoms, then a relation between the spectra of the
positive electrons and of the wave-radiations from the
source is to be expected. But Alikhanov and Kosodaev
find the spectra of the positrons from the two sources are
quite different. Hence the mechanism of the direct emission of positrons from the radioactive source must be of
another sort. They have suggested two other hypotheses;
that the positrons are emitted from the atomic nuclei with
an appropriate change in the nuclear charge. This
mechanism would not require the emission of an electron.
According to the second hypothesis, the energy of an
electron emitted from the nucleus will be transformed into
a positive and negative electron. They could not decide
from the data before them which process occurs. But the
first process would lead to serious difficulties.

Alikhanov is about twenty-five years old, and a native of
Armenia. His future researches will be awaited with high
expectation.

I. W. Kurtchatov is another young physicist of exceptional ability. He has published a number of papers on
the properties of Rochelle salt, or sodium potassium tar-
tarate, and recently on artificial radioactivity.

The electrical properties of crystals of Rochelle salt are
unusual. The dielectric constant rises to 20,000, and is
four times the normal figure. If the intensity of the
electric field is varied, the dielectric constant diminishes
with intensity, and gives a curve similar to the saturation of
the magnetization curve in iron. Thus the dielectric constant
of Rochelle salt has a parallel with the permeability of iron.
This suggests that its dielectric behaviour is due to a dipole
effect. The dipoles in the crystal are orientated by the
electric field. Kobeko and Kurtchatov have shown that
Debye's dipole equation, established by experiments on
various gases, may also be applied to Rochelle salt.

If the dielectric constant is investigated in relation to
temperature it is found to be at maximum values at $-15°$ C.
and $+22.5°$ C. It is suggested that these maxima occur
through the disappearance of spontaneous orientation. The

maximum at 22·5° C. is due to the heat movement of the dipoles, and that at — 15° C. is due to a reciprocal action between the dipoles and the lattice.

Similar effects are observed when an ammonia ion is substituted for the potassium ion in Rochelle salt.

The effect of high pressures applied by Bridgman's technique has been investigated.

It is found that a uniform external field of twenty volts per centimetre is sufficient to change the orientation of the dipoles in Rochelle crystals. Weak fields change the orientation in about one minute, and powerful fields change it in a hundred-millionth of a second. These figures are in general agreement with Landau's theory of the effect.

Debye's formula is not applicable to other solid substances because the dipoles tend to pair, and remain unaffected by the orientating forces. J. D. Bernal has suggested that the distance between the atoms in Rochelle crystals is large enough to allow easy orientation.

In his recent researches, Kurtchatov has investigated artificial disintegration and radioactivity.

His laboratory contains a 500,000-volt Cockcroft disintegration apparatus, and a Lawrence apparatus is being tested. The protons are accelerated in a field of 12,000 to 15,000 volts, up to an energy of 500,000 volts. Difficulties have been experienced in the elimination of high-frequency fields, and in the operation of measuring instruments.

The Cockcroft apparatus gives a current of 100 microamperes at a uniform potential. The protons are obtained as canal rays from a 50,000-volt tube. Only 3 per cent of them are scattered in the accelerating-tube.

Boron was bombarded with protons, with the production of triplets of helium nuclei. The sum of the energies of these particles has been estimated by different observers to be 9 million, and 11 million electron volts, respectively. Sinelnikov and Kurtchatov believed they had detected a two-million volt wave-radiation, with 200,000 volt protons. They confirmed the existence of the wave-radiation by absorption experiments in lead. Lauritsen found no wave-radiation when bombarding with million-volt protons. Perhaps the processes of disintegration are different at different voltages.

The spread of the group of helium nuclei is not quite in one plane, so perhaps the wave-radiation is perpendicular to the plane.

Bombardment of lithium with protons gives helium nuclei of mass four and three respectively. The lithium was exposed to a proton current of ten micro-amperes at 350,000 volts for fifteen minutes. No evidence of induced radioactivity could be detected.

It was assumed that the wave-radiations observed during the bombardment of the lithium are due to the capture of an electron by the helium nuclei of mass three, and subsequent disintegration of three protons and a wave-radiation.

Kurtchatov has recently published papers on the Fermi effect. In collaboration with Myssovsky, Eremeyev and Shtchepkin he has examined the radioactivity induced in aluminium, silicon, phosphorus, bromine, silver and iodine by neutrons ejected from fluorine and beryllium. They have shown that whenever the nucleus is formed by the capture of a neutron without the emission of a heavy particle, it becomes radioactive irrespective of whether the neutrons are from fluorine or beryllium. In addition, they have shown that the neutrons from fluorine can produce radioactive phosphorus.

With G. Latishev he has investigated the number of positrons and electrons emitted in the disintegration of radioactive bromine, and the passage of neutrons through substances containing hydrogen. The experiments were made with a Wilson chamber, surrounded by a magnetic field of 450 gauss. The emission of positrons from the radioactive bromine was shown to be small, and probably due to the formation of pairs of electrons by fast electrons escaping from the radioactive nucleus.

Fermi has shown that if neutrons are surrounded with compounds containing hydrogen their velocities may be reduced to the order of thermal velocities, that is, of a few kilometres a second.   Kurtchatov and Latishev have shown that nevertheless a considerable number of fast neutrons from a beryllium source pass through a water filter 10 to 15 inches thick.   He has investigated the scattering of slow neutrons in collaboration with Eremeyev and Shtchepkin. A beryllium neutron source was surrounded with various thicknesses of water.   The neutrons moving at any point in the water were detected by a probe consisting of a silver plate in which they could induce radioactivity.   It is clear that if the silver plate is put at any point in the liquid facing the neutron source, some neutrons will strike its face, and others, that have collided with protons in the water molecules behind the plate, will strike its back.   The number of neutrons striking the back of the silver plate is related to the thickness of water behind the plate, and to the mean free path of the neutrons that have rebounded after collisions. Using this relation, Kurtchatov and his colleagues found that the figures obtained in their experiments indicated that the mean free path of the thermal or slow neutrons was 1·2 centimetres.   The effective radius of collision of a thermal neutron with a proton was found to be two-million-millionths of a centimetre.

The Institute of Agricultural Physics has rooms in the Physico-Technical Institute.   The chief members of its scientific staff are F. Kolyasev, B. Alexandrov and A. Kurtener.   They work on the physical properties of soil, biophysics, and the influence of physical forces on living organisms.

They have investigated the effects of ultra-violet radiation on yeasts, white mice and other organisms, and in particular the retardation of growth by these rays.   The mice are exposed to ultra-violet rays of low intensity for long periods; the reverse of the medical practice.

The feeble rays are measured with an instrument devised by Reyanov for measuring the absolute value of the intensity of ultra-violet rays.   This was used on the Mount Elbrus expedition for measuring the rays at a height of 4000 metres, and it is also useful for measuring biological spectra.

In their researches on the physics of the soil they have

studied soil structure, with the object of changing and regulating it. One of the various methods of doing this is to mix it with suitably treated industrial wastes, and straw, turf and dried grass. The structure of manure is studied, and the nutrition of plants by mineral manures. The effects of the radiation of heat from the soil, especially in districts such as Leningrad, may be large. The temperature, moisture and nitrate content are studied.

Suitable physical treatment can help to convert sand into soil, and increase the size of crops. For instance, crops of oats may be increased by 15 per cent by physical treatment of the soil alone. This has been demonstrated in experimental fields.

The temperature, moisture and dielectric constant of the soil is registered hourly by automatic apparatus. The temperatures are registered from thermophiles on the surface of the soil, and at depths of 5, 10, 20 and 40 centimetres. The dielectric constant is measured by a radio-wave method.

The radiation from the soil is regularly measured. The mechanical effort necessary for breaking clay has been investigated. The physical properties of the clay are changed by mixing it with a gum prepared from turf and the waste products of paper and artificial silk factories. Acids are prepared from this waste. The turf is boiled with alkali. This gummy preparation has a disintegrating effect on soil.

The influence of the colour of soil on the degree of heat-radiation from it has been studied. In hot Central Asia the soil should be covered with white material in order to reduce the absorption of heat, and evaporation. In the cold Leningrad climate the soil should be blackened, in order to increase the heat absorption. They change the colour of the optical properties of the soil by dyeing it with aniline colours. A suitable soil dye may produce at a depth of 20 centimetres the temperature previously existing at 5 centimetres.

For blackening the soil they use an emulsion of bitumen.

The albedo or reflecting power of the soil is measured

with a photo-electric cell with a photo-element filtered for one wave-length.

In their field experiments with oats they have found that treatment of the soil with a black bituminous emulsion has increased the crop by 11 per cent, owing to the increased warmth of the soil.

The moisture content of the soil has been investigated by surface action. A unimolecular film reduces filtration, hile thicker films do not.

The previous pages will give an idea of the range and variety of researches in progress at the Leningrad Physico-Technical Institute. Many interesting workers and researches have not been mentioned. For instance, nothing has been said about the distinguished theoretical researches of A. V. Fock and J. Frenkel, and the researches of Fredericks on anisotropic crystals. As these are highly technical, it is not easy to give a general impression of them here. Frenkel has written on very many subjects and has an encyclopædic knowledge of modern theory, shown by his large volumes on Wave-Mechanics, which have been translated into English. He has an extremely rapid understanding and memory, and is able to write almost verbatim reports, not merely of ordinary speeches, but of the various mathematical papers at a conference on theoretical physics. The instant understanding and remembering of the varied mathematical arguments in different branches of physics is a remarkable gift. The Russian editions of his volumes on Wave-Mechanics sell in tens of thousands. Very few books in the English language on this subject achieve a sale of even one thousand. The general desire of the young students to have a treatise on wave-mechanics shows their desire to have some acquaintance with modern physical ideas. The English student rarely studies wave-mechanics until he has completed a long course on the classical theoretical physics.

Fock is a theorist of another type. He has attacked the problems raised by Dirac's theory of the electron, and recently has improved Hartree's methods of calculating the strengths of atomic fields.

The strength of the Leningrad school of physics is in its variety. This is partly a reflection of the mobile intelligence of its creator, Joffe. The Soviet Union owes much to Joffe for organizing this great school. The variety of subjects of research has led to the discovery of a large variety of talent. In the first decade of the revolution the discovery of variety of talent was the chief task in the creation of a culture of physics in the Soviet Union. Before the Revolution there were few physicists in Russia, and immediately afterwards there were almost none. Thus the first task was the training of a variety of good, not necessarily great, physicists, who would be able to organize physical laboratories of all types in every sort of university and large factory. Under Joffe's leadership, the Physico-Technical Institute accomplished this task splendidly.

Now that the first task of Soviet physics has been accomplished, it is possible to consider where the weak points of Soviet physics may be strengthened. The variety of researches at the Leningrad Physico-Technical Institute, which has been for a long period a foundation of the institute's value, is now, perhaps, tending to produce some avoidable weaknesses. Greater concentration on fewer lines of research would probably produce discoveries of still more profound importance. Many of the highly gifted young physicists there tend to fly after the latest exciting world-discovery, and add a few embellishments to it, and then turn to the next, and add something to that. This produces a body of useful modern work of wide range, and a group of very well-informed investigators, which is of great educational value in the Soviet Union, where the quality of general education requires much improvement. But this spreading of interest makes the discovery of entirely new regions of physical knowledge more difficult. Until the Leningrad physicists concentrate more on a few regions of research it is improbable that they will become the world masters of any region.

The Physico-Technical Institute is at Lesnoe, which is about thirty-five to forty-five minutes on the tramway from the centre of Leningrad. With the old Polytechnical

Institute, now the Industrial Institute, and the Institute of Chemical Physics, and the Electro-Physical Institute it forms an academic colony in the suburban pine-woods.

Many of the heads of departments live in a fine block of flats in the adjacent woods, and others live in blocks of new flats at a distance of about quarter of an hour on the tramway. The contiguous institutes and residences provide a large and varied scientific life. Numerous discussions and lectures can easily be organized, and researches can be done in more than one institute, according to the suitability of the equipment for particular investigation. Members of the staffs often do not go into the city more than once or twice a week. A magnificent secondary school has been erected near to the other buildings, and a scientist's club-house is being erected.

CHAPTER 6

THE PHYSICO-TECHNICAL INSTITUTE OF THE UKRAINE, KHARKOV

I

THIS institute was one of the first off-shoots of the school of physics created by Professor Joffe at the Leningrad Physico-Technical Institute. It was opened in a splendid new building about 1930. The first director of the institute was Professor Obreimov. He was succeeded by Professor Leipunsky, and is now the leader of the Physical Seminar. Leipunsky has recently been succeeded by Professor Davidovitch, and is now devoting himself entirely to research on atomic physics and the phenomena of high-tension electricity. Research physicists in the U.S.S.R. are not at all anxious to obtain directorships. These give them much administrative work, and distract them from the pursuit of physics. The democratic social relations between the members of the staffs of institutes also reduces the attraction which directorial position possesses for some types of person. The difference in standard of living between the scientific members of the staff is not great, so the directorship is not attractive for that reason. Again, many men dislike being directors because this entails many journeys to Moscow and attendance at many committees. The acceptance of directorships is often due to a desire to serve the wishes of the Communist Party. Communist directors will often speak wistfully of their desire to return to the laboratory bench, but that this is not yet possible, because their political and administrative experience is deemed necessary in solving the difficult problems that arise in the development of the new institutes, so few of which are yet ten years old.

The nature of the organization of any institute is partly related to the qualities of the director. For instance, the present director of the Physico-Technical Institute of the Ukraine, Professor Davidovitch, is an administrator accustomed to scientific work, and not a physicist who continues to follow his own line of research besides conducting the administration. Like so many of the new directors and leaders, he is in the thirties, and was educated under Joffe. The training of so many younger men in Joffe's institute has made most of them known to each other. This gives a peculiar homogeneity to the group of the younger Soviet physicists.

Davidovitch studied at Leningrad at the same time as Leipunsky, Hey, and other leaders of his departments. His acquaintance is particularly broad, as he began his physical studies three times. They were continually interrupted by the call of the Communist Party, of which he is an old member, to undertake some onerous special task. He had been an active Communist before the revolution and had been exiled from Russia on account of his political activities. He spent part of his exile in Australia and there he acquired a knowledge of British institutions and the English language. Before he came to Kharkov he was engaged in the Leningrad Laboratory for Research in Road-making.

As Davidovitch is primarily an administrator, the scientific lead in research will come from Leipunsky, who now devotes himself to pure research. Leipunsky has recently spent a year at the Cavendish Laboratory, Cambridge, in research on atomic physics.

In many laboratories there have been two or three leaders: the director, the secretary of the branches of the Trade Unions to which the members of the staff belong, and the secretary of the group of Communists in the laboratory. These formed what is known as a "red triangle". Formerly, the leadership was collective, and had the good points of collective action, but tended to be too slow. The scientific director is now given definitely more power than the others, so that individual responsibility in the chief director has been increased. As the chief of the administrative side of any organization tends to obtain most of the power, the administration chief has often had most influence. Even when the administrative director, or secretary, is not the chief director, he usually has much power because he is generally a member of the Party. Some of these "red directors," or secretaries, of institutes, owe their position more to Party membership than to technical qualifications. When the chief director of an institute is not a member of the Party he usually seeks an administrative director who is a member. A Party member knows other Party members outside the circles of the institute. If he is an old member he probably has known the chief political personalities of the district for years. He has fought in the civil war with colleagues who may now occupy the highest positions in State departments in Moscow. A Communist administrative director with moderate intellectual powers may be able to help an institute much by merely securing the attention of influential persons, who happen to be old friends, for its problems.

This phenomenon of bureaucracy is well-known in Britain, where Oxford and Cambridge graduates, and more particularly, men who have been educated at the most famous boarding-schools, are given administrative appointments, especially by North of England business men, because they have access to influential old school-fellows in London. But the parallel to the "old school tie" phenomenon is weakened in the Soviet Union by the rapidity of changes. Some contend that it will be more serious in the future, when the machinery of life is more settled, and persons have the opportunity of preserving more continuous contacts.

As the number of well-educated young Communists increases, the number of "red directors", whose chief qualification is membership of the Party, decreases. There has been a decrease in the number of purely "red directors" during the last year or two.

The relations of the Kharkov Physico-Technical Institute with industry are close. The Institute in some instances engages in the manufacture of special apparatus for sale to other laboratories and works. Partly owing to these relations it is convenient to have a chief director, such as Professor Davidovitch, who has had industrial scientific experience.

Apparatus being made on an industrial scale includes large Dewar vessels of fifty-litres capacity, and electrostatic condensers. They have engaged in this work to help themselves rather than industry. As soon as industry can supply them with this equipment they will be glad to stop making it.

Various apparatuses are invented in the laboratory, and then a suitable form for industrial use is worked out. For instance, Strelnikov has perfected in the laboratory the industrial design for his rotating anti-cathode X-ray tube.

The engineer Sinelnikov, of the Kharkov Electrical Machine Factory, has worked in the laboratories of the Physico-Technical Institute on the design of an electric motor whose speed can be regulated by changing the frequency of the secondary current.

Another investigation has been concerned with the application of thyratrons for controlling the motors of rolling mills.

A principle of the Soviet policy is the rapid introduction of scientific inventions and ideas into industry. This is facilitated by industrial experience on laboratory directorates, and it is desirable that directors should understand the industrial point of view.

A part of the work of the Kharkov Physico-Technical Institute arises from requests from factories and trusts to investigate certain general problems.

Besides undertaking a certain amount of industrial research, the Institute assists in the training of a number of senior students. During 1935 about twenty students will be given some work in the laboratories in order to see whether they have an interest and aptitude for research.

At present there is not very keen competition for positions

on the research staff of the institute. This is due to the present line of public policy. During the period of the construction of industry there is a special urgency for engineers in new works and plants. The student feels the social urgency of completing the foundation of the new socialist industrial economy. Owing to his special importance at the present time, the engineer enjoys much prestige, so the student feels it would be a specially fine thing to be an engineer.

There is another reason why students should be biased in favour of engineering. Nearly all of them are of proletarian origin and have grown up in contact with industry. Many of them have secured their secondary education while already working in industry.

One of their ablest young men, Vereshtshagin, left the institute and worked in industry for two years. He has returned to research, but nevertheless would like to return to industry.

When the vast numbers of students at the universities and technical high schools have completed their courses, more graduates will be available, and there will be more competition for places in the research institutes. The supply of specialists should begin to become more adequate by the end of the third year of the Second Five Years' Plan.

II

The Kharkov Physico-Technical Institute has a total staff of between two and three hundred workers. About fifty of these are fully qualified research workers, and about twenty more are research students. There is no systematic tuition, but there are seminars. The general Physics seminar is conducted by I. V. Obreimov, and the Theoretical Department of the institute is directed by L. Landau.

About six of the fifty research workers are Communists. Many more Communists are found among the large workshop staff. Some account of the rôle of the Communists in the life of the laboratory will be given later.

The institute has ten departments. The laboratory workshops count as departments, and have a higher standing than in institutes in other countries. This is an important point of difference between many Soviet institutes and Western institutes.

There are three workshops under one manager, who has the same standing as the director of a research department. The workshops are for woodwork, metalwork, and glass-blowing. The glass-blowing workshop has two foremen, while each of the others has one. The metal shop has a staff of about fourteen, and the glass-blowing shop about ten.

The procedure of a physicist who requires a piece of glass-blowing is as follows: he writes a description of his requirement on an order addressed to the glass-blower's workshop, but takes it to the manager of the workshops. The manager writes his own version of the order, gives an estimate of the time it should take, signs it, and gives it to the foreman of the workshop. This system prevents the workshop staff from being disorganized by the importunities of individual physicists. In many Western laboratories there is considerable competition between research workers for the services of the skilled staff in the workshops. The Kharkov system ensures that the work is distributed evenly among the workshops and their staffs, and that no physicist is able to monopolize the best mechanics.

The high degree of the development of workshop organization is partly a reflection of the condition of science in the U.S.S.R. when the Republics were formed. In 1917 there were very few instrument-makers and shops in the country. Instruments had been mainly imported. The revolutionary wars destroyed the trade and communications with foreign countries, so instruments could not be brought into the country, and the destruction of wealth had removed the means for paying for the instruments if they could have been brought in. If physicists wished to do research in the early years after the revolution they had to make their own apparatus, or arrange for it to be made in their laboratory workshops. The relatively large part of laboratory workshops in instrument manufacture remained after the social economy had been stabilized, and begun to grow,

PLATE 4

The Physico-technical Institute of the Ukraine, Kharkov

Scientists' flats in the Institute's
grounds

View from the balcony of a flat

and the laboratory workshops shared in the general growth. At present the Soviet laboratory's workshop resembles a combination of a British laboratory workshop with a British scientific instrument firm. The standing of the manager of the laboratory workshop resembles that of a combination of the chief mechanic of a British laboratory workshop and the proprietor and senior staff of a British scientific instrument firm. In England the senior staff of a firm such as Adam Hilger often act as collaborators and advisers in research.

The Kharkov workshops have sections for wiring, plumbing and fitting. Besides serving the needs of the research physicists, the workshop staff have to make repairs to the laboratory's buildings and fittings. This detail illustrates one of the interesting features of the institute. Its organization and operation is remarkably self-contained. The life of the institute also has this quality.

When the institute was opened in 1930 it had one large laboratory building. This had been built on the side of a hill, from which most of the city of Kharkov could be seen. A large piece of ground had been appropriated and fenced off. Within this area, two large blocks of flats had been built for the accommodation of the institute's staff. One of these blocks contained a kindergarten for the staff's children, and a simple sort of communal restaurant for those who required it.

Two very large extensions to the institute are now being built. One of these is a very large high-voltage laboratory. It should accommodate a 7-million volt generator and discharge apparatus comfortably. A block of flats is attached to this building, which is in the same grounds as the original laboratory. The director of this laboratory, Leipunsky, says he will be quite happy if they can build a two- or three-million volt generator. He is anxious to improve the quality of research in the U.S.S.R., which is now the instruction of the Party to scientists. Stunt research is to be avoided, and investigators are to learn to be more critical and exact. During the next years there will be less enthusiasm for monster apparatuses, and more for accuracy. Leipunsky will continue his experimental search for the neutrino. His first aim will be the construction of more exactly controlled apparatus. The well-known physicists Lange and Houtermans have recently joined the staff of the high tension laboratory.

A very large laboratory for technical and pure research on low-temperature problems and industrial gas separation is also being built, not within these grounds, but on a site at a distance of several kilometres.

These extensions will probably grow into independent laboratories, but as yet they are still part of the original organization.

The grouping of the original laboratory with its workshops and blocks of flats in a self-contained unit within its own grounds has given the social life of the institute some interesting features.

III

The members of the staff live within a few metres of each other. They can walk from one flat to another, and to the laboratories and home again, without wearing a hat or coat, in moderate weather. They can easily meet together in each other's flats, for entertainment and discussion. As they live close together, they have no difficulty in going home late at night. This is an important detail, because the travelling facilities in Soviet cities are not always convenient, and colleagues who live at considerable distances from each other are apt not to meet partly because they do not care to face long journeys in over-crowded tramcars when they are tired. Even with many travelling facilities, as in London, colleagues are apt to have little contact with each other if they do not live in the precincts of their institute. The lack of collective feeling in institutes in big cities, especially in London, is a serious problem.

There is a magnificent view from the flats of the Kharkov Institute. These buildings are three and four stories high, and designed in a functionalist style. Every flat has one or two balconies. During the long hot summer it is delightful to sit on these balconies in the evening. There is enough room on them to eat supper in the open air, and to talk with one's friends afterwards. The position on the side of the hill allows the balconies to receive most of the cool evening breezes. On a summer night the thousands of electric lights in the city make a marvellous blaze in the valley. The sky and air are generally clear, owing to the absence of house and factory smoke.

During the hot summer daytime sunbathing can be enjoyed on the balconies. At Kharkov the summer sunshine is a powerful irradiating agent, and many people swiftly become deeply tanned.

Besides having one or two balconies, each flat has much window area; they are light. The internal design of the flats is admirable. It would be difficult to find in Britain dwellings as beautifully designed, as comfortably arranged, and as finely situated as the flats of the staff of the Kharkov Physico-Technical Institute. Most of the flats have three rooms, with two balconies, kitchen, bathroom, and small hall. There are doors between the rooms, and between two of the rooms and the hall. These are hinged in two halves, and open in the middle, similar to the entrance doors seen on many public buildings in Britain. The paint is usually white or grey, and the walls are distempered white or pale grey. This decoration gives a light airy effect.

The lighting is electric, and gas is laid on for cooking. The chief difficulties in these flats arise from water shortage. The water-supply of Kharkov is inadequate. The small stream that runs through the city is nearly dry during the summer, and water has to be pumped from deep wells in the surrounding chalk hills. It is very hard, owing to the salts in solution and the quantity is insufficient to meet the needs of a city whose population has trebled since the revolution, and whose industry has increased on an even larger scale. In addition to the shortage of water, the high situation of the flats prevents the water flowing up to their supply pipes. These difficulties often prevent the occupants from using water freely during the daytime. At night the industrial consumption of water decreases, and the flat cisterns fill up. As a consequence many domestic workers do their household washing at night, and also have their baths then. Some water is often run into the bath afterwards, in order to guard against shortage during the next day. This water shortage and hardness is a cause of some domestic discomfort. The considerable amount of minor summer ailments, such as slight fevers and diarrhœa, is probably connected with it.

The plans for the development of the city of Kharkov contain arrangements which will ultimately solve the water problem. It is proposed to dig a large canal which will connect Kharkov with the Donetz, a tributary of the River Don, and bring an unlimited supply of water.

Though the water shortage is inconvenient for domestic workers, there are some particularly convenient features of the conditions at Kharkov. In summer the hot dry air dries clothes very quickly, and in the winter this is done by the hot air from the centrally heated radiators. This makes the washing of clothes much easier in Kharkov than in London, where the summer air is relatively cool and damp and in winter rooms are at the low temperatures provided by the usual coal fire.

There has been a general movement for beautifying cities, factories, institutes, and all organizations of Soviet life. Groups of students and workers adopt a street and improve its appearance by planting trees and flowers in it. This method of improvement develops a collective proprietary sense. It is often possible to go for a walk with an acquaintance who will stop you in a street before a tree and say: "Look, this is my tree, I planted it."

The same policy has led to the improvement of the institute's grounds. Many trees and shrubs have been planted in it, and they have been encircled by a handsome wall. Some members of the staff cultivate elaborate gardens. Gravel tennis courts have been laid out. Tennis and other sports are much cultivated in the U.S.S.R. In the winter, groups of the staff go ski-ing.

The institute possesses a large radio-gramophone. This can be borrowed by members of the staff who want to give small dance-parties. Jazz dancing is now popular.

IV

The concentration of all this activity within the institute creates a lively and attractive atmosphere. The homogeneity of the social life is increased by the uniform youth of the staff. The whole of the research staff is less than forty years of age, with one or two exceptions of men about forty-one or two. The majority are under thirty years of age. This cannot be paralleled by any research institute of comparable size outside the U.S.S.R.

The youth of the responsible members of staff is one of the most remarkable features of the scientific life of the U.S.S.R. Young people in no other country receive such opportunity for holding responsible positions. It will be interesting to see the results of all this experience in ten or twenty years' time, when the young directors of thirty years of age have grown into mature administrators of forty to fifty years. In Britain men rarely have full administrative and creative responsibility until they are over forty years of age. British people are tending to forget how young men, with their first charge of energy and enthusiasm, would attack the deep problems of the government and organization of contemporary civilization.

V

The most original feature of Soviet laboratory organization is the planning of research. The general plan for the Kharkov institute is drawn up in collaboration with NIS, as already explained. The details of the plan are worked out by the laboratory staff. Each department makes a plan for the year, from January 1 to December 31. This is divided into sub-plans for each quarter.

These plans must receive adherence in principle from every research worker, but they are not intended to be interpreted in a mechanical manner. They are guides which prevent any worker from being uncertain what problem he should be attacking.

The research worker cannot change the subject of his researches without wide discussions by the staff of the institute. He has to report on the progress of his work after periods of about one month. Formerly at certain times the worker had to estimate what percentage of his plan had been accomplished. This has now been discontinued and the performance of each worker is assessed by the director, the departmental director, and the worker himself in collaboration.

The planning of work introduces a rhythm into the performance. After three-quarters of a planned period is past, the worker is usually behind the schedule. He spurts during the last quarter, in order to complete his programme. In December there is intense activity in Soviet laboratories, as everyone is anxious to return the best possible report on the accomplishment of his part of the year's plan.

The workers engaged in the study of the same problems or groups of problems are organized in a brigade. This provides collective control and energy. An individual in the brigade can have his colleagues' help and advice, and he feels the impulsion of the collective spirit. The brigade holds frequent meetings to assist in the solution of the problems of its members, and to discuss its attitude towards orders received from the chief laboratory direction, and how they can be most effectively performed.

The personal desires of the individual members of a brigade receive little consideration. If an individual can convince his brigade and the laboratory direction that the problems he wishes to investigate are important and suitable to the laboratory's equipment, his proposals are officially adopted, and he receives all possible assistance for his research. He receives this assistance not because he happens to want it for his own ends, but because the institute has decided that it wants the research to be done. In practice, a competent person with a practicable proposal can usually have it officially adopted. Thus the Soviet research worker does not count much as an individual; the collective aims of the institute and Soviet society in general have the first importance. The individual who helps his brigade and institute to achieve their collective ends receives high honours and publicity, but more as a representative of the group to which he belongs, than as an individual who has demonstrated his own cleverness. Nevertheless, the praise he receives may be for the accomplishment of a research which he had himself proposed. This is how the growth of personal fame is combined with communal ideals in the U.S.S.R.

The brigades are not of equal size. In the Kharkov institute those for low-temperature and high-voltage work are particularly large, and have a special workshop. The brigades are responsible for the economics of their activities, and have to keep records of their expenditure. A special cheque-book is provided for each research problem. The cost of all equipment and workshop services is recorded by the cheques paid out for them. In this way, it is possible to make an exact comparison of the cost of any research with the cost which had been estimated for it in the plan of research. Individual departments and work-shops buy and sell from each other, and the economic results are balanced in the institute's office, which acts as a clearing house. This cheque system gives interesting information on the time of making apparatus, and the comparative speed of various workers. It provides the data for much rationalization.

The size of the office organization for dealing with this system is large. The director who manages this part of the operation of the planning system has an important position in the institute. His status is of the same order as that of the administrative and scientific directors, and much greater than that of the secretary in a British institute. At Kharkov he is assisted by eight accountants, a cashier and clerks. Besides managing the laboratory economics, this director controls the economy of the whole institute. He acts as steward of the institute's flats and grounds. He supervises repairs, and supplies the chief pieces of furniture. The supply of electricity, water, and gas is controlled by him, and he sees that the plumbing is kept in order.

His work has resemblances to that of a bursar in a college at Oxford or Cambridge. The self-contained life of the Kharkov institute is similar in several ways, though vastly different in others, to the life of a Cambridge college. Apart from the difference in political ideals and class composition of the staff, the mixture of the sexes is notable. The research worker's wife lives within the grounds of the institute, and often works in the laboratories.   The relations between the sexes customary in Soviet life rule also among scientists.   There is equality for all persons of equal ability, irrespective of sex, and there is the usual emancipation from the Western European laws which oppress relations between the sexes.   The marital relations of Soviet scientists are much freer, but on the whole not much less stable than those of Western European scientists. The status and presence of women scientists prevents the development of the celibate forms characteristic of Oxford and Cambridge intellectual life and acquired by them from the monastic tradition of the Middle Ages.

VI

The financial accounts of the Kharkov Physico-Technical Institute illustrate the methods of arranging the finances of a Soviet laboratory.   The total budget for running the institute, apart from fresh capital expenditure, was 1,500,000 roubles during the year 1934.   The cost during 1935 was more.   Thirty-five per cent of this sum was spent on the management of the laboratory apparatus, heating, electricity, etc., and purchasing and making equipment.

The total number of persons working in the institute was two hundred and thirty, a smaller number than in recent years.   There has been a general movement in Soviet institutions to prevent overstaffing.   Like other institutes, the Kharkov laboratory has benefited from this movement, as the removal of overcrowding makes the conditions of work more comfortable.

Of the total staff, forty-seven are qualified research scientists.   Seventy-eight are laboratory assistants and auxiliary workers, and seventy are on the workshop staff. There are thirty-five persons which include janitors, doorkeepers, handymen, etc., who are not engaged in work directly concerned with research.   During 1935 there were slight increases of staff in all categories, owing to the extension of the laboratories.

Ninety per cent of the funds are provided by NIS, from the Commissariat of Heavy Industry. About 10 per cent of the funds come from fees for technical researches conducted for industrial trusts.

The capital expenditure on the new Low Temperature Gas Separation Laboratory was about 2 million roubles during 1934. In 1935 about 1 million roubles were needed for capital expenditure on the High Tension Research Laboratory. The total capital cost of the High Tension Laboratory will be about 4 million roubles. The cost of the building alone will be about 1,800,000 roubles.

The general expenses of running the laboratory are about 15 per cent of the budget. The number of researches conducted in the institute during 1934 was sixty-two, and the plan for 1935 contained sixty-five.

About 120,000 roubles were spent in 1934 on training aspirants, i.e. graduates starting research and aspiring to high qualifications. This sum is not included in the institute's budget.

VII

Western students are naturally interested in the rôle of the Communist Party in the life of Soviet institutes. Different investigators of this question will return different answers, and the impressions described here must be clearly accepted as those of an individual observer. The writer has spent considerable time and effort on attempting to learn the nature and scope of this rôle, and the following account is the result of his inquiries. Most of the Communist scientists and directors questioned by the writer did not give a definite picture of the Party's work in scientific institutes. This may be due to the difficulty of explaining a rôle which is complicated and subtle. Part of the obscurity is almost certainly due to the absence in some "red directors" of a clear conception of the Party's rôle in the life of an institute. Some of the Communist directors and scientists who appear unable to give a clear account of the Party's work in an institute, seem in practice to interpret it as mainly loyalty to bureaucratic instructions.

Discussions with more explicit Communist scientists suggests the following account.

The Communists on the staff of an institute form a Party cell or group. This cell is concerned particularly with two questions, that of political leadership, and that of the output and performance of the institute.

In its task of political leadership the Party cell has to explain to the staff of the institute the meaning of Party and Government policy and orders. For example, when Stalin on behalf of the Central Executive Committee of the Communist Party speaks on the general line of policy, and suggests some modifications, the institute's Party cell would immediately begin to explain the pronouncement, and how its suggestions should be applied in the particular conditions of the institute. Following the Party cell's lead, meetings of the whole staff, and of the departmental staffs, would be held to solve the problem of introducing the modifications.

The Party cell in the Kharkov institute organizes sets of lectures on political questions and literature. Attendance at these lectures is voluntary. The lectures are given by a Party member. He receives help in his conduct of them from the District Party Committee. If the Party cell in an institute or factory has no good lecturer, the District Party Committee supplies one.

In the Physico-Technical Institute about eight persons who are not Communists attend the lectures. These are given on three subjects : (1) the history of the Communist Party ; (2) on political training for new and backward members of the Party and for candidates for admission to the Party; and (3) on the classics of Marxism. Early in 1935 the number of persons attending the lectures on these subjects were respectively twelve, ten, and twenty-two. The third group, studying the classics of Marxism, contained the eight non-Communist attendants.

The staff of the institute has 230 regular workers, and there are also 100 who do some part-time work. Out of this total, 34 are members and candidates for membership of the Party.   Of the 47 of the qualified scientists 4 are full members of the Communist Party.   Of the 23 aspirants or post-graduate research students, 7 are Communists, and among the qualified scientific staff, there are 4 Young Communists.   The Young Communist League is a youth organization.   Only a small percentage of its members qualify for membership of the Communist Party when they have reached the age of entry.

Most of the meetings of the Party cell are open to all members of the staff.   The subjects of discussion include the organization of socialist competitions between departments or with other institutes.   Each side in a socialist competition undertakes to complete a certain research within a shorter period than that allotted in the official plan.

Socialist competition may apply also to the undertaking of research obligations, economy in work, taking part in seminars, coloquiums, making something cheaper or better or quicker; or the training of aspirants or post graduate students.

Questions of management and economy are discussed, and the significance of changes in policy, such as the abolition of the bread-card system, and on international affairs.

The directors of the institute explain their plans for the institute at staff meetings.   Every member of the staff is expected to understand the general reasons why the particular plans of work have been chosen, and the general reasons for the choice of the particular methods of organization.

The staff enters into collective agreements concerning payments and conveniences.   Such tasks as the beautification of the institute's grounds, the construction of new roads, and the supply of new towels to the worker's club are discussed.   At a recent staff meeting the agenda contained ten pages of items of this sort.

If a worker disagrees with his treatment by the directorate on personal and political questions he has many possibilities of appeal, and finally he can appeal to the Central Committee in Moscow.   Personal, research, administrative and financial questions are settled by NIS.

The choice of personnel is made chiefly by the scientific director.

The group of the Party members in the institute is responsible to the Party for the success of the institute. If the Party notices that the progress of the institute is not satisfactory, it asks its group in the institute to give an explanation.

The rôle of the Party group in helping the institute may be illustrated by its present activity concerning the construction of a large Van der Graaf apparatus. Such an apparatus is needed for the progress of the researches on high-tension electricity. The necessity for the apparatus has been explained to the Party group by the chief Communist scientists on the staff. The Party group and the administration then called a meeting of the staff. The scientific importance of the apparatus was explained. The resultant strengthening of physical research in U.S.S.R. from the possession of such an apparatus would have political importance, as increased scientific strength would confer increased material and hence political power.

These meetings and propaganda make all of the members of the staff feel that they have a part in the government and development of the Institute, and in the development of Soviet science.

The promotion of discussions of philosophical questions is of much importance. It deepens the workers' understanding of the nature of science, and its rôle in social affairs. It reveals, too, often unconsciously, the tendencies of the participator's thoughts. Saboteurs may be discovered through the suggestiveness of their philosophical opinions.

VIII

A large physico-technical laboratory, for the investigation of the separation of industrial gases at low temperatures, is being erected in another part of the outskirts of Kharkov. The site is near a large coking plant, so that a large supply of the gases produced during coking will be available for experimental research on a semi-industrial scale. The laboratory is being built as a department of the Physico-

Technical Institute, but its great size and situation suggests it will soon become an independent institute. The laboratory is given the abbreviated title of OSGO. In January, 1935, 300 building workers were engaged in the erection, and a large part of the foundations and walls had been completed.

The building operations are managed by an independent building committee. The assistant-director of this committee is A. Weissberg. The committee has its own office and book-keeping organization, but the latter is responsible to the book-keeping department of the Physico-Technical Institute. It possesses a special fund for training a group of workers to become members of its future staff. This semi-independence of the new laboratory is a frequent feature in Soviet scientific development. New institutes bud off old ones. At Leningrad, for instance, the director of the physico-technical institute being erected at Sverdlovsk in Siberia has rooms in the Leningrad Physico-Technical Institute. He is superintending the plans and the training of the future staff for the new institute being erected thousands of miles away. The Leningrad Physico-Technical Institute is, as it were, budding in Siberia. As will be described in another chapter, the Physico-Technical Institute in Dniepropetrovsk has already budded off the Kharkov institute, which in its turn budded off from the original Leningrad institute.

The Kharkov institute has been charged with the training of the staff for OSGO. The director of the scientific training is M. Ruhemann, the low-temperature physicist, who is of British nationality.

Ruhemann is a member of the staff of the Low Temperature Department of the Kharkov institute. This department is directed by L. V. Shubnikov. Two or three workers have been provided as a nucleus for the OSGO staff from the Low Temperature Department, and other workers are added to the group as suitable candidates appear. As assistant scientific director for OSGO, Ruhemann is responsible for the training of the prospective staff, and he has to obtain material and equipment for the laboratory.

The Physico-Technical Institute pays the working expenses for the workers being trained. These receive a salary during training. The instruction is half scientific and half technical, and is given in lectures by Ruhemann, Dr. Barbara Ruhemann, Ryabinin and Steckel.

The total budget for the construction of OSGO is 7,500,000 roubles. It is impossible to express this sum accurately in English pounds, but judging from the size of the new buildings and equipment, the writer estimates that it must be equal to at least £100,000.

The budget is in several parts. One section is for the bricks, concrete and building on the site. Another section is for laying gas-pipes, plumbing, equipment and furnishing. A third section is for training future staff. A quite large sum, 200,000 roubles, has been set aside for beautifying the site and grounds. Refuse is to be cleared and trees planted.

The total cost of the laboratory is very large, but there is less difficulty in obtaining the money than in spending it. The sum due each quarter for the construction of the laboratory is absolutely fixed. The building committee must arrange its expenditure in each quarter exactly within this sum. The money for the laboratory is held by the Communal Bank of Kharkov, which controls the transfer and expenditure of money very thoroughly. Before the money can be transferred from the bank to a factory supplying equipment, the building committee must satisfy the bank that the objects bought are in the category stated, and that the prices are quoted correctly. With scientific apparatus this is difficult, as prices change rapidly. Further, the committee cannot buy goods where it likes, but only in specified types of shops. There are at least three sorts of shops selling more or less the same articles at different prices. There are the SNAB shops that are distributing centres for supplying groups, factories, institutes, etc. Then there are the TORG shops that supply articles to private individuals, and then there are the UNIVERMAG shops that supply goods at luxury prices. The SNAB shops sell at what are named "hard" prices, while the other two sorts sell at "soft" prices. If a person has a permit to purchase a scientific instrument at a SNAB shop on behalf of his institute, he will obtain it at a much lower price than if he bought the same sort of instrument in a TORG shop for his private use. The OSGO building committee must buy its equipment at "hard" prices. If the "hard"-price shops happen to be short of the articles required, which may happen if the directorate of a manufacturing or distributing trust is trying to improve its balance-sheet by increasing the percentage of its goods sold at "soft" or high prices, the building committee may have much difficulty in obtaining the things it wants. The controlling rôle of the banks in expenditure on construction has much increased during the last two or three years. By the time this account is published these methods of purchase may have been modified or abolished.

The main building of OSGO consists of four parts ; the laboratories, the workshops, the experimental factory, and the administration. The workshops are larger and more complete than in ordinary institutes, as the facilities for building new low-temperature plant, besides repairing, are required. They will have large lathes and machine tools capable of taking large pieces of machinery. The laboratories contain several large rooms for physical and chemical work. Some have been designed for housing large experimental models. These have thick walls with light roofs, and no cellars, so that accidental explosions will do the minimum amount of damage. The nucleus of the research staff consisted early in 1935 entirely of foreigners. The directorate desire to engage more Soviet scientists and to acquire a well-trained Soviet staff. About ten research workers will be necessary to undertake the work for which the laboratory has been designed.

There will be two blocks of flats for the staff; one for the research workers, and one for the technical staff. These flats will have a kindergarten, and, it is hoped, a refectory designed in the style of a Viennese café, and provided with modern steel furniture. Unfortunately, it is improbable that these embellishments will be obtained.

An iron and copper foundry is put in a separate building, which also houses the boilers for steam, and the central heating for the whole group of buildings.

Gasometers will be erected in open ground at a distance of fifty metres, or so, from the next building.

The OSGO institute has been founded for three objects. Firstly, to solve the problems of gas-separation; in particular, of the low-temperature-method of separating the constituents of the gases from coke-oven plants. This is required in the large-scale production of mixtures of hydrogen and nitrogen for supply to synthetic ammonia plants. The method is due to Linde, and has been introduced in the Soviet synthetic ammonia factory at Gorlovka.

In this method nitrogen is separated from the air by cooling rectification and pumped into the coke-gas supply at a pressure of 180 atmospheres, in order to produce cooling, and to wash out the carbon monoxide which is very poisonous to the catalysts used in the ammonia synthesis.

It is possible that the Claude method may be better. This will have to be settled by experiment.

The Laboratory may also conduct researches on the design of compressor pumps, and on the chemistry of catalysts, but this is improbable.

The difficult task of manufacturing the copper cooling-tubes is accomplished with considerable success at the Tambov copper factories. For generations there have been copper works in that district, and the copper workers have an acquired skill in copper-working. This helps them to overcome the problems of the construction of gas liquefiers, and enthusiasm completes their success. The Soviet workers will work twenty hours a day in order to make an installation operate successfully.

The necessity for an institute such as OSGO became clear several years ago. The Soviet synthetic ammonia industry has designed and begun to erect several very large synthetic ammonia factories. Some of these are to have low-temperature coke-gas separation machinery three

times as large as the largest built by Linde.   When such
a huge increase in the scale of design is made, alterations
in the details of the design and operation are always necessary.   The OSGO experimental plant can collect the data
required for the calculation of these alterations.   It is a
form of insurance, as the expenditure of 7 million roubles
on an experimental plant may insure the successful operation of a factory costing 100 million roubles.

The existing synthetic ammonia factories have frequently
consulted the staff of the Low Temperature Department
of the Kharkov Physico-Technical Institute on their
problems.   This spasmodic consultation on particular
points is not satisfactory, and wastes time.   A systematic
investigation of the phenomena of coke-gas separation by
the low-temperature process would enable most of these
questions to be settled immediately.

The first object of OSGO is, therefore, to collect the
data of low-temperature coke-gas separation.

The second object is to study the general methods of
rectification, or purification, of gases, and to suggest
improvements in the design of machinery and processes.
The methods of preparing the rare gases, such as xenon,
are to be studied.

The third object is to investigate the general possibilities
of low-temperature physics in industry.   Research will not
be restricted to work on gases.   They hope to investigate
ultimately such problems as the possibility of operating
electrical transformers at low temperatures.   At first they
will try to answer questions put to them by industry, and
in a few years they hope to be able to suggest profitable
new methods to industry.

There is considerable difficulty in collecting persons of
initiative for the staff.   The graduates of the high school
system often have less sense for practical work than the
manual workers.   It is sometimes better to find manual
workers with practical aptitude and train them for the
scientific work, rather than engage graduated students.

Persons who are members of the Communist Party often
have more initiative, and are less biased.   The non-party

man is sometimes more anxious than the party man in making suggestions, as, if they prove to be bad, he may be suspected of ill-will.

Old party men may be very useful at the staff, even when they have little scientific knowledge. They have often gained much experience of how to acquire things, and get things done. They possess the spirit of the partisans during the revolutionary civil war, when scrounging and living by the wits was necessary for survival. If an old partisan is told, for instance, to find a special sort of lathe, he will campaign for it as if he were ambushing a White detachment, and appear with it triumphantly, when others would have believed that the acquisition would have been quite impossible.

IX

The workshops of the Kharkov Physico-Technical Institute manufacture a certain amount of apparatus for sale. This includes vacuum flasks. Ten-litre copper vacuum flasks are manufactured for sale at 700 roubles, compared with the German price of 200 marks. The copper hemispheres for these flasks used to be made by Caucasian coppersmiths, who hammered them out by hand. They are now spun in lathes. Fifty-litre flasks have been made satisfactorily, and were manufactured for sale in 1935. These large flasks are evacuated for five days at a temperature of 120° C.

The rate of evaporation of liquid air from the 10-litre flasks is 1·2 litres in twenty-four hours.

One-hundred-kilovolt electrical condensers are also manufactured for sale. These have a capacity of half a microfarad. There are forty-six sheets in each group, with one hundred groups. The size is 21·6 mm. by 50 cm². The condensers with their paper sheets are evacuated for ten days in order to draw out the moisture held in the paper. When the sheets are dry the case is filled with oil which has been filtered, deaerated and dried.

They can purify oil for five condensers in twenty-four hours.

The resistance and capacity of the condensers are measured during the preparation.

These condensers are sold to scientific institutes such as the Leningrad Physico-Technical Institute and factory laboratories in Donbas. They are used in the construction of impulse generators.

X

Before describing some researches in more detail, the general lines of the work of a number of the staff will be mentioned.

Obreimov continues his studies of the optical and other properties of solids.

Prikhotko has examined the fluorescence of naphthalene at liquid hydrogen temperatures and has obtained a very fine line absorption spectrum.

Strelnikov has perfected the design of his 10-kilowatt rotating anticathode X-ray tube. It is now worked out for factory production. The beam of electrons is projected at the rim of the wheel along a radius, and the X-rays are taken off along a line perpendicular to the plane of the wheel. As the wheel is rotated in a vertical plane, the beam of X-ray emerges in a horizontal direction. The apparatus is cleanly designed. There are few external gadgets, and it looks a practicable routine apparatus.

Brilliantov has been extending Obreimov's researches on the deformation of crystals. He has also studied the discoloration of rock-salt by X-rays, which turn it brown. He has obtained results in good agreement with Landau's theory of the effect.

Gorsky has observed that when mercury iodide is crystallized from acetone, orange crystals besides red and yellow crystals are formed. It is metastable at temperatures between 15° and 140°, and can be transformed into the red by touching with the finger.

In the low-temperature laboratory Shubnikov and Ryabinin are studying the penetration of magnetic fields into supra-conductors.

Trapeznikova has investigated the magnetic properties

of iron chloride. It is quasi-magnetic. Landau suggested that sheets of atoms in a crystal, two-dimensional structures, may have ferro-magnetic properties. Trapeznikova's results agree with Landau's theory.

She has also investigated the heat capacity of para-magnetic salts at low temperatures.

Sinelnikov and Walter are experimenting with models for a large Van der Graaf apparatus.

Fomin and Kisilbash have been designing a Wilson chamber for research on cosmic rays.

Papkov and Leipunsky have designed a Tessla transformer for producing 1 million volt-accelerations.

Garber is extending G. I. Taylor's measurements of the energy of plastic deformation of metals to crystals of rock-salt.

Hey and Kahn have extended the work of Kautsky on the fluorescence of dyes, and phosphorescence when adsorbed on gels.

Yussak has ingeniously adapted a thermopile for measuring low temperatures in factory processes.

M. Ruhemann and A. Prikhotko have been studying the absorption spectrum of solid oxygen in layers one-fifth of a millimetre thick. There is a splitting of electron levels probably due to electron exchanges in oxygen molecules containing four atoms.

M. Ruhemann has investigated the melting curves of mixtures of methane and ethylene, and other gases.

B. Ruhemann has designed a special form of X-ray camera for use at low temperatures.

The researches of I. W. Obreimov, who was the first director of the institute, have mainly been concerned with the properties of solids.

In 1924 he published in collaboration with Shubnikov a method of preparing giant single crystals of metals. The metal is held in graphite or hard glass tube. If the metal is prevented from solidifying normally by lowering the tube into a furnace, so that it cools from one end only, and the end of the tube is tapered, one crystal nucleus tends to form, instead of more. Single metal crystals 12 inches long and 1 inch in diameter have been prepared by this method, or variations of it.

Obreimov has investigated the change of colour in crystals at low temperatures. At these temperatures the absorption spectra of all crystals are probably line spectra, and the wide absorption band of most well-known crystals should split into fine lines like the bands of the rare earths, or the wide bands of benzene.

In collaboration with W. J. de Haas, Obreimov has examined the absorption spectra of azobenzene crystals at temperatures within 20° of absolute zero. They show a line spectrum which may be approximately described by a simple formula.

In another research he has investigated the splitting strength of mica. The flakes, of thickness about one-tenth of one millimetre, were split off from a specimen of mus-covite from Chupa, with a fine glass wedge. On the assumption that Young's modulus for the material was 20,000 kilograms per square millimetre, the work done in splitting was determined by an optical method to be 1500 ergs per square centimetre in air, and 2000 in a vacuum. If the wedge is withdrawn the split-off portion of a flake partially split off unites perfectly with the main portion, provided the surface remains uncontaminated. The split-ting is accompanied by triboluminescence.

With A. Prikhotko he has extended the studies of the absorption spectra of crystals at low temperatures. They have investigated the absorption spectra of solid naph-thalene at temperatures of 20° C. and — 190° C. They chose this series of substances because they are homologous, and the foundations of most of the aromatic compounds, and the spectra of their crystals can be compared with that of their vapours. The preparation of very thin crystal layers of the substances was accomplished very skilfully by a process of sublimation. With thin films and low tem-peratures more similarities with the vapour spectra are observed.

With N. A. Brilliantov, Obreimov has investigated the

H

effects of annealing plastically deformed rock-salt crystals. This followed earlier work with Shubnikov in which it had been shown that residual strain remains in a plastically deformed crystal of rock salt, and that its magnitude can be estimated by means of the double refraction (piezo-electric effect) that it produces. They expected that at each temperature the strain cannot exceed the flow limit, and that the residual strain below the flow limit would not diminish, and that in the course of time a rapid diminution of strain down to the flow limit would occur. These expectations were derived from the view that the diminution of strain by annealing was the result of lowering of the limit of plasticity at high temperatures. But neither of these expected results was found. This conclusion appeared to conflict with the results of the investigation by Joffe and his collaborators of the plastic flow of rock salt by X-ray methods. In a further paper, Brilliantov and Obreimov brought their results into relation with those of Joffe. It was shown that during the plastic deformation of rock salt the crystal lattice is rotated, producing the phenomenon of twinning ; and that gliding, if it occurs at all, has a secondary rôle.

The director of the low-temperature department is L. V. Shubnikov. In the period of five years he has evolved an efficient organization, and, with the assistance of his colleagues, is publishing first-class research. The Kharkov low-temperature laboratory has achieved a place beside the half-dozen other low-temperature laboratories in the world. Shubnikov is in the early thirties, and has studied at Leiden. He has absorbed the Dutch quality for mastering of detail, and combines it with Russian enthusiasm. His laboratory should have an important part in the future of Soviet science. It contains seven rooms and a special workshop. He has six research colleagues, and twelve mechanics. The equipment includes a large liquid air plant which provides 25 litres per hour, and an average daily production of 150 litres, a liquid hydrogen plant in which the gas is thoroughly purified, and liquid helium apparatus of the type invented by Simon and Ruhemann. An electric magnet which will give a field of 30,000 gauss over a cylindrical volume 20 centimetres long and 20 centimetres in diameter is being constructed. The special iron for the core has been successfully made in a Soviet ironworks.

Shubnikov has recently been studying the behaviour of the magnetic field in supra-conductors. It is well-known that many pure metals become perfect conductors near absolute zero. How do they behave magnetically when in the supra-conducting state? In 1933 the German physicist Meissner and his collaborators published the results of exploring the distribution of the magnetic field around solid and hollow cylinders of metal in the supra-conducting state.

If a magnetic field of small strength, not large enough to destroy the condition of supra-conductivity, is produced around the cylinder, the latter behaves as if its magnetic permeability were zero. This in accordance with the simple electrodynamic theory.

If the transition to the supra-conducting state takes place while the cylinder is in a magnetic field, other phenomena occur. If the cylinder is solid, part of the magnetic field becomes locked inside it, on transition to the supra-conducting state. If the cylinder is hollow, some of the original magnetic field remains in the hollow, after the transition of the metal to supra-conductivity. A piece of the magnetic field seems to have been caught, and isolated in a stable state.

This extraordinary discovery has stimulated much research. K. Mendelssohn and J. D. Babbit at Oxford showed that the magnetic induction in tin spheres, cooled in an external magnetic field until they became supra-conductive, did not vanish entirely, but that part of the electric field remained in the body, frozen in, as it were. Shortly afterwards Shubnikov and Ryabinin published the results of similar experiments on a long thin cylinder of lead. They measured the magnetization curve for the cylinder at 4·2° absolute in fields of increasing strength. They found that the relation of induction to field strength was simple in an increasing field, and as expected in a supra-conductor, but complicated in a decreasing field. They found the induction remained at about 20–30 per cent of its maximum value, when the field was reduced to zero; in other words, the supra-conducting cylinder retained a magnetic moment. It follows from these observations that the induction in the supra-conducting cylinder can have two values for a particular strength of magnetic field, depending on whether the particular strength has been reached by a rise or fall. In these experiments the lead cylinder was 5 millimetres thick and 50 millimetres long. It was put in a magnetic field whose direction was parallel to its axis. A layer of thin lacquered wire was wound round it, and connected with a ballistic galvanometer. The throw of the galvanometer with sudden changes in the magnetic field was observed.

The cylinder was cooled with liquid helium produced in the apparatus itself by Simon's method.

They followed these experiments with similar ones on a lead single crystal, and obtained somewhat different results. The quantitative differences between the inductions produced by increasing and by decreasing fields was much less, and the induction rises slightly with time in a constant magnetic field. This dependence on time and the small hysteresis in single crystals led them to suggest that all states of a supra-conductor with an induction differing from zero are unstable.

They have also examined the magnetic behaviour of supra-conducting alloys of lead and thallium, and lead and bismuth.

The high skill of Shubnikov and his colleagues, and the large resources and organization which have been produced in such a short time, should ensure a fine extension of low-temperature research at Kharkov, and its achievements will be watched with special interest.

M. Ruhemann and Barbara Ruhemann are the low-temperature physicists who formerly worked in the laboratory of Simon in Berlin. They migrated to Kharkov, and are now British citizens.

Ruhemann will be the research director of the new

laboratory for technical and pure research on the low-temperature method of gas separation. He and his wife are members of the staff of the low-temperature laboratory. During the last three years he has been investigating the behaviour of mixtures of gases at low temperatures, and working out their phase diagram. He has obtained the cooling curves, specific heats, and equilibrium curves of methane-ethylene mixtures. The eutectic point (the statement of the temperature and other conditions at which the constituents of the mixture may simultaneously exist in either the liquid or gaseous state) was found at $84 \cdot 55°$ A., when the mixture contained $12 \cdot 2$ per cent of ethylene. The limit of solution of ethylene in methane was found to be $2 \cdot 5$, within a possible error of $0 \cdot 3$ per cent. These data appeared to provide the reason why this particular mixture of methane and ethylene had been patented by an industrial concern.

Barbara and Martin Ruhemann have pointed out that the computed curves of the specific heats of mixtures of various strengths, as determined by the cooling curves of the methane-ethylene mixtures, have features which resemble the specific heat anomalies in pure substances. There are resemblances to the effects of the transition to supra-conductivity, the specific heat of ferromagnetic substances near the Curie point, and other phenomena. They suggest that all of these phenomena might be interpreted in terms of changes of state (phase changes) in mixtures of two substances.

In collaboration with A. Prikhotko and A. Federitenko, M. Ruhemann has been continuing research on the optical properties of solid oxygen. They have described several methods of preparing the three forms of solid oxygen, and have examined their absorption spectra with visible light. The absorption spectra of two of the forms in the near ultra-violet have also been examined, and a detailed examination of the absorption spectra in the infra-red and ultra-violet regions is being made. The general distribution of the spectrum remains the same in all forms, but a number of single lines and doublets appear in two of the modifications.

The theoretical explanation of the origin of these lines is not yet clear.

M. Ruhemann has been studying the structure of solid air. He has shown that it consists of two sets of solid solutions, one of oxygen in nitrogen, and the other of nitrogen in oxygen. The structure of oxygen is different from that of nitrogen. Seventy per cent of solid oxygen will dissolve in the crystal lattice of solid nitrogen. Mixtures of nitrogen and carbon monoxide give good solid solutions.

Barbara Ruhemann has devised a special type of vacuum X-ray camera for use at low temperatures. The material to be examined is kept in the vacuum, but not the photographic film. Two designs of the camera have been made for different purposes. One is for Debye and rotation crystal pictures. She has designed a small cooling apparatus that can be put on any vacuum camera instead of a Dewar vessel. Any temperature between room temperature and that of liquid hydrogen can be preserved with a constancy of one-tenth of a degree during photographic exposures of many hours.

With this equipment she has measured the variation in the size of the crystal lattice of manganese oxide at temperatures between $77°$ above absolute zero, and room temperature, especially in the region $115.9°$ A. At this temperature manganese oxide has an anomaly in its specific heat.

The high-tension research laboratory in the original building had a considerable amount of space, and much experimenting has been done with a variety of types of high-tension apparatus. Most of the work may be regarded as preliminary investigation for deciding the type and design of equipment to be put into the new high-tension laboratory that has recently been erected. As already mentioned this very large building is one of the biggest high-tension research laboratories in Europe. It is directed by A. Leipunsky, who has recently been working in the Cavendish Laboratory at Cambridge for a year, and probably will become an independent institute. The new laboratory is large enough to accommodate a seven million-volt apparatus. It is proposed to adopt the Van der Graaf type of statical machine.

Sinelnikov, Walter, and others have been experimenting with smaller Van der Graaf machines in the original laboratory. The Van der Graaf machine consists essentially of a driving-belt running between two drums, and made out of an insulating material. One drum is fixed inside a discharging sphere, and the other at a distance. Static electricity is communicated to the side of the belt that is running into the sphere, and a collector in the sphere transfers the electricity from the belt on to the surface of the sphere. The charge on the surface of the sphere can be increased to immense values in this way.

It is calculated that the strain on a belt for a big machine will be over one ton, owing to the electrostatic attractions.

The potential difference may be doubled by charging two spheres with positive and negative electricity, respectively. If they are charged to potentials of half a million volts each, they will give a difference of 1 million volts, and be able to produce a million-volt discharge.

The belt may be made of reinforced rubber of the sort used for making babies' waterproof bedding, or material of the sort used for making the envelopes of airships.

The various experimental models that have been made include one that operates at 1,800,000 volts. It contains two spheres each charged to 900,000 volts at an opposite sign. The discharge tube is erected horizontally between the two spheres. Owing to the horizontal position, the strains on the tube owing to its weight are not uniformly distributed. This is a serious difficulty. The tube in use has been cracked. They thought it would not work after that, but patching with jointing material has enabled them to make it usable. They do not propose to have a horizontal tube in the big machine. This will have one big sphere, and discharge from this to earth. A possible difference of some millions of volts will be lost, but the machine will become much easier to use and more reliable, as the discharge will be vertical and downwards. The existing 1,800,000-volt apparatus gives a current of 1 microampere. The electron beam is difficult to focus. It penetrates 8 metres of air. The observer is stationed inside one of the spheres. Owing to focusing difficulties, Walter's face and Sinelnikov's fingers have been burned by the electron beam. On the advice of a doctor, Walter tried to cure his burns by dipping his face in a bucket of alcohol. The results of the treatment, in various ways, were unexpected and unsatisfactory.

The observer is inside the sphere for four or five hours, during one experimental run. The air becomes uncomfortable through the production of ozone.

Two horse-power motors are used for driving the belt for each sphere. The efficiency of the apparatus is rather high. The current remains constant, and the voltage varies. The apparatus is not easy to work in summer owing to the humidity of the air. During winter, when the temperatures are very low, the air becomes very dry and the problems of insulation become simpler. Perhaps their difficulties have been increased owing to the apparatus not being entirely enclosed.

The ancillary apparatus for observing atomic disintegrations and bombardment phenomena are Wilson cloud chambers, scintillation screens and counters. These are mounted inside one of the spheres.

They have investigated the disintegration of lithium atoms of mass six with this Van der Graaf apparatus. When beams of lithium ions are used, protons are always present. They deflect the protons out of the beam. Lisa Meitner and Szilard showed that when beryllium is bombarded with wave-radiations from radium, it emits neutrons. These reactions can be measured by reactions with iodine. Meitner could not measure the threshold of this effect, and they are trying to find it with their apparatus.

When they bombarded lithium with beams of lithium nuclei, the apparatus was filled with a blaze of scintillations. Its power as a radiator is equivalent to that of 10 grams of radium.

In 1932, soon after Cockcroft and Walton had shown that lithium could be disintegrated by swift protons, Sinelnikov, Leipunsky, Walter and Latishev made similar experiments with an apparatus constructed on the same principles as that of Cockcroft and Walton. They were the first physicists to repeat the great experiment of Cockcroft and Walton.

The Kharkov workers have made various studies of the properties of rock salt and photoelectric substances. Borissov, Sinelnikov and Walter have made copper-oxide photocells which reproduce their behaviour. They have examined the influence of the thickness of the electrode and that of the nature of the gas in which it has been precipitated.

They found that the photoelectrical qualities were apparently not connected with unipolar conductivity, according to the theory of Frenkel and Joffe.

Sinelnikov, Walter, Kurtchatov and Litvinenko have studied the effect of irradiation with X-rays on crystals of rock salt at low temperatures. They found the irradiation produced almost no yellow discoloration if done at a temperature of — 180° C., and no internal photoelectric effect. They attribute this behaviour to the passage of the electrons torn away by the X-rays from their normal energy level to that of the conduction electrons. On their movement in the atom lattice they become bound to the positive sodium ions. This catching of the conduction electrons is influenced by the heat movements of the atoms in the lattice.

Kisilbash, Kondratiev and Leipunsky have investigated the extinction of atomic fluorescence and its connection with atomic and molecular collisions. They have made experiments on the extinction of sodium fluorescence by nitrogen and carbon monoxide. The fluorescence was produced by the excitation of the vapour of sodium iodide by sparks from zinc and aluminium electrodes.

CHAPTER 7

A CONFERENCE AT KHARKOV

CONFERENCES have an important rôle in Soviet scientific affairs. In this feature the Soviet habit resembles the continental European rather than the British habit. There is still much dislike among British scientists of conferences. They say the papers at a conference are rarely of interest to more than three or four workers, and the other members of an audience find papers from subjects apart from their speciality are boring, and their time is wasted by listening to them. There is some truth in this opinion. Badly managed conferences contribute little to the progress of science. The British tradition of individual work is also against the cultivation of conferences. According to it, research is conducted by a few individuals in various places, who can easily arrange private meetings between themselves. No public arrangements are necessary for their discussions. This attitude, which in fact has some justification, is partly a product of the period when scientific research was a voluntary occupation of gentlemen. They could arrange meetings in their own large private houses, without the assistance of a permanent secretarial body.

The British backwardness in the cultivation of conferences is partly a reflection of the aristocratic traditions that still influence the habits of British scientists.

The degree of the survival of these traditions in British scientific affairs is greater than many British scientists would suppose. Foreign observers notice it more clearly. When an eminent German experimental physicist was asked a few years ago what he considered was the most interesting feature of the character of British physical research, he referred to the conditions of research enjoyed by the late Lord Rayleigh, who had a laboratory in his country mansion. This German physicist longed for wealth and leisure in which he could follow his desires without deference to the requirements of any other person or body.

The aristocratic part of the British tradition is against public conferences and in favour of informal parties. The recent increase in the number of national and international scientific conferences in Britain is an indication that the pursuit of scientific research is passing more and more to persons who are less and less under the influence of the old aristocratic tradition, and its forms preserved in Oxford and Cambridge. This does not imply that fewer scientists are being educated at Oxford and Cambridge, but that those who have been educated there are coming more under the control of public bodies and national trusts. The growth in the number and scope of conferences is partly a reflection of the increasing influence of governments and trusts on the pursuit of scientific research. Large conferences could not generally be financed without direct or indirect subsidies. At many conferences there are exhibitions of apparatus and books. The charges to the exhibitors may cover an important part of the costs of organization. Sometimes large firms give donations towards the expenses of conferences. Industrialists who have made vast fortunes out of the exploitation of science sometimes present endowments to scientific societies which enables them to finance conferences.

The modern well-organized scientific conference has much value. When the organizers have sufficient means, they can arrange that the lectures and discussions are in small groups of definitely interested participators. They can invite the most important workers from all parts of the world.

If the discussion groups are small and carefully chosen, and the hours of discussion are short, say from 11 a.m. until 12.30 p.m., and from 2.30 until 4 p.m., the participators may learn much from a conference. Under these circumstances they have energy and time for informal discussions between the sessions.   Meeting workers at the same problems from all parts of the world is stimulating, and provides the opportunity for elucidating in conversation obscure passages in published papers.

In large countries, such as America or the U.S.S.R., conferences are more important than in small countries, such as England, because personal contact between specialists is more difficult.   The generous hospitality to visitors in large countries is a reflection of the importance of travelling.   Scientists in England can easily meet owing to the small distances.   Some important scientific discussion clubs held in London, have the character of periodical informal conferences.

In May, 1934, the Kharkov Physico-Technical Institute organized an international conference on theoretical physics. The foreign visitors were Niels Bohr of Copenhagen, L. Rosenfeld of Liége, I. Waller of Upsala, M. S. Plesset of Pasadena, J. Solomon of Paris, E. J. Williams of Manchester, W. Gordon of Stockholm, Tisza of Budapest, and the writer.   The majority of the visitors were married, and their wives were included in the invitations.   The Kharkov institute advised the visitors to enter the Soviet Union at Leningrad, and sent a representative to that city to arrange for their reception.   In the course of a few days most of the party gathered in an excellent hotel, and those who arrived earliest had opportunities of seeing Leningrad. When the party was as complete as possible it left by train for Moscow, travelling in a tourist third-class carriage, which, if not luxurious, was clean and comfortable.   On arrival in Moscow it waited in the station for some time, as the arrangements for travelling to Kharkov were not yet clear.   Presently it was taken to the offices of NIS, the Scientific Research Sector of the Department of Heavy Industry.   Further waiting increased pessimism among the inexperienced members of the party concerning the successful continuation of the journey.   After an hour or two the party was informed that they would be taken to the station for Kharkov, and that there was not very much time to spare.   They were by this time so anxious to continue on the journey that they would willingly have accepted the hardest hard seats in the earliest available train. At the station they were conducted with haste to a platform where their train was standing. Within a minute it began to move, and the party threw itself and its baggage into the nearest carriages, without inquiring the whereabouts of its reserved seats. In the train it was learned that an international sleeping car had been attached to the end of the train for the party. The members walked through a dozen carriages to their car, and found, after all, that they would complete the train journey to Kharkov in the most comfortable conditions.

The Kharkov railway station was packed with deputations of young workers waiting to receive the Austrian Schutzbündler, who were expected to arrive at about the same time.

During the period of the conference the weather was extremely hot, about 80° to 100° F., in the shade.

The visitors stayed in a hotel in the centre of Kharkov, and were supplied with sets of tickets that entitled them to have meals in the hotel, and also in the café of the Park of Culture and Rest in the outskirts of the city.

On the evening of their arrival the party was entertained at an open-air supper in the Park. The dry heat and breezes suggested reflections on the advantages of a climate where it is possible frequently to take meals with complete comfort in the open evening air.

The conference sessions were held in the building of the VOKS organization. At that date, Kharkov was still the capital city of the Ukraine, and VOKS, the Society for Cultural Relations between the Peoples of the Soviet Union and Foreign Countries, had fine offices in what had been before the revolution the mansion of a wealthy man. The morning session lasted from about 11.30 a.m. until 1 p.m., and the evening session from about 6 p.m. until 8 p.m.

The chair was taken by L. Landau, the director of theoretical studies in the Kharkov institute, and the discussions on papers were opened by Niels Bohr.

The Soviet physicists at the conference included I. Tamm, V. A. Fock, and J. Frenkel. A number of advanced students were invited to listen to the papers and discussions, but the number was limited. The total attendance did not exceed fifty persons.

The discussions were conducted chiefly in English, and partly in German and Russian. The leading Soviet physicists exhibited a brilliant command of languages. Occasionally they lapsed into Russian when they desired to argue with exceptional vigour among themselves. The traditional style of debate in the U.S.S.R. is more violent than in England.

The papers of E. J. Williams were received with particular interest. He described the general state of research on the scattering of hard γ-rays by matter, and his recent experiments on scattering with thin sheets of material. He found that if the sheets of foil are sufficiently thin, the range of the electrons produced out of the γ-rays by interaction with the atomic nuclei in the foil is sufficient for them to avoid annihilation except at a considerable distance from the foil. In this way the annihilation radiation can be separated from the other part of the radiation. The existence of the annihilation radiation can be proved by this method, and is found to constitute the whole of the scattered radiation of energy 0.5×10^6 volts. The energy of the positive electrons can be estimated approximately from the variation of the intensity of scattered radiation with the thickness of the scattering foil. The fraction of positive electrons with a low degree of energy proves to be unexpectedly large, and may be explained as due to the production of double pairs of electrons.

In another paper Williams described an analysis of observations by Kunze on cosmic rays, which suggested evidence for the existence of a negative proton, or negatively charged particle of mass equal to that of the nucleus of a hydrogen atom. Kunze took photographs of cosmic-ray tracks with a Wilson cloud-chamber apparatus, surrounded by a powerful magnet through which the current from the Rostock town electric power station could be sent early in the morning before the daytime demand for current began. His photographs showed tracks of particles of high energy, which appeared to produce about 20 ions per centimetre in normal air. If the particles had been electrons about 35 ions per centimetre would have been expected. It is difficult to be sure that the spots of all of the ions were registered on the photographs, but if they were, then the tracks must have been due to particles heavier than electrons. As the direction of the curvature of some of the tracks indicated that they must be due to particles with negative electric charges, Williams suggested tentatively that Kunze may have secured photographs of the tracks of negative protons, or negatrons.

Plesset discussed Dirac's theory of the positive electron, and the extensions of the theory by Fock and by Carlson and Oppenheimer. He explained that these formulations involved difficulties of invariance. In another paper he described an application of quantum electrodynamics to the determination of the proper energy of a vacuum in the theory of filled states of negative energy. Transitions from the initial state of the vacuum distribution to the intermediate state in which an electron-pair and a quantum of radiation are present, are considered, and then transitions from these intermediate states back to the initial state. The intermediate states may be given the picturesque interpretation of representing fluctuations in the vacuum distribution.

Fock explained that his contributions to the extension of Dirac's theory were purely mathematical. He had simplified the treatment but had not amended the difficulties in the physical conceptions of the theory. His work merely brought the physicist to the conceptual difficulties more quickly.

Waller showed that a simple device based on Dirac's theory of rays enabled certain mathematical difficulties in the problem of the scattering of rays by free electrons to be avoided. The theories based on the conception of electrons as points do not give a satisfactory account of the phenomena.

Tamm discussed the deduction of the size of exchange forces between protons and neutrons, according to Fermi's theory of the emission of electrons in radioactive disintegration.   In this theory it is assumed that transmutations of neutrons into protons, and the reverse, are possible, and are accompanied by the birth or disappearance of an electron and a neutrino.   If two heavy particles are respectively in the neutron and the proton states, there will be no change of energy if they are suddenly changed into the proton and the neutron states respectively.   The first particle, the neutron, may emit an electron and a neutrino, and become a neutron.   The emission and reabsorption of a positron and neutrino may also occur.   In this way the two degenerate states of the system considered are split into two energy states differing by the sign of the exchange energy.   Calculation shows that if the difference between the masses of the neutron and the proton is larger than the sum of the masses of an electron and a neutrino, the emission of light particles by a heavy particle may occur without a violation of the conservation of energy.   But the corresponding value of the exchange energy may be shown to be far too small.   The result indicates that either the Fermi theory requires revision, or that the origin of the forces between neutrons and protons does not lie in their transmutations, as originally suggested by Heisenberg.

Rosenfeld described researches in mathematical astrophysics, made in collaboration with Cambresier.   They have investigated the dissociative equilibrium in stellar atmospheres.   With this assumption the number of molecules of a given sort in the atmosphere of a star can be calculated as a function of the effective temperature and surface gravity of the star.   The calculation requires an allowance for the variation of pressure in the different layers in the atmosphere.   The pressure at the base of the atmosphere can be calculated from the general absorption, by a method first used by Milne and Chandrasekhar.   The treatment of concrete cases requires assumptions on the relative abundance of the atoms taking part in the reactions, but the results are not much affected by such assumption. the equilibria of titanium oxide, zirconium oxide, and the combinations of single carbon atoms with single atoms of nitrogen, oxygen, and also with another atom of carbon, have been computed in different cases ; when oxygen is either much more or much less abundant than carbon. The first case corresponds to the main sequence of stars, and the second to the branch of carbon stars. Simply on this assumption a satisfactory agreement is obtained between the obscured variations of intensity of the corresponding bands with spectral type and surface gravity, with the giant or dwarf characteristics of the stars.

Besides these technical discussions some lectures of a more popular character were arranged for students and other interested persons. The local press gave prominence to the existence of the conference and published portraits and short interviews with the most distinguished participators.

Professor Niels Bohr gave a lecture on Causality in Physics to a packed audience in the lecture theatre of the Röntgen Institute. He spoke in German, and the audience included Zatonsky, the commissar of education in the Ukraine.

The objects and results of the conference were explained by Professor J. Frenkel to a large public audience, in a lecture of three hours' duration.

These events show the importance attached to the conference by the State authorities, and the degree of public interest in it. It was not regarded merely as a meeting of persons engaged in researches of no interest to others. The arrangements showed that theoretical physics, however recondite, was considered to be a matter of State, and some popular interest.

In the afternoons the guests visited various institutes, factories and farms; and after the evening sessions they were frequently entertained at private parties given by the Kharkov scientists.

A group of the members of the conference visited the Kharkov Tractor Works. It produces wheeled tractors of the McCormick type, in two models, of 50 and of 30 horse-power. The Chelyabinsk and the Stalingrad Tractor Factories are producing caterpillar tractors. The normal output of the Kharkov works is 140 tractors per day ; the variation being from about 133 to 147. There is a staff of 12,500, of whom about 30 per cent are women. Work is organized in two shifts per day.

The design and production is directed by about four hundred qualified engineers. There are about 160 foreign workers in the factory. Most of them are Americans, and nine only are qualified engineers. Of the staff about 3000 are Communists, and about 35 per cent of the qualified engineers are Communists.

The average salary of qualified engineers is about 350 roubles per month, and the highest salary is about 900 roubles per month. Unqualified engineers receive about 180 roubles, and labourers about 120 roubles, per month. Piece-workers earn up to 300 roubles per month. Shock-workers are not paid extra for voluntary overtime, but have their own restaurants and holiday sanatoria in the country.

The average life of a Kharkov tractor up to the first overhaul is about 900 hours, or three working months. They are overhauled twice a year, at the end of the two three-month periods of continuous use. The overhauls are made at repair stations in the country, or at the Kharkov factory. The manufacture of spare parts is an important department of the production at Kharkov, and their value reaches 1 million roubles per month.

The amount of spoilt work in the engine department of the Kharkov works is about 5 per cent.

The organization of the factory would compare favourably with Western European factories of similar size. Such departments as the tool stores are orderly and clean. This represents a notable triumph over old Russian habits.

The assembling is done on a conveyor. During the last 10 yards of its journey, the new tractor comes to life, as it were. Mechanics test the various controls, and the engine is started by a portable electric motor. After a few adjustments the tractor's motor begins to cough and spit. While the engine is being coaxed into its first uneasy action the whole tractor is being carried stealthily to the end of the conveyor. A driver sits on the driving-seat and tests the controls. By this time the front wheels of the tractor will have been gently lowered by the conveyor into contact with the floor, and the tractor runs off, like a newly born animal, to a yard outside the shop. A new tractor runs off about every 7 minutes.

The Kharkov Tractor Factory no longer presents any of those quaint features that used to be seen in Soviet factories. There were none of those entertaining but unindustrious groups so often seen gossiping in corners. The beautifying of the grounds of the factory had already begun. Amid enormous pipes for new water mains under construction, there were large beds of geraniums, and many trees had been planted.

In order to learn something of the new Soviet farming, a party of the physicists visited the Hope Kolhoz, near Kharkov.

This collective farm is situated near the railway about 25 kilometres from Kharkov. Its area is about 3000 acres, and it supports about 700 persons, 420 of which have a part in the farming work. Fifteen of the workers are Communists and 36 are young Communists. The population lives in a neighbouring village containing 300 families. Only about 20 of these families have not joined the collective farm. The whole of the village's population lives in ordinary peasant houses, one or more families to a house. During difficult times some families leave the *kolhoz* and fend for themselves. At the worst time, they have never lost more than thirty families, and nearly all of these have returned to the *kolhoz*. At present, six families are on the applicants' waiting list. Fresh families cannot be taken in now without some preliminary arrangements.

This farm was founded in 1921. Its social life is organized around a large old country house that had been empty since 1903. The old orchards had survived and made a useful part of the present farm. The big house contained a communal restaurant open to all members of the *kolhoz*. The visitors were served with a meal in this restaurant. It consisted of a vegetable soup, black bread, mashed potatoes with boiled meat, and glasses of fresh milk. It was more wholesome than the much more elaborate meals provided in the large tourists' hotels. The communal house contained a large clubroom suitable for meetings and theatrical performances, with newspapers, radio and table-games. Smoking was not allowed in this room. The school and crèche were two of the most striking features of the social organization. About 100 spotlessly clean infants were seen sleeping during the afternoon heat. The managers of the children, like so many young women in Soviet Russia, made an exceptionally good impression. Near the communal house, by the orchard, there was an open-air cinema.

Twelve hundred and fifty acres of the farm lands were used for corn-growing, 250 acres for vegetables, and 75 acres for fruit. The remainder consists of meadows. The orchards contained many beehives. The live stock consisted of 293 cattle, of which 150 were mature cows. The milch cows were divided into two groups, one of which averages 8 litres of milk per cow per day, and the other 12 litres. The calves were very carefully tended. An old peasant house had been converted into a little veterinary hospital. In one room the new-born calves were reared, until strong enough to enter the calves' paddock. In another room there was a stock of veterinary medicines in the charge of the cattle superintendent, who had taken a veterinary course. This rough veterinary hospital was thoroughly swept and cleaned. The cowsheds were of rough construction, but well kept. The cattle superintendent deeply impressed us by his knowledge and love of his work. He spoke with affectionate detail of the lives and careers of the various cattle whose births he had superintended. In addition to the other live stock the farm possessed 112 horses.

The appearance of the fields was interesting. They were in a condition which might not be expected in a country of large units such as the U.S.S.R. They were not large and presented a variety of crops, and looked as if they had received much detailed cultivation. This was the fact, as groups of twenty to thirty girls were engaged in hoeing and weeding. The majority of them were barefooted. During our visit in May the weather was very hot. The Kharkov district had had almost no rain for two months. The fields were still green, and the crops were not yet spoilt, but a few weeks' more drought must have done serious damage. Fortunately, rain came in the following days. English people are not usually in the position to feel the terrifying oppression of fierce drought. While walking through the fields of this *kolhoz* an Englishman could learn again the weakness and the uncertainty of the life of the pale green vegetation upon which humanity depends. A month's excess of sunshine could burn up all the products of half a year's intricate labour. Several groups of men and women were irrigating plants and young trees with water brought in a water-cart from a neighbouring stream. Experiments were being made on the distribution of water from the stream onto a large cabbage field. The water was pumped to a height of 30 or 40 feet with the aid of a tractor, and run through wooden channels over the field. The Kharkov fire-brigade visits farms in the district and pumps water onto them during drought.

The workers are paid in money and produce by the working day. The share is 3 roubles, $2\frac{1}{2}$ lb. of bread, and 17 lb. of vegetables. The recipient can sell as much of his allowance of vegetables as he wishes. He does this in the special markets established in the towns for the sale of the products of collective farms. The value of this *kolhoz's* annual production is assessed at about 1 million roubles. It is the product of 140,000 working days (420 workers working about 330 days).

The visitor notices that the standard of life in such a *kolhoz* is primitive compared with that on many Western European farms. The majority of Soviet agricultural workers are still culturally primitive compared, for example, with those of Denmark. But they are learning to conduct agriculture on lines ultimately capable of the highest development. At present they are primitive people, and although using a good method, their average efficiency is low. They cannot instructively be compared with the agricultural workers in Western countries. They belong to another sort of civilization, and more instruction is to be had from comparisons of the ideals of these two civilizations. The Russians are in the first stage of a new civilization and the Western peoples are in an advanced stage of a different civilization. The common denominator is not easy, and may be impossible, to find.

On the way from Kharkov to the Hope Kolhoz there is a sanatorium for patients suffering from diseases of the stomach. A spring which produces water containing salts with medicinal value rises in a small wood on a hill. The sources are surrounded with a concrete and glass structure that holds the rising water. Through the glass windows the little swirls made by the rising water may be watched. Patients can take water from the overflow. The excess runs down to a depression, and forms a lake in the grounds. The majority of the patients in this pleasant sanatorium are shock-brigade workers from the Ukrainian steel works, suffering from stomach disorders.

A visit was paid to the Dzerzhinsky School for Orphans in the outskirts of Kharkov. It contains 400 girls and boys, who live with a large degree of freedom and self-government. The terrible loss of life in Russia during the War and the revolution left vast numbers of children without parents or homes. Soon after the Bolsheviks had seized the government they had to manage this immense problem. The direction of the salvaging of the orphans was undertaken by Dzerzhinsky, the famous organizer of the Bolshevik Political Police. In honour of their founder, the Political Police have voluntarily continued this work. Their members have built the school at Kharkov and institutions in other places, from their own subscriptions, and also supply the money for conducting them. The Kharkov school has three workshops organized for the manufacture of cameras on the Leica design. They are magnificently equipped. It is not at all easy to make cameras of this type, and the idea of re-educating orphans in these laboratories seems very bold and expensive. There was a considerable staff of adult mechanics for helping and teaching the most difficult jobs. The school was having considerable difficulty with the manufacture of the camera lenses. The orphan child frequently has a definite sort of temperament. He is quicker and more independent than the ordinary youth. He is familiar with many adult experiences. Sometimes he is unable to learn the habits of a regular life, even when he wants to.

The director of the Kharkov school was a quiet man of exceptional charm ; an officer of the political police. There was some difficulty in obtaining permission to take a photograph of him out of the U.S.S.R., as photographing officers of the political police is not usually allowed.

CHAPTER 8

THE PHYSICO-TECHNICAL INSTITUTE, DNIEPROPETROVSK

I

THE city of Dniepropetrovsk was formerly named Ekaterinoslav. It lies on a hill beside the River Dnieper, which is of a magnificent size at this place not far from its mouth in the Black Sea. Like the river, the city's main street is broad. It runs straight up the hill overlooking the river, and at the top of the hill there is a splendid view. A number of fine buildings, including a College of Mining, had been built in pre-revolutionary days. Many more fine buildings have been added lately.

The population of Dniepropetrovsk is about 400,000. Before the revolution there were large metal works in the district. These have been greatly extended, and many new ones have been founded. The largest of these works, which is about 40 kilometres from the city, has a staff of about 36,000 workers.

The immense hydroelectric power station and dam at Dnieproges is about 100 kilometres away. Dniepropetrovsk will be the chief city of the new industrial region growing around Dnieproges. It has been of great agricultural importance for generations, as it is one of the chief grain markets of the Ukraine. In pre-revolutionary days many grain merchants had offices and warehouses in Ekaterinoslav. Their cargoes of grain were dispatched down the Dnieper to the Black Sea, and thence to Western Europe. The taste of these merchants may still be recognized in the furniture of Dniepropetrovsk hotels. One may see suites of furniture not more than twenty or thirty

126

years old, covered with excessively elaborate carving. The chairs are of various shapes, and their frames look like congealed vines decorated with grapes. They were probably covered with gilt when new. The spirit of these old designs is in contrast with the relatively simple lines of the new buildings and houses.

In winter, the air of Dniepropetrovsk may be extremely clear. Frost fixes all the dust, and the sunshine is brilliantly reflected from the snow. As the power for the city is electricity, transmitted on line from Dnieproges, there is a notable absence of smoke. The scientific institutes in Dniepropetrovsk are among the cleanest and neatest in the Soviet Union. These qualities were particularly noticeable in the laboratories of the Physico-Technical Institute. The institute is only four years old and has not yet received the large new building designed for it, the foundations of which have been already laid. Its laboratories are spread among several old buildings. The rooms for the X-ray investigation of the structure of metals are in the University building. Before the Revolution this building was a school for young ladies. Researches on electrical waves are conducted in another building which also contains the administration, and researches on the explosion of gases are made in this building, and in rooms of the Mining Institute. Despite the modest housing arrangements, the Dniepropetrovsk Physico-Technical Institute is one of the most attractive and best managed institutes in the Soviet Union. This appears to be due to the ability of the director, Professor Finkelstein, and the young and able staff he has collected. Much care has been given to the choice of a staff that can work together harmoniously. The Director has the advantage of being a physicist and a Communist. He is one of the post-revolutionary graduates of Professor Joffe's institute, and is a mathematical physicist who specializes on the electron theory of metals. Some of his chief colleagues were fellow students at Leningrad.

The friendly staff entertains its guests very pleasantly. One may arrive at Dniepropetrovsk at midnight in winter, when the train is seven hours late and the temperature is

— 32° C. (57 Fahrenheit degrees of frost), and be met by a group of the chief members of the staff and their wives. A Rolls-Royce car transports one to a restaurant, where an excellent meal relieves an appetite sharpened by hours of waiting and anxiety in the train.

The lateness of trains in winter is partly due to the excessive radiation of heat from the locomotives at low temperatures. On the journey from Moscow to Dniepropetrovsk, the temperature was about — 34° C. at Moscow, and fell as low as — 38° C. (68 Fahrenheit degrees of frost) at Kursk. The locomotives lack sufficient steam, owing to the extra radiation of heat and to inferior coal. The railway authorities try to arrange for better coal to be available in very cold weather.

The traveller does not notice this very cold weather unless he is inadequately clad or the heating fails. Fur coats are necessary for travelling in the open air, and frost-bite, particularly of the ears, must be cautiously avoided. After a few days of temperatures between — 30° C., it is possible to see many people with bandages round their ears. These are frostbitten Russians, who, after having lived all their lives in Russia, have carelessly left their ears exposed and not tucked them under their fur-lined caps.

When the clothing and heating are adequate, life in the Russian winter is comfortable. It is possible to return to England and shiver frequently in under-heated, draughty English rooms, after weeks of agreeable warmth in the centrally heated rooms, and fur coats, of Moscow. When the Moscow heating fails, and proper clothes are not available, the cold is petrifying. The British traveller, accustomed to short punctual train journeys, becomes anxious on the long unpunctual train journeys in Russian winters. He is not sure whether his hosts can be expected to wait at a railway station several hours for the late arrival of his train. He wonders whether he will be met, and if not, whether he will be able to find a room in a hotel at midnight, or whether he will have to spend the night in the open at a temperature of — 32° C.

The staff of the institute at Dniepropetrovsk relieved these fears splendidly. It is not in fact difficult to arrange to meet late trains as there are not many main line trains, and it is customary to enquire from the station by telephone the expected time of arrival of the Moscow train. Everyone stays at home until he learns from the station that the train is due, and then he goes to meet it. Like so many of the details of life which differ in the U.S.S.R. from those in other countries, the technique of railway travelling in cold weather is simpler and less inconvenient than one might have expected.

The atmosphere of a Soviet long-distance train is different from that of a train in Britain. It is perhaps chiefly due to the very much longer distances of the average journey in the U.S.S.R. Fellow travellers know they must be together for at least half a day, and often several days. Social intercourse cannot be avoided, so they usually start the journey by being civil and conversational. Train journeys in Britain are on the average too short for the cultivation of an agreeable conversation, so social habits have not grown among ordinary British train passengers. The British passenger considers the train a rather boring necessity that lies between him and the object of his journey. He can easily spend the hour or two, thinking about the things he has just left behind, and then about the things to which he is going. The impersonality due to short-distance travelling is illustrated by the behaviour of passengers in the London Underground Railways. The very short period of contact prevents the growth of social intercourse, and produces a remarkable atmosphere of social frigidity among closely packed crowds of passengers.

The reserve of British people is partly due to the small size of their country.

The long distances and spaces and the large scale of things in the U.S.S.R. have led to the building of broad-gauge railways, with spacious rolling stock. The soft category, or second-class, compartments on long-distance trains have four passengers, and are much larger than similar compartments on British railways, and the corridors are also much broader.   These have tip-up seats, on which one may sit and smoke and converse.

As the train passenger in the U.S.S.R. is prepared for long distances, a few hours more or less do not usually make much difference to his arrangements.

In spite of delay, uncertain catering, and dirty lavatories, the soft-class train travelling is generally interesting and comfortable.

The Dniepropetrovsk institute is not self-contained, as at Kharkov, but most of the staff live near the institute, and have a pleasant social life.

The Director's wife and the wives of his colleagues organize charming parties and informal dances in his flat for the entertainment of guests.   In winter, farewell parties may continue into a considerable number of early hours, as trains do not always depart punctually.   Instead of leaving at midnight, it may leave at 3 a.m., so it is possible to remain cheerful and warm at the party, and periodically telephone to the station to discover whether the train is yet ready to depart.

II

The director, Professor B. N. Finkelstein, has published papers on such questions as the virial theorem in wave mechanics, on the ionization potential of atomic configurations with two electrons, and on the viscosity of electrolytic solutions.

Professor A. E. Malinovsky has made extensive researches on the phenomena of gas explosions ; in particular, the effect of electrical forces on the propagation of flame in explosive gas mixtures.   J. J. Thomson was the first to point out the connection between the electrical condition of a flame and the direction of its movement, first in 1893 and again in a report of the British Association in 1910.

It is interesting to note, in passing, the important contributions of J. J. Thomson to physical chemistry.   His investigations of the nature of the phenomena of chemical dissociation in compound gases preceded his discovery of the electron, and it is not improbable that his thoughts on chemical dissociation prepared his imagination for the conception of the phenomena of ionization.

Thomson suggested that the process of combustion, and its propagation, was due to the emission of electrons from the front of the flame. This suggestion was not investigated at the time, but during the last decade it has stimulated much research. In 1924 Malinovsky published a paper on the movement of ions in the flame of combustible mixtures of gases. He found that the explosion wave in a mixture of benzene and air was arrested if directed between two metal plates with a potential difference of several hundred volts. He was unable at the time to obtain a similar result in other gaseous explosive mixtures. He attributed the result to the removal of electrons from the explosion wave. The flame travelled some distance before it recovered its former condition. Other workers were at first unable to obtain similar results. In 1930, in collaboration with Lavrov, he published a demonstration that an electric field perpendicular to the direction of the movement of the flame, impedes the propagation of the flame and may even extinguish it. Malinovsky and Lavrov explain the phenomenon by the hypothesis that the electric field removes the electrons supposed to be responsible for the propagation of the flame. If they are removed from the front of the flame, immediately after being emitted, they cannot produce the conditions for the advance of the flame.

The facts of their experiments agree with results published by F. Haber in 1929. But Haber gave a different interpretation of the effect. He supposed that the electric field affects the ions due to the high temperature of the flame, and hence interferes with the front of the flame and its propagation. In Haber's opinion, the determination of the propagation of the flame is not due primarily to the ions and the electric field, but to the mechanical movements of the ions due to the electric field. Semenov considers Haber's explanation is the more correct. But Malinovsky disputes this, and continues to publish further experimental results in support of his opinion.

With the collaboration of B. N. Naugolnikov and K. T.

Tkatchenko, Malinovsky has recently made a photo-record of the speed of an explosion wave in an electric field.

The apparatus consisted of a glass tube into which acetylene and air could be passed. The inside of the tube was lined with thin tin strips in two places, so that an electric field could be produced. Two cylindrical rods bearing metal rings were inserted from the opposite ends of the tube, so that the inside of the tube was provided with two cylindrical condensers. Ignition of the mixture of acetylene and air produced in the tube was made by an electric spark produced by an induction coil. The primary winding of the coil was connected with the control of a photographic plate for recording the movement of the explosion flame, so that ignition and camera were simultaneously controlled.

The tube was mounted horizontally, and covered with black paper, but leaving a horizontal slit which coincided with the position of the burnings of the condensers. Two strips were glued over the slot to mark the beginning of the first condenser and the end of the second. On the photographs they came out as parallel dark strips crossing the flame as it passed the respective condensers.

As the photographing was done according to the method of Mallard and Le Chatelier, the photographs show a combination of the horizontal path of the flame and the vertical path of the plate.

The photographs show that the speed of the flame increases markedly between the rings of the first condenser.

As it comes out of the first condenser the flame deviates slightly upwards, but when entering the second condenser it bends again and becomes nearly horizontal. The transmission of the explosion wave is observed through the throw of a galvanometer connected to the second condenser. The percentage of ions transmitted, and the speed of the explosion wave through the second condenser, can be calculated from the throw of the galvanometer, the number of revolutions per minute of the photographic plate, and the shape of the photographic pictures. It was found that the speed of the explosive wave when the electric field was present in both condensers, and when absent from the first, was in each case of the same order of magnitude, and equal to 25 metres per second.

The voltage communicated to the condensers was 1000, and the speed of the photographic plate was 2·8 metres per second.

The authors concluded from an examination of their photographs that the transmission of ions by the explosive wave was according to their findings in their earlier papers. They deduced that the electric field does not influence the expansion of the explosive wave. Thus the argument of Semenov, that the effect of ion-transmission is only apparent, and is due to the change in the speed of propagation of the explosion wave in connection with the electric field, is in their opinion invalid.

They conclude that these experiments show that the effect of the electric field in arresting or extinguishing flames in mixtures of hydro-carbons and air occurs only at slow speeds of flame expansion, at the preliminary burning stage with constant speed, and in the unstable region when, changing into a detonation wave, the electric field does not produce any apparent effect.

The arresting effect is observed only in mixtures rich in hydrocarbons.

Malinovsky and K. A. Skrinnikov have investigated the possibility of the ignition of explosive mixtures of gases by electrons produced by X-rays. In 1913 J. R. Tompson had found that certain explosive mixtures of gases appeared to be ignited by electrons produced by X-rays. Malinovsky and Skrinnikov have concluded that his results were probably due to the catalytical effect of freshly heated platinum. The experiments are not a proof that ignition of a gaseous mixture by electrons is impossible. It is quite possible that much larger current densities than are obtained by the photoelectric effect are needed for ignition.

With V. S. Rossikhin and V. P. Timkovsky, Malinovsky has investigated the influence of high-frequency electrical fields on the burning speeds of gases.

They have observed that the spreading speed of flames

in mixtures of acetylene and air decreases when the flames pass through direct-current fields of a strength of 200 to 1500 volts per centimetre, and in alternating fields of a frequency 60,000 per second and tensions of 300 to 2900 volts per centimetre.

The percentage decrease of the spreading of the flames was 1·40 per cent to 100 per cent in the direct field, and 1·8 per cent to 100 per cent in the alternating field. The influence of the alternating field was 1·5 to 2 times as feeble as that of the direct field. As the speed of the flame increases, the influence of both sorts of field decreases. With increasing dilution of the mixtures rich in acetylene (23 per cent acetylene, with air), the difference between the effects of both sorts of fields decreases, and both sorts have almost no effect on the burning speed. They were unable to observe any influence by either sort of field on the speed of the flame in mixtures of hydrogen and air.

Malinovsky and I. A. Klass have investigated the influence of temperature on the arrest of gas explosions by electric fields. They passed mixtures containing 25 per cent of acetylene and 75 per cent of air, and 20 and 80 per cent, through the field of a highly charged air condenser. It was found that if the mixtures were exploded at the same initial temperature, a smaller field tension served to arrest the explosion in the mixture rich in acetylene. The arresting tension increases with temperature.

The effect of the temperature on the tension necessary to arrest explosions is less in the mixtures rich in acetylene. It increases roughly in proportion with the increase of temperature, while in the poorer mixture an influence of the temperature is noticeable only at about 40° C., and increases strongly above 100° C.

With Rossikhin and Timkovsky, Malinovsky has investigated the influence of field frequency on the combustion of gases. Working with a mixture containing 25 per cent of acetylene and 75 per cent of air, they found that the arresting effect is the less the higher the frequency. Above frequencies of 8 million per second the arresting influence of an alternating field is scarcely observable.

III

The X-ray investigations of metals at Dniepropetrovsk are directed by G. Kurdumov, one of the ablest physicists in the U.S.S.R. He studied physics under Joffe at Leningrad, and began important researches on the crystal structure of steel by X-ray methods.

The properties of iron and its combinations with carbon are very complicated. Pure iron at room temperatures consists of an aggregate of tiny crystals of a certain shape, and is named alpha-iron. If it is heated gradually, it becomes non-magnetic at 767° C., though the arrangement of the atoms in its crystals remains unaltered. This non-magnetic iron with the same crystal shape as alpha-iron is named beta-iron. It was erroneously believed to be the cause of the hardening process. At 900° C. the iron crystals change their shape. This rearrangement of the atoms absorbs much heat, and produces a contraction of $1\frac{1}{2}$ per cent in the volume of the iron. In the alpha-iron crystals eight atoms are arranged at the corners, and one atom at the centre, of a cube. With the change of shape at 900° C. the atoms are arranged at the corners of the cube, with an atom also at the centre of each face of the cube. This face-centred cubic form of crystal is named gamma-iron. At 1400° C. the crystals change back into the alpha-iron form, but are non-magnetic and stable at high temperature, and are named delta-iron.

Steel consists of iron containing small quantities of carbon. If any steel is annealed to a temperature of 1130° C. and quenched rapidly, its appearance under the microscope resembles that of a pure metal. The iron absorbs the carbon in an intimate manner, and is said to hold it in a state of solid solution, a uniform dispersion of atoms of one element amongst atoms of another element. The iron atoms are arranged in the face-centred cubic system, within which the carbon atoms are packed, inside the crystal lattice. The iron at 1130° C., which is in the gamma condition, holds a maximum amount of carbon in solution at that temperature.

K

A solid solution of carbon in iron is named austenite, after the metallurgist Austen.

Crystals of pure iron are named ferrite.

The chemical compound of iron and carbon, iron carbide, is named cementite. Pearlite is an intimate mixture of crystals of iron and of iron carbide; that is, of ferrite and cementite.

Rapidly quenched steels with a relatively high content of carbon show when polished a surface criss-crossed with needle-like crystals. In this condition the steel is named martensite, and is in the hardest and most brittle condition.

When martensite is slightly tempered it shows black rounded areas, and is then named troostite.

Owing to this multiplicity of states the explanation of the properties of steel is very difficult. It depends fundamentally on the properties of the minute crystals of which steel is composed. As these crystals are far too small to be visible under a microscope, little progress could be made until some method capable of elucidating the shapes of sub-microscopic objects became available. This occurred with the discovery of the method of crystal analysis by X-rays. Besides being able to investigate the shapes of objects of atomic size, the new method, owing to its utilization of X-rays, could probe substances such as steel, opaque to ordinary light.

The application of the methods of X-ray crystal analysis to the study of the crystal structure of hardened steel has been described by Öhman.

The first investigations of hardened steel with this method made by Westgren in 1921 and Wever in 1924 failed to reveal any difference between the crystal structure of martensite and alpha-iron. In 1926 Fink and Campbell published the excellent discovery that hardened carbon-steel crystals contain a substance with tetragonal structure —a deformation of body—centred cubic alpha-iron crystals. Selyakov, Kurdumov and Goodtzov in Leningrad independently made the same discovery, and published their account in 1927. The former authors found an axial ratio of 1·5 per cent, while the latter found that the axial ratio as well as the volume of the unit cell increased with the content of carbon.

The eminent Japanese metallurgist Honda, and Sekito, obtained a constant axial ratio of about 1·07 per cent, irrespective of the content of carbon. Selyakov pointed out that this was due to surface carburization caused by heating the specimens in graphite powder. The Japanese researchers had in fact investigated a variety of steels with approximately the same content of carbon. They also stated that the axial ratio continuously diminished with increasing distance from the surface of the quenched specimen. Kurdumov disproved this and explained their results as probably due to a tempering effect produced by incautious grinding.

The most reliable X-ray investigation of the variation of the dimensions of the lattice of tetragonal crystals of martensite according to its content of carbon was made by Kurdumov and Kaminsky. They found the dimensions of two of the axes of the crystal unit to be functions of the content of carbon, and the lines intersect at a point corresponding to the elementary cube edge of pure alpha-iron. This result indicates that the tetragonal structure revealed by the X-rays is that of crystals of alpha-iron holding carbon in a supersaturated solution.

Ferrite and tetragonal martensite are in the same phase, but as they are often together the latter is labelled α'.

Kurdumov and Sachs showed how the transformation of γ into α iron may be conceived to take place by means of simple displacements of the atoms. They considered tetragonal martensite to constitute an intermediate stage. Their theory is based on a very beautiful investigation in which they prepared single crystals of austenite. They found that the crystallites of α-iron besides the martensite needles were orientated in a regular way in relation to the form of the crystal planes of the original austenite.

Öhman comments that as newly formed crystals generally orientate themselves in relation to existing crystal planes, this is hardly a sufficient foundation upon which to build a theory of transformation.

Hanemann and Traeger found a contraction on tempering hardened steel at 100° C. Kurdumov and Kaminsky showed this change is due to the decomposition of the α' phase into α-iron free of carbon, and cementite.

An expansion that occurs at 235° C. is due to the decomposition of austenite.

Kurdumov showed that in the decomposition of the α' phase, the tetragonal martensite decomposed gradually. With increasing duration of the tempering time, the axial ratio was diminished, and simultaneously the interference figures produced by the X-rays became more and more diffuse. This indicated that some parts of the specimen decomposed faster than others. Later, with Sachs, Kurdumov found evidence of a spontaneous decomposition into α-iron free from carbon, and from the intensities of the X-ray lines he estimated the percentage of alpha-iron formed by decomposition of the α' phase after temperings of different durations at 100° C. After two hours of tempering at that temperature the specimen was found to consist of 95 per cent alpha-iron free from carbon.

Öhman agrees with Kurdumov's earlier work. He concludes that the phase is not decomposed after tempering for several days at 105° C. The decomposition occurs more rapidly at 125° C., and at 150° C. the α' phase is decomposed in 15 minutes. In his review of the causes of the hardness of quenched steel, Öhman remarks that in 1920 Maurer suggested martensite is a supersaturated solution of carbon in iron. Hardness is due to the forced solution of carbon in the iron, which causes appreciable decrease in volume and a deformation of crystal structure.

Kurdumov and Sachs showed that martensite consists of fairly large units, or crystallites.

Solid solutions are always harder than pure metal, and the first explanation of hardness is to be found in this phenomenon. The hardness of quenched steel is explained partly by its condition as a supersaturated solid solution, but the phenomena that affect the hardness of other alloys also contribute to the hardness of steel.

Kurdumov describes the process of hardening in steel as chiefly due to change in the structure of its constituent crystals, and to fusion. The cooling must be done so that both processes go on together. The first occurs quickly, while the other occurs slowly. At room temperatures the second process is very slow. When solid iron at a high temperature is cooled suddenly the fusion process occurs very quickly. In 1926 the nature of martensite was still obscure. Sauveur made twenty-nine experiments which gave different answers. This situation was changed when the shape of the crystal lattice for each phase was determined by X-ray analysis.

Kurdumov joined the staff at Dniepropetrovsk in 1932. He and his colleagues are working on the liquid stage and the ageing of metals. They are investigating the influence of third substances on alloys of two metals and the determination of the internal tension in metals by X-ray methods.

There are large deposits of non-magnetic ferric oxide ore in the province. The technological problems of exploiting these deposits are being studied.

The ore contains only 30–40 per cent of iron and is mixed with quartzite. In order to be smelted satisfactorily the percentage of iron must be increased. This cannot be directly done by magnetic separation, as the iron in the form of ferric oxide is not magnetic. How can the non-magnetic ferric oxide be turned into the magnetic ferrosoferric oxide? Some chemical authors believed this occurred at about 700° C., but they did not know that ferric oxide becomes magnetic at 700° C. At 500°–700° C. ferric oxide gives a structure similar to that of ferrosoferric oxide. The magnetic susceptibility is 20 per cent greater in the special ferric oxide form.

The metallurgical laboratories are staffed with one technological expert, three research workers and three laboratory assistants. The work is conducted in three shifts between 9 a.m. and 9 p.m. Each worker works in three-hours shifts. This is due to the social legislation in the U.S.S.R. governing workers in dangerous occupations. The use of X-rays is classified as dangerous, and workers are not permitted by law to work with X-rays more than four hours daily.

Persons who work with X-rays receive an addition to their annual holidays, and are entitled to an extra daily milk ration free of charge.

While the staff work in short shifts the X-ray tubes are arranged to work in daily periods of twelve hours.

Coolidge tubes are not in general available for X-ray research in the U.S.S.R. as the Soviet Government has an agreement with foreign electrical firms not to use their inventions without payment. This presumably was made by the foreign firms before they undertook the construction of many of the vast new electrical plants in the U.S.S.R.

The Dniepropetrovsk X-ray laboratory works with gas tubes. With the ingenuity to be expected from Kurdumov, their vagaries have been minimized and they give surprisingly good results.

In the Physico-Technical Institute at Leningrad each investigator works with the tube in his own room. At Dniepropetrovsk all the tubes are in one room, and exhausted by a common pumping system.

They have the usual ovens for preparing single crystals.

Kurdumov is much interested in the methods of Weffer of Düsseldorf, who can produce cooling rates of 10,000° C. per second. Extra rapid cooling is of great value in the study of the process of hardening. The usual hardening change occurs at about 700° C., but with very swift cooling it can be done at 200° C. or 300° C. Working with air, they can produce cooling rates of 1000°–1500° per second. Swifter rates may be obtained by using hydrogen.

The study of hardening in copper-aluminium alloys does not require cooling as swift as that necessary in the study of the hardening of steel.

In their studies of the internal tension in steel they find that a tension of 70 kilograms per square millimetre produces a displacement in X-ray photographs of one millimetre.

W. Danilov has made interesting investigations with X-rays on the structure of liquid metals. Debye found that mercury atoms are capable of a very close geometrical packing, and it is therefore interesting to examine the structure of liquid mercury near the point of crystallization. Danilov investigated the behaviour of reflected X-rays from a mercury surface at room temperatures; then at 1° C. and at — 39·6° C. He found that the change in intensity of the X-ray figure at the low temperature, as the point of crystallization is approached, is continuous. This is in contrast with the discontinuous changes that occur in the state of solid solution.

They take the X-ray photographs in periods of three minutes. The exposures must be short, so that no significant warming or cooling can occur during them. In previous experiments these exposures usually lasted several hours. The reduction in time of exposure was due to improved focusing in tubes and camera.

Danilov and his colleagues have followed the work of J. A. Prins on the investigation with X-rays of the distribution of heavy dissolved molecules in high liquids. He confirmed the theory that such heavy molecules would behave like a gas by obtaining from them X-ray diagrams characteristic of a gas.

One may expect to find two diagrams on the photograph, one due to the pseudo-gas formed by the heavy molecules, and one due to the solvent liquid.

With this technique it is possible to determine the structure of various molecules, in some cases better than with the Raman spectrum.

Danilov has obtained some experimental results which seem to confirm the theory of J. D. Bernal and R. H. Fowler on the mobility of hydrogen ions.

Much experimental research on short radio waves is being done at Dniepropetrovsk. Malinovsky and his school study the effects of high-frequency fields on explosions and combustion.

The biological properties of high-frequency fields are being investigated. It has been found that cotton seeds treated with 18-metre waves for 15 seconds grew to maturity in 27 days less than the normal period. Tomatoes matured in 9 days less than the normal period, and gave a bigger yield.

The growing experiments are controlled by setting treated and untreated seeds in alternate rows of beds.

They find there is a relation between the tension and the degree of stimulation. High-tension fields are more stimulating than low-tension fields.

The seeds were treated in the laboratory. They are first soaked in water, and then exposed to the electric fields. Without the water soaking the fields do not have much effect.

These and other experiments of the sort suggest the development of an electric method of vernalization, or stimulation of early growth. Other methods of vernalization, of stimulating the growth of seeds and young plants so that they will not be exposed so long to the normal climate, have been much studied by Soviet agricultural botanists.

IV

The Mining Institute and Technical High School at Dniepropetrovsk has 3000 students. The Chemical Institute and the Metallurgical Institute have grown out of two of its departments.

The physics department has a 250-k.v. high-tension set for X-ray work. Malinovsky occupies a chair in the school, and some of his researches are made in its laboratories.

The school has an excellent library of 68,000 volumes. It is efficiently managed, and must be of much help to research workers in Dniepropetrovsk.

The Engineering Department is directed by Professor Dinnik and is well equipped, especially for work on the strength of materials. Research is conducted on the elastic qualities of building materials from the Donbas. Theoretical and experimental investigations are being made on the elasticity of wire hawsers, and the results are used for correcting Hütte's tables.

There is a section for aerodynamics. A group of eight post-graduates works on the theory of vibration in aeroplane wings. The growth of scientific work in Dniepropetrovsk has tended to concentrate the teaching of scientific and technical students in the Technical High School, and to move the research work into new independent research institutes. The chief members of the staffs of the research institutes also hold teaching professorships in the High School. Some research is done in the High School laboratories, but that appears definitely to be a secondary activity. There are advantages in this system in which professors do most of their teaching in one institute and most of their research in another. There is an additional stimulus to do properly in each institute the appropriate work. When a professor does all of his teaching and research in the same department he is often tempted to sacrifice one duty to the other, according to his taste. This is not so liable to happen if his research is judged alone in one institute, and his teaching is judged alone in the other. He enjoys the stimulation of working in two institutes where the spirit of research, and that of teaching, are respectively predominant. If he works in one institute only, he must adapt himself to one atmosphere, which may or may not be most suitable to him. Two places of work offer more than twice as much possibility that his gifts for research or for teaching will receive the fullest scope.

CHAPTER 9

THE PHYSICAL INSTITUTE OF THE UNIVERSITY, MOSCOW

THIS institute is directed by B. Hessen, whose well-known researches in the history of science, especially concerning the origin of Newton's ideas, are described in another chapter.

As it is a university institute, the staff lecture on physics, and do not give the whole of their time to research.

The chief departments are for physical optics, electrical oscillations, theoretical physics, magnetism, and thermodynamics.

I. Tamm is the leader of the department of theoretical physics; Mandelstamm and Ruhmer of optics and electrical oscillations; Psedvoditelev of thermodynamics; Arkadiev and Akulov of magnetism; Konoseevsky of the X-ray analysis of metals; and Landsberg of optics. Landsberg is senior professor of physics in the university.

Mandelstamm and Landsberg independently discovered the Raman effect. They were investigating the relations between the refraction of crystals with the thermal energy of their molecules. They found much larger disturbances than they had expected. They obtained these results in February, 1928, and spent two months on control experiments in order to obtain complete information, before publishing their results. Meanwhile, in March, 1928, Raman had published his observations.

They were interested in the optical effects connected with the Debye part of specific heat, and the comparison of the movements connected with heat motion.

Landsberg is studying selective absorption near mercury-vapour lines, and the effects of pseudo-molecules.

He has done researches in applied spectroscopy for the control of metallurgical processes. He has designed various optical instruments now used in industry. He has designed a new form of light source for beams of high intensity, polarizers for studying fluid flow in liquids, and simplified forms of industrial spectroscopes.

The chief difficulties in experimental research are due to the lack of small accessories, such as adequate supplies of Ilford photographic plates, and quartz. The situation is improving rapidly. Five years ago there were no Soviet-made rheostats, galvanometers, etc., and now these are made here. Scientists who are in serious need of special books and instruments, housing accommodation, etc., can apply to the Scientists' Aid Society, the K.S.U. The need for its services is rapidly disappearing.

Landsberg usually gives two days a week to teaching. During the year 1935 he had no teaching, and was able to give the whole of his time to research.

W. Zehden is a young German physicist. He designs, builds and tests apparatus for spectral analysis. He has designed special spectroscopes for use in factories. His spectroscopes for estimating chromium and silicon in metallurgical routine analysis will give a result in twelve to fifteen minutes. Other spectroscopes are for steel analysis, and for deciding qualitatively the sort of steel in various samples.

He has worked out a quantitative spectroscopic method for analysing steel, and has designed and constructed the appropriate spectroscopes.

His apparatuses are to be manufactured by mass-production methods in a Leningrad scientific instrument factory.

Mandelstamm is considered by many to be the most brilliant physicist in the Soviet Union. He is very modest and does not enjoy good health. His critical sense is deep, and he is not easily satisfied with his own work. He has never lost his feeling for self-criticism, even in his lectures to students. It is said that his tendency towards caution and thoroughness was acquired from his teacher Braun, but it seems clear that it is also natural. His critical temperament has prompted him frequently to decline directorships of institutes.   He is not a scientist of the organizing type.

His independent discovery of the Raman effect is only one of many researches.   His work on non-linear vibrations is considered to be the most original, and he has started a new line of research in this direction.   In Western Europe important contributions to this subject have been made by Van der Pol, and in the Soviet Union, Liapounov has made fundamental contributions to the mathematical theory.   In the theory of vibrations one is usually concerned with linear vibrations because their mathematical analysis is relatively easy.   In nature, however, vibrations are frequently non-linear, as in radio-communication. Until about 1925 problems in vibration were usually solved by analogy to linear vibrations.   But the laws of practical vibrations are often without analogy to those of linear vibrations.   The creation of the appropriate mathematical analysis for dealing with the non-linear equations for describing non-linear vibrations was begun about a hundred years ago, in the study of the mathematical analysis of the perturbations of planetary orbits.   It was continued by Poincaré.   The results were not applied to physical problems.   This has been begun by Mandelstamm during the last eight or ten years.   New physical notions have to be developed, and new conceptions of resonance, etc.   A radio transmitter is an example of a machine which produces non-linear vibrations.   A direct current is made to produce oscillations.

In electrical engineering Mandelstamm's studies of non-linear vibrations have inspired the invention and construction of a new type of dynamo for producing electricity. A model is under experimental test in Leningrad Electro-Physical Institute, as mentioned in Chapter 17.

The non-linear electric generators consist of a condenser whose capacity is varied.   It is put in a circuit with a self-inductance.   If the distance between the plates of the condenser is varied, a current is produced, whose period is one-half that of the changes in the condenser.   This form of generator gives a very high voltage. The efficiency in laboratory models is at present about 80 per cent. The efficiency can be increased by keeping the condenser in a high-pressure atmosphere. One can expect a higher ultimate efficiency than is obtained from the ordinary electromagnetic induction motor. The new type of generator does not short circuit. It is very light. The amount of metal required in its construction is much less than in an electro-magnetic induction generator of equal power.

The Mandelstamm-Popalexi dynamo is one of the most original contributions to electrical engineering since Faraday's invention of the first primitive dynamos employing the principle of electro-magnetic induction.

The early designs contained a variable self-induction consisting of seven pairs of coils fixed face to face around the circumferences of two parallel discs. A toothed metallic disc rotated between the fields between the coils. The teeth had been cut out so that the fields between the coils were simultaneously unoccupied. As the disc was rotated, the self-induction of the circuit decreased as the teeth passed through the space between the bobbins, and increased as they passed out. They used a disc of duralumin that could be rotated at a peripheral speed of 220 metres per second, and obtained a frequency of 1700 to 2000 per second. The coils were filled with iron cores in order to increase the self-induction and concentrate the field. This arrangement excited oscillations in the circuit, without the assistance of any current or voltage, whose frequency was exactly equal to one-half of the frequency of the variation of the self-induction.

The amplitude rapidly rose to a value sufficient to disrupt the insulation in the condenser and in the conductors of the circuit. In these experiments the tension rose to 12,000–15,000 volts.

According to the theory, the production of a stationary state requires the introduction of a non-linear element. In the first experiments, a group of 100-watt incandescent lamps were attached as a shunt to the oscillating circuit.

V. Lazarev has extended these researches at the Leningrad Electro-Physical Institute. He has used an apparatus with a modulation of 40 per cent instead of 14 per cent as in the first experiments, and a power-consumption of up to 4 kilowatts. The rotor has eight teeth and is made of hard aluminium. The self-induction was varied with a frequency of about 1900 per second, giving oscillations of about 950 per second. The stationary state, in which the machine produced electricity steadily, was obtained with the help of non-linear self-induction from either the iron cores of the coils of the stator, or from coils with cores of special iron which reacts in a particular way to the continuous current of magnetization of the iron.

Electrical oscillations in another machine were obtained by the periodic variation of the capacity by mechanical means. An oscillating circuit is formed by a condenser with periodically changing capacity shunted with a condenser containing oil, and a self-induction. The first condenser has two systems of armatures, one fixed, the stator, and the other rotating, the rotor. The stator consists of 26 square aluminium sheets, each having 14 radial symmetrically disposed indentations. The rotor consists of 25 circular aluminium sheets perforated in the same manner as those of the stator, and rotated by a continuous current driving motor at 4000 revolutions per minute. If the motor rotates n times per second, the capacity varies with the frequency $14n$ per second.

Six neon tubes requiring 220 volts, and a static Hartmann-Brown voltmeter were used to detect the existence of oscillations, and measure their intensity. The neon tubes also served to limit the growth of the oscillations.

If the neon tubes are left out, the system becomes linear, and the oscillations increase until the insulation is disrupted. The neon tubes maintained a tension of 600–700 volts, but without them the voltage rose to 2000–3000, which produced sparks in the armatures of the condenser.

H. Sekerska has studied a new process for producing Melde's phenomenon, the parametrical excitation of a vibrating cord. The normal nodes of a wire may be adjusted to different frequencies by the suspension of a variable weight. The wire is connected with an alternating current circuit with a frequency of 50 per second. This makes the temperature and consequently the tension of the wire vary with the frequency 100. When one of the normal nodes of the wire approximates to the frequency of 100, one finds, if the intensity of the current is sufficient, the parametrical excitation of this node.

In a radio receiver the resonance vibrations are of the same frequency as those of the transmitting wave. With non-linear systems the resonance vibrations of the receiver have twice the frequency of the transmitting wave. Such a system has practical advantages. The reception is much quicker, and the interference by atmospherics is much reduced. The ordinary receiving set has a period twenty to fifty times that of the incoming wave. It is constructed to be very selective, and takes much time before its resonance grows to a maximum. But the second type of resonance reaches its maximum much more quickly with the same selectivity.

The first type of multiple non-linear problems is presented by the phenomena of auto-oscillation, the oscillations created by the oscillatory system itself, without the participation of external forces, and at the expense of a constant source of energy, such as an accumulator battery. The non-linear methods for describing the effect of gentle and abrupt excitation, transitory phenomena, etc., have been given, and methods for giving quantitative approximations to the amplitude and frequency of almost sinusoidal oscillations. These methods give rigorous proofs of results previously known. Also, in some cases, they indicate the existence of periodical solutions and establish their stability. The proof of such existence theorems can have practical importance. The conventional differential equations used to describe phenomena are frequently idealized, and have a false simplicity.

Sometimes experiment shows that periodical solutions exist, of which the conventional theory gives no hint. An adequate theory would have exposed these properties without experiment.

In many of the older standard textbooks there are inadequate expositions of such elementary phenomena as the
operation of an electric bell or switch. The armature,
in a state of equilibrium, closes the circuit containing the
electro-magnet. The electro-magnet attracts the armature,
the current is interrupted, the magnet loses its attraction,
and the spring restores the armature to its original position;
and then in the words of a well-known German treatise,
"the game continues". But if the differential equations
for these actions are written down, it is easily proved that they
will not permit the game to continue, that they do not
permit a periodical solution. This shows something
essential has been neglected. In fact, the theory of the
switch is less simple than it appears. The self-induction
is essential in order that the oscillations may be possible.
Leontovitch has shown that self-induction is not only
necessary for the phenomenon, but it also intervenes in the
period of the oscillations, which is different from that of
the armature.

In their treatment of the theory of the oscillations of
relaxation, the Soviet school use analogous methods in
electrical and mechanical problems, similar to those used
in the analysis of elastic impacts. At the moment of impact
the speed changes discontinuously. The conservations of
energy and momentum permit the deduction of the speeds
after the impact from those that existed before. This
process excludes by principle the possibility of analysing
the speeds during the extremely short period of impact.
Attempts to do this, such as those of Hertz, show that the
problem is extremely complicated. So they have simplified
the mathematics of their theory of the oscillations of relaxation by a similar idealization, and in consequence, cannot
explain how the system jumps from one state to the other.

They have applied this process to electrical systems
possessing one degree of freedom, where the self-induction
has a secondary part, and also to mechanical auto-oscillatory
systems having a small mass and large friction.

Van der Pol has discussed the Abraham-Bloch multivibrator, with two degrees of freedom. He assumed the

phenomenon to be symmetrical, and avoided the discussion of the transitory phenomena following an initially unsymmetrical state. This restriction enabled him to obtain one equation of the second order. But in the general case he would have obtained two equations of the second order, which would have led to severe complications. The Soviet school with their method have obtained two equations of the first order, and have analysed the stationary conditions, calculated from the amplitude and period, and the asymmetrical transitory phenomena, of the Abraham-Bloch multivibrator. The results are confirmed by experiment.

No rigorous mathematical theory of the oscillations of emitters with antennæ, or Lecher wires, Grechova ultra-short wave valves whose grids form an oscillating system, telegraph wires that sing in the wind, the vibrations of aeroplane wings, musical instruments with strings, organ pipes, etc., exists. An approximate theory can be constructed by analogy with the rigorous theory for a system with a finite number of degrees of freedom, which will permit the calculation of amplitude, stability, etc., but it must be used cautiously. It gives several different solutions for the same conditions, and the correct one must be chosen by a consideration of the initial conditions or history of the system. Bendrikov and Brailo at Moscow, and Grechova at Gorky have confirmed the results experimentally. It is possible to make an excited wave in a Lecher-wire auto-oscillator disappear by touching with a finger. The system then begins to oscillate on another wavelength. When the finger is removed, the system does not return to the first wave, but remains on the length of the new wave. This phenomenon can also be produced by absorbing the energy with a resonance circuit. Analogous phenomena appear in musical string instruments. Similar experiments with a string vibrating under the impact of a jet of air or water, have been made by Strelkov. They are very simple, and excellently illustrate the phenomena of multiple auto-oscillatory systems.

Experiments have shown that resonance of the second order can be successfully applied for the demultiplication of frequencies, very strong amplifications where the frequency must remain very constant, and in reception. It can be used as a selective filter. Prolonged trials at Sagaredjo near Tiflis, where atmospherics are very severe, has shown that the filter separates a prolonged harmonious operation from an impulse very efficiently.

Mandelstamm and his colleagues are making experiments on the statistics of small variations in the electron movements in a circuit without electromotive force. These are amplified in secondary circuits and produce small currents and disturbances. The number of statistical electrical impulses may be counted, and their variation with temperature, etc., may be studied.

If two similar voltmeters are put in parallel in a circuit, there are slight differences in the voltages registered by them. The changes may occur in a second or a minute.

A variation of this arrangement is made by constructing a circuit where the current has a predilection for one of a pair of valves in parallel. If the predilection is high, the current will always flow through this valve. But if the predilection is reduced the current will sometimes flow through the other, and the number of changes may be compared. If the predilection and the rate of the changes is known, the size of the statistical variation may be calculated.

Ultra-sonic waves are another subject of research at the Moscow laboratory. The time of these vibrations is comparable with that of two consecutive effective collisions of molecules, so that the laws of dissipation of ultra-sonic waves among molecules are different from those for the dissipation of ordinary sound waves.

This leads to new methods of investigating absorption, etc.

It is possible to deduce from the interaction of gas molecules at very low pressure with ultra-sonic waves of very high frequency the efficiency of the transfer of translational into internal molecular energy.

Tamm's recent researches have been concerned with the theory of metals and solid bodies, in collaboration with

Shubin; general problems of quantum theory and nuclear physics, and statistical mechanics.

Ruhmer has given special attention to quantum chemistry.

Tamm and Shubin have recently published papers on the theory of the photoelectric effect in metals.

Shubin has made important contributions towards the explanation of ferromagnetism and conduction. Ferromagnetic metals have important electrical peculiarities. Slater has suggested similar ideas, and Shubin has worked them out.

Blochinov is studying phosphorescence. He found that an electron is always torn away from an atom in this phenomenon. Phosphorescent bodies are always impure. The loose electron becomes attached to one of the foreign atoms, and is then thrown off by the atom's heat vibrations. The problem then was: how can the walking electron attach itself to any atom? Blochinov showed it depended on a quantum mechanical sticking effect, combined with a deformation of the lattice.

In nuclear physics, Tamm and his colleagues have been studying the magnetic moment of the neutron. The hyper-fine spectral structure gives information about the nucleus, and Landé showed how the magnetic moment of the proton could be calculated.

They have studied, also, the forces of interaction between protons and neutrons. These are not electromagnetic. Heisenberg suggested they were due to interchange of charges.

Fermi's researches on the theory of electron-emission in radioactivity implied that this interchange might be possible.

Tamm has calculated the size of the forces that might be due to this interchange and finds it far too small. He has heard that Heisenberg obtained the same result.

In the quantum theory fields of force are associated with particles. He believes the interaction between protons and neutrons may be due to neutrinos. The interaction of electric forces can be caused by photons.

He has deduced the law of force between protons and neutrons, and finds it a fifth-power law. He supposes two protons and two neutrons repel each other, but one proton and one neutron can attract each other. Tamm has recently published some interesting calculations with J. D. Bernal, on the deduction of the properties of water from its molecular structure.

Arkadiev in the J. C. Maxwell laboratory of the institute has demonstrated the direct photography of radio-waves. He can fix the track of the waves along a sheet of white paper. The apparatus consists of a coherer with two electrodes that rest on moistened paper, impregnated with a chemical indicator. The colour of the paper changes owing to electrolytic decomposition of the chemical substance when the waves fall on the coherer and send a current between the electrodes through the paper. The track of the waves may be followed by putting a large number of small detectors on the paper and joining the series of coloured spots that appear on it. Arkadiev has succeeded in reflecting and refracting the rays with mirrors and lenses, and has obtained a diffraction image of their source.

Researches on hysteresis losses, ferro-magnetism, the Hall and Thomson effect and the magnetic properties of alloys are made by N. Akulov in the magnetic laboratory.

He has given theories of the hysteresis losses in ferro-magnetic materials in alternating and rotating magnetic fields. The losses that occur when they are rotated in weak fields disappear, however, when the materials are rotated in strong fields. The cause of the disappearance is the same as the cause of the Paschen-Back effect. The theory shows how the maximum hysteresis losses in any metal may be calculated, and various results concerning the Barkhausen effect in rotating fields may be deduced.

Experiments are made on the magnetic microscopic properties of single crystals. The structure of a magnetized mixture of iron powder and alcohol has been studied.

Apparatus for the industrial testing of machinery by magnetic methods has been designed, including magnetic apparatus for testing and rejecting defective articles from mass-production conveyors and travelling belts.

A collective attack is being made on the Thomson effect. It was discovered eighty years ago, and 2000 papers on it have been published, but no adequate theory has been given. Akulov believes that simultaneous observations of magnetic properties by a number of observers might provide the necessary data.

They have investigated the effect of cold working on the orientation of the crystals in steel by their behaviour in magnetic fields. The percentage of the orientation can be calculated.

The magnetic laboratory was organized three years ago, and employs no foreign apparatus.

The laboratory buildings are old, and situated in the centre of Moscow, on the university site by the Mokhovaya. Several of the chief professors live within the precincts. The extreme convenience of the situation has probably had a happy influence on the institute, as the charm and cultivation of its distinguished staff may partly be due to living in such an accessible place.

The Moscow University students of physics are fortunate to have their studies directed by such men as Hessen, Landsberg, Mandelstamm, and Tamm. Tamm's powers of scientific exposition in the medium of the English language are exceptional, and in the Russian language he must be a superb teacher.

The chief characteristic of the work of the institute is quality. They do not aim at publishing very many results, but a smaller number of more original and profound results. This is a very proper ideal for an academic institution. The institute is making an excellent contribution towards the creation of the culture of the new Soviet society.

CHAPTER 10

THE PHYSICO-TECHNICAL INSTITUTE OF THE URAL, SVERDLOVSK

THE director of this institute, which is being established at Sverdlovsk, is Professor Dorfmann. His description of its objects will be followed here.

The Ural Mountains are one of the richest centres of natural wealth in the world. Under the plans of industrialization, the district is being provided with industries of size appropriate to this wealth, and it will become one of the world's chief industrial centres. The methodical development of industry requires a system of research institutes not far from the factories and works.

When industry has been established, its growth always suggests new theoretical problems. These can be investigated most conveniently in neighbouring institutes.

The Sverdlovsk Physico-Technical Institute is intended to be a centre where problems of general physical interest may be investigated, and also where special attention can be given to the sort of physical problems that arise in the chief Ural industries. The Urals are particularly rich in metals of many sorts, so special attention will be devoted to the physics of metals, including the ferrous and non-ferrous sorts.

In the past, metallurgy has not received much theoretical development. Authorities such as Rosenhain and Hume-Rothery have explained the necessity for a closer collaboration between metallurgy and physics. But their exhortations have not had the desirable effect, partly owing to the patent-monopolies in Western countries, which create barriers between empirical industrial research, and science.

In the Western countries the throttling effect of patent-monopolies on the application of new scientific discoveries is very prominent. Scientific discovery continues at a swift pace, but becomes more separated from industrial development owing to the state of economic crisis.

This contrast of relative scientific advance does not occur under a socialist economy. The proper connection between industry and science can be established in a planned economy, so in the U.S.S.R. it is confidently hoped that an institute for the cultivation of the physics of metals will be successful.

The physics of metals is a wide subject. The following aspects will therefore have to be studied, such as the laws of the formation of alloys, and the problem of the valency forces between the constituent atoms ; the changes in phases of metals and the dynamics of these changes, which form the core of the theoretical treatment of alloys, which, in spite of several beautiful researches, remain largely obscure ; the problems of cohesion, and the quantitative theory of plastic deformation and twin-formation which are of great importance to technology ; the mechanism of electrical conduction and supra-conduction, which remains obscure; and the theory of magnetism in metals which is of great electro-technical importance.

While the institute was being built in Sverdlovsk, the nucleus of a staff was formed in Leningrad, with rooms in the Leningrad Physico-Technical Institute. This contained about forty-five persons, and prepared plans of research, and equipment, and engaged in training for its future activities. The skeleton organization contained departments for the study of electrical and magnetic properties, phase changes, mechanical qualities of metals, and theoretical physics.

The area of the rooms of the Sverdlovsk building is about 5000 square yards. There are large laboratories with the latest X-ray equipment, with apparatus for strength of materials investigation, for metallography with first-class optical, electrical, magnetic and thermal and other physical equipment. By 1937 the scientific and technical staff is expected to number about 200.

PART III

CHEMISTRY

CHAPTER 11

THE KARPOV INSTITUTE OF PHYSICAL CHEMISTRY, MOSCOW

THIS institute was founded in 1922. It has two large laboratories. The first building near the centre of Moscow is an old mansion in a large garden on the side of a hill. A second large new building has been erected at the bottom of the garden. These houses with gardens near to the centre of the city resemble, on a larger scale, the houses in St. John's Wood in London. They were formerly the town houses of country landlords, and other members of the richer classes. A large part of Moscow has this pleasant mixture of houses and gardens.

The director of the Karpov institute is Professor A. N. Bach. He is a biochemist, not a physical chemist. He also directs a neighbouring institute of biochemistry, named after him. He lives in a flat at the top of the Karpov institute. His daughter, Natalie Bach, is also a chemist, and as she is an excellent linguist she frequently acts as the foreign secretary of chemical conferences. Bach's own researches have been concerned with ferments and enzymes, especially catalase and amylase. (The former exists in the blood and promotes the oxidation of the tissues, and the latter splits the starch in food, in order to promote digestion and assimilation.)

Bach is an old revolutionary, and knew many of the exiles when he was living in Switzerland. His combination of scientific eminence and political knowledge has made him one of the most important leaders of the new scientific development in the Soviet Union.

The leaders of research in the Karpov institute include the well-known physical chemists A. Frumkin, who works on surface chemistry; A. J. Rabinovitch on photochemistry and colloid chemistry; I. Kasarnovsky on metallurgical chemistry; and S. S. Medvedev on combustion.

Frumkin works in laboratories at the top of the old building. There is a fine view of the district from the windows. He has about fifteen collaborators.

The German quantum chemist H. Hellmann has a study in this building. The main laboratories of the applied physical chemists are in the new building. This is spacious and of modern design.

Frumkin's researches have mainly dealt with the principles of electrocapillarity, and adsorption. These principles have a fundamental part in the explanation of the phenomena that occur at the surfaces of contact between substances. The production of electricity by electric batteries and accumulators depends on the actions at the surfaces between the metal plates and the salt solutions.

This is evident because the electric potentials throughout the metal plates and the solutions themselves are constant. If the metal plates and solutions are individually connected to a galvanometer, no production of current is registered, but if they are arranged in contact, a current may be obtained.

The nature and theory of the conditions at the surface between the metal electrodes and the electrolytes in voltaic batteries has been extensively investigated. The fact that voltaic cells possess a difference of potential and can produce a current shows that a differential of potential must occur across the surfaces separating the metal and liquid components of the cell.

W. Thomson, Varley and Helmholtz discussed the implications of this fact during the latter part of the nineteenth

PLATE 5

Photo. Planet News Ltd.

The Laboratory for applied chemistry at the Karpov Institute

[face p. 160

century, and deduced the electrical properties of the surfaces on the assumption that these consisted of two electrified sheets facing each other. Helmholtz supposed that one of these sheets was in the metal surface and the other was parallel to it and in the electrolyte. This conception did not suggest any detailed picture of the structure of, and distance between, these two sheets, or double layer, as they were named. It is now believed that the position of the layers of electric charge are not exactly defined, but diffuse through a small distance from the interface between the surfaces.

When the strengths of the salt solutions in a battery become weaker, the voltage falls. Nernst showed that this could be deduced from what he described as the ionic solution pressure of the ions in the solution.

The influence of the potentials existing at surfaces is suggested by the behaviour of metals in contact. Different metals have a different affinity for electrons. It is known, for instance, that copper attracts electrons with a force measured by about 4 volts, whereas zinc attracts them with a force measured by about 3·4 volts. The difference between these is 0·60 volts, and is of the same order (1·10 volts) as the voltage given by a Daniell cell, which consists of plates of copper and zinc in a solution of sulphuric acid.

These roughly successful explanations of the origin and variation of the voltage produced by voltaic cells confirmed the existence of electrical activities at the interfaces between different substances.

It is well known that surfaces have physical peculiarities. For example, the surface of water is in a state of tension which enables it to support relatively heavy objects. A steel needle will float on the surface of water. If electrical forces may also operate at the surfaces of liquids, reactions between these forces and surface tension should not be unexpected. The existence of such electro-capillary phenomena, as they are named, was demonstrated by Lippmann in 1875. He showed that if the potential difference across the surface separating mercury and dilute sulphuric acid was changed then the tension at the surface between the two liquids changed. As the potential difference is increased, the surface tension gradually falls to a minimum and then rises again. Lippmann derived an equation to describe these results.

From discussions of these phenomena by Helmholtz in 1881 it follows that the surface of the mercury possesses a positive charge, and opposite to it, at a small distance in the liquid, is a negatively charged layer, presumably produced by an array of the negatively charged particles or ions in the solution.

When the increase in the potential difference through the surface is begun, the positive charges in the surface of the mercury accumulate, and repel each other. This reduces the surface tension.

These remarks may help to give some idea of the sort of problems investigated in the study of electro-capillarity. Those who desire further elucidation should read E. K. Rideal's *Surface Chemistry*.

Two of Frumkin's earliest papers were written in 1917, on the form of the electro-capillary curve and Lippmann's equation, and included criticisms of Nernst's theory of ionic solution pressures. He was then at Odessa University, and about twenty years old. The papers were published in English in the *Philosophical Magazine* in 1920.

In 1922 Frumkin gave an experimental proof of Lippmann's equation. He measured the current produced by dropping mercury through various solutions. The number and the surface area of the mercury drops was known, so the size of the electric charge on the mercury surface tension with potential difference was also measured. He found that the data fitted Lippmann's equation within an error of about 5 per cent.

Gouy had observed that the addition of organic substances to the electrolyte altered the shape of the electro-capillary curve. It has also been observed that if other electrolytes were used instead of sulphuric acid, the agreement was no longer good. Frumkin has proposed a quantitative interpretation of these results. In his papers of 1920 he had explained that Krüger's attempt to describe the anomalous results obtained from solutions of iodides and cyanides by a modification of Lippmann's equation, did not give a sufficiently large correction, and proposed another modification which gave closer agreement between experiment and theory.

Frumkin has given a theory of the displacing effect of neutral molecules, such as those of organic substances, on the electro-capillary curve. He has calculated the effect of replacing a water molecule in the interface by an organic molecule, and has compared the calculated effects for molecules of tertiary amyl alcohol, caproic acid, pyrogallol and other substances, in sodium chloride solution with those observed by experimental measurement. In these cases the agreement is good, but with other substances, such as those containing halogens and sulphur, it is not so good, owing to the adsorption of these substances by the mercury surface. He has found that betaiodo-proprionic acid is adsorbed thirty-six times more strongly than betachlor-proprionic acid at the surface between mercury and water. This large difference is not observed in the adsorption of these acids at the surface between water and air.

Frumkin has made important researches on the electrical conditions existing at the surfaces between gases and liquids. Studies of these conditions provide information on the orientation of molecules at these surfaces.

He has improved the experimental methods. He has shown that the difference of potential produced by fatty acids at a gas-liquid surface is, for a given surface concentration, independent of the length of the acid molecule. He has shown that the surface adsorption of water increases with the increase of the number of chlorine atoms in sodium chlor-acetates. This indicates that energy is required to pull a chlorine atom from the surface into the interior, and provides data for determining the orientation of the chlorine in the surface.

If a water surface is covered with a unimolecular layer of acetate molecules, the tops of the molecules will form a sheet whose charge will depend on the atoms in the tops. If hydrogen atoms in the tops are replaced by chlorine atoms, the total charge in the sheet of tops will be lowered. If electrical measurement shows the charge has decreased, then the positions and orientations of the various atoms in the acetate molecule may be deduced.

Frumkin and the Karpov school have made extensive researches of electrolytes by charcoal. If sugar charcoal is activated by heating it for five hours in carbon dioxide, it behaves as a gas electrode in water solutions. The sign of the charge on the carbon surface is determined by the nature of the gas in the carbon. If air is present, hydroxyl ions pass into the solution, leaving the carbon positively charged, and acid is adsorbed. If hydrogen is present, the carbon may send hydrogen ions into the solution. The addition of a little platinum to the carbon enables it to remove oxygen, and it can then adsorb alkali. Carbon which has been activated by heating in hydrogen at 1000° C., adsorbs alkali in air-free solutions. This is the reverse of the effect observed in air. When this carbon is exposed to air it recovers oxygen and again adsorbs acids.

Frumkin and Cirves have shown that the Lippmann-Helmholtz equation applies to the change of the potential difference between electrolytes and mercury when thallium and cadmium are added to the latter to form amalgams.

The spraying of liquids leads to the separation of electric charges. This electrical effect of water-dropping or bubbling has been named ballo-electricity. The ballo-electrical capacity of the majority of molecules is influenced by their orientation at the surface. The substances may be divided into two classes, according to whether the positive end of the molecule in the surface is directed towards the liquid or the gas. In water the positive ends of the molecules are pointing towards the water, and not towards the gas.

Frumkin, Levina and Zarubina have shown that every point on the surface of activated charcoal has the same potential. This contradicts the view that some points are negatively, and others positively charged.

B. Kabanov and Frumkin have examined the size of the gas-bubbles produced by electrolysis. They suggest that it is determined by the marginal angle at the boundary between the electrode, the solution, and the bubble. It is also dependent on the potential of the electrode. Up to the moment of rupture the equilibrium of the bubble is entirely determined by the surface forces, hydrostatic pressure and the gas pressure within the bubble. The results are of practical importance, and Kabanov and Frumkin have explained their application in the industrial electrolysis of zinc.

Natalie Bach and I. Levitin have studied by microphotography the changes in the form of crystals of Ceylon graphite during combustion in carbon dioxide. The hexagonal faces are reactive at the edges but not in the middle. Ash from natural graphite and potassium, catalyse the reaction with carbon dioxide at 1000° C.

When the graphite is burned in mixtures of carbon dioxide and hydrochloric acid, the holes are hexagonal, but in pure carbon dioxide they are round or irregular.

N. Bach is at present investigating the electrokinetic and thermodynamic potentials of surfaces between gases and liquids.

S. Levina is continuing the studies of the effects of platinum on charcoal adsorption. She has found that if 200 per cent of platinum is added to the charcoal, the increase in the adsorption stops. The active places on the charcoal are due to contact processes.

Burstein is investigating the catalytic effect of charcoal on the conversion of ortho- and para-forms of hydrogen. The poisoning of the surface with hydrogen is influenced by the temperature. She found that atomic hydrogen poisoned the conversion effect.

Temkin and Sirkin are studying the oxidation of nitric oxide at liquid air temperatures. At room temperatures and low pressure there is no reaction. At the temperature of solid carbon dioxide there is no reaction. At liquid air temperatures the rate of the reaction doubles for changes of 2°. The reaction occurs on cold walls only, and it is proportional to the area of the tubes. It is a catalytic effect.

They are studying dipole moments, and precise methods

of measuring the angles between chemical bonds, and the shape of the water molecule.

Hellmann is applying the theory of wave-mechanics to the explanation of chemical bonds. It is necessary to allow for the kinetic energy of electron changes, besides the work done against static forces. He has investigated the increase of kinetic energy through overlapping of the fields from adjacent particles, and his calculations of the magnitudes of the forces binding two potassium atoms into a molecule, have given promising results. He has results also for the binding between atoms of potassium and hydrogen.

Rabinovitch and his colleagues have made extensive researches on the nature of colloidal solutions. These consist, in the simplest form, of mixtures of two substances, one being distributed throughout, the other in particles of a certain range of diameter. This range of diameter is from about one ten-thousandth of one-millionth of an inch. Fluids containing particles of this size often differ considerably from simple fluids. For instance, soap solution is considerably different from water. It consists of particles, or micelles, of sodium stearate distributed through the water. The elucidation of the properties of solutions of this sort is the task of colloidal chemistry. This science is of great importance, as all of those applied sciences, which have to deal with colloidal substances must utilize its principles more or less consciously. It happens that most animal and vegetable tissues are colloidal. Thus the science of medicine, which has to keep living tissue healthy, must frequently employ a knowledge of the science. All of those industries which employ animal and vegetable products, such as wool and cotton, require a knowledge of colloid chemistry.

The most characteristic colloids are sticky or jelly-like substances. That is why they are named colloids, as the word is derived from the Greek word for glue, *kolla*. It is not surprising that sticky substances should be made of relatively large particles spread through a fluid. Solutions which contain no particles larger than molecules are not much more viscous than the liquid with which they are made. But if the molecules bunch together and make larger particles, the solution becomes viscous. If the particles become very large, and can be seen, the solution loses its colloidal properties, and begins to resemble a bag of sand. If the particles were exceedingly small, the solution would not be sticky, and if they were very large, it would also not be sticky.

As colloids derive their properties from their possession of particles of a certain size, the constancy of their properties, their stability, depends on their retention of this size of particle. If the particles are dispersed into molecules, the colloid becomes an ordinary solution. If the particles stick together, or coagulate, and form heavy lumps, these fall to the bottom and settle out, and again the colloidal character is destroyed.

Why do the particles in colloidal solutions not settle when the solution is left to stand? This is due to the movement of the molecules, whose effects were first observed by the botanist, Robert Brown, in 1827. They continually bump into the colloidal particles. If these are not too heavy they are never able to settle. Thus colloids are made stable if the size of their particles can be fixed.

One of the ways of stabilizing colloids is to add substances that cover their particles with layers of molecules, which prevent the particles from sticking together when they collide. Another way is to stick electrically charged particles on to the colloidal particles, so that all of them have a considerable electric charge of the same sign. As electric charges of like sign repel each other, the colloidal particles repel each other, and resist the tendency to coagulate.

The effects of this coating and charging of the particles in colloids are of immense practical importance.

For instance, bread is a colloidal material. To a large degree it consists of colloidal particles of starch bound together by water. It is well-known that new bread is soft, and has a greyish, slightly transparent appearance. Old bread is hard, white and opaque. It is commonly believed that it is stale because it has become dry. This is not so.

M

There is little difference between the amount of water in new and in old bread. The change is due to colloidal coagulation. The starch particles begin to stick together and form larger particles. These become too large to transmit light, so the transparent appearance disappears. The large hard particles reflect the light and appear white. They give the bread a gritty structure and a dry taste.

Evidently the preservation of the size of the colloidal particles in starch is essential if the newness of the bread is to be preserved. This is done by putting fat into it. Fat or butter enables rich cakes to preserve their flavour because they give the starch particles a coating of fat which prevents them from coagulating and forming large white stale particles.

The stability of London fogs is due to the same cause as the keeping power of rich cakes. The fog consists of water particles of colloidal size. If these were pure water they would tend to stick together and condense. But they collect a layer of oil from the smoke from all the coal fires in London. This enables them to preserve their size, and behave like stabilized colloids, to the discomfort of the inhabitants.

Another important example of the behaviour of colloidal solutions is seen in the formation of deltas at the mouths of rivers, such as the Mississippi or the Nile. It is known that the amount of mud deposited at the mouths of such rivers is greater than the amount of visible mud carried down in the river-water. Where has the mud come from? Much of it has been carried down the river in the form of a transparent colloidal solution. When it has passed into the salty water of the sea, the invisible colloidal particles have been coagulated by the salt into visible particles of mud, that settle on the sea-bottom and form mud-banks. The molecules of dissolved salt in the water are dissociated into pairs of electrified particles. Some of the electrified particles stick to the colloidal particles, and neutralize their electric charges and destroy their mutual repulsion or protection. The colloidal particles are then free to coagulate, and form visible mud.

These simple examples are sufficient to illustrate the importance of colloid chemistry in industrial processes and those of daily life, and the importance of obtaining a complete knowledge of how the colloidal particles hehave, and all the different methods by which they may be stabilized or coagulated.

Rabinovitch and Kargin have discussed the fundamental conceptions of that sort of colloidal solution in which the particles do not attract the fluid which supports them. In some ways such colloidal solutions resemble electrolytes, which contain salt molecules that have dissociated into ions bearing electric charges. In colloidal electrolytes numbers of these ions stick together in groups, and so form abnormally large particles which confer on the solution its colloidal behaviour.

They have described a number of observations which seem to show that colloids with particles which do not attract the fluid supporting them, i.e. lyophobic colloids, contain mechanisms of a sort different from those found in ordinary electrolytic solutions, such as that of common salt in water. They had made some experiments on the dilution of colloidal acids, such as vanadic and tungstic acids. In these colloidal solutions, the particles of acid appear to act as a reservoir of acid material which is gradually emptied into the liquid as the dilution proceeds. The solutions behave like buffer solutions. This property appears to be different from those of electrolytes.

Their analysis of measurements of the electrical properties of the solutions, which provide information concerning the electrical state of the ions, indicates that these measurements refer chiefly to the ion in the liquid between the particles, and do not allow any conclusion to be made concerning the concentration of compensating ions, i.e. of ions of sign opposite to that of the particle, surrounding the latter, in the double layer.

They have pointed out that considerable amounts of both ions of stabilizing electrolytes have been detected in the liquid between the particles of most colloids of the type in which the particles do not attract the liquid.

When electrolytes are added to these colloids, they may

produce insoluble salts, which must influence the stability of the system.

They have explained that the exchange of ions held, or adsorbed, by the particles of the colloid, may produce forces of attraction between the particles.

As already mentioned in connection with the formation with river deltas, the addition of electrolytes, such as common salt solution, to colloidal solutions, often makes the particles in the latter coagulate. The electrified ions of sodium or chlorine are adsorbed by the colloidal particles, and this may help the particles to stick together, and become too large not to settle in the liquid.

Rabinovitch and Kargin consider that both of the ions produced by the dissociation of the salt in an electrolyte may be adsorbed by the colloidal particles. One of them may diminish, and the other may increase a colloidal particle's electric charge and stability.

If a stabilizing electrolyte has already been added to the colloidal solution, which has the effect of increasing the independence of each of the colloidal particles, by, for example, increasing their electric charges, so that they repel each other more rigorously, then the addition of a second electrolyte for the purpose of producing the reverse effect, will lead to exchanges between the four ions which will now be adsorbed by the particles. These exchanges will determine whether, and how far, the stability of the colloid will be increased or decreased.

They have found that the addition of potassium chloride to arsenic trisulphide and selenium colloidal solutions or sols increased the stability. The addition of sodium sulphate to ferric oxide sols had a similar effect.

Their conception of exchange adsorption suggests the possibility of attractional besides repulsive forces arising from the exchange of adsorbed ions. They depart from the current conception of a colloidal particle as a multivalent ion with a constant number of charging ions that confer on it a permanent electric charge. They suppose all of the sorts of ions present may be adsorbed by the surface of the particle. The surface itself must be variable, and the variation in the attractive forces towards other particles must be due to this.

The Karpov school of colloidal chemists have made important researches on the properties of colloidal silica. The usually accepted theory of colloidal solutions of silica (known commercially as water-glass, and used for preserving eggs and many other purposes) was proposed by Pauli and Valko. It has been shown by titration with alkali that pure silicic acid sols have a very high acidity, and if the conceptions of Pauli and Valko are correct, these acids must be very strong and entirely dissociated into ions.

But Rabinovitch and Kargin have shown, as already mentioned, that the methods used by Pauli and Valko for determining the concentration of ions entering into the double layer is not correct. This method gives only the concentration or activity of the dispersing, or peptizing, ions in the liquid between the colloidal particles.

Thus the measurements of Pauli and Valko prove only that a strong acid exists in the liquid between the particles.

If a colloidal silicic acid is made by polymerizing a pure silicic acid solution, i.e. making its molecules or ions clump together until they produce groups of colloidal size, its acidic properties prove to be quite different. This shows that the structure for the silicic colloidal particles cannot in all cases be that proposed by Pauli and Valko.

Kargin and Rabinovitch suggested that this and other contradictions could be resolved if the high acidity of the silica sols is due not to the dissociation of colloidal silica as a colloidal electrolyte, according to Pauli's theory, but to the admixture of a common acid in true solution which is distributed in the liquid between the particles.

In order to test these ideas, A. J. Bybaev studied extremely pure silica sols made from silicon tetrachloride. No difference in conductivity was noticed between these sols and that of twice-distilled water.

Very pure silica sols were prepared by a new method. Silane, or silicon tetrahydride, was oxidized by ozone in water. These sols had no acid properties, and it was concluded that pure silica sols are neutral. Their stability is attributed to the water-attracting properties of the colloidal particles of silica.

Bybaev found that the concentration of ions of hydrogen in highly acid silica sols was equivalent to that of the ions of chlorine.   This indicated that acidity found by electrical methods was due to hydrochloric acid in the liquid between the colloidal particles of silica.

Thus it is concluded that the apparent high acidity of silica sols is due to hydrochloric acid, that has not been removed by sufficient purification.

These researches indicate the general high importance of the condition of the liquid between the particles in colloidal solutions.

Other researches conducted in the colloidal laboratory have been concerned with the optical properties of the surfaces of colloidal particles.

The diffraction of slow electrons of 50 to 400 volts has been used for the investigation of dispersed tungsten sols.

They have shown that the viscosity of colloidal solutions may be increased by 50 per cent, if the solutions are exposed to an electric field by placing them between the plates of an electrical condenser, in the form of a capillary viscometer.   This is due to the orientation of the particles by the field as they slip through the capillary tube, and the change in orientation alters the speed with which they travel.

They have investigated the effect of ageing on colloidal solutions.   S. A. Katz has shown that the viscosity of alkaline silica sols of similar chemical compositions and concentrations increases very much with age.   Thus these sols cannot be in complete equilibrium.

They use Shalnikov's method of preparing colloidal ices by directing two beams of molecular rays on to a bulb cooled with liquid air.   The colloidal ices melt and may be collected inside a tube.   It is possible to prepare many interesting colloidal mixtures by this technique.

They are experimenting with ultra-sonic waves for the preparation of colloidal solutions.

Attempts are being made to harden soil by hardening the silica through colloidal treatment.

Experiments have been made on 1 to 3 per cent solutions of rubber which have a high electrical orientation.

Rabinovitch also directs the laboratory for the chemistry of photography, which conducts pure research and also is consulted by the industry on technological processes. He has made interesting experiments on the colloidal theory of the development of the latent image in the photographic film. The problems of sensitization, the surface of bromide grains, etc., are studied.

Kargin is studying the quantum yield of the oxidation of iron salts under ultra-violet irradiation.

The laboratory for the study of the catalysis of organic compounds is directed by S. S. Medvedev. The kinetics and mechanics of this process are studied, especially the kinetics of the oxidation of hydrocarbons.

They have found that the reaction occurs through a chain mechanism, not only in gases, but also in liquids.

They have demonstrated that hydrocarbon oxidation proceeds through the formation of peroxides, which act as catalysts. The hydrocarbon is first activated. Then it combines with oxygen to produce a peroxide. The peroxide while still active attacks more molecules of the hydrocarbon, and leaves them in an activated condition. The cycle of reactions is then repeated. A formula for calculating the velocity of the reaction has been deduced.

The polymerization of butadiene for the production of synthetic rubber has been investigated. It is promoted by sodium, and was believed to proceed homogeneously. They have found that the reaction is heterogeneous.

With E. N. Alexeyeva he has used the original method of Baeyer and Villiger for preparing the higher akyl peroxides. They have obtained isopropyl hydrogen peroxide by treating di-isopropyl sulphate with hydrogen peroxide and alkali. This compound gives a salt which can be converted into a peroxidic ester by terephthalyl chloride. They have prepared peroxidic compounds of the camphoric acid series, and have used percamphoric acid for the determination of unsaturation.

Wood-spirit oil has been investigated in collaboration

with S. I. Rybin, and the catalytic hydrolysis of alkyl halide vapours with A. Abkin.

They have studied the progress of chemical reactions with variable activation energies.

The oxidation of methane has been investigated by Medvedev.   Much methane in the form of natural gas escapes from the earth in various parts of the Soviet Union, and methods of employing it as a raw material are of great industrial importance.   A method of converting it into formaldehyde has been worked out.

I. Kasarnovsky has made researches of great industrial importance on processes of aluminium extraction.   He has devised a method of obtaining aluminium from clays, and carbonized aluminium chloride residues left in the process of oil-cracking.   Aluminium chloride is used as a catalyst for breaking crude petroleum into lighter oils suitable for use as petrol and motor spirit.   The Soviet Union is not rich in bauxite, the high-grade ore which is the usual source of aluminium, so the possibilities of extracting the metal from clays and oil-cracking residues were investigated.

The aluminium chloride for the cracking catalysts is prepared from kaolin.   The deposits of kaolin, the petroleum refineries, and the hydroelectric plant at Dnieproges, are within convenient transport distances of each other.   An immense factory for extracting aluminium has been erected at Dnieproges and will draw electric power from the hydro-electric plant.   It is twice as large as the largest aluminium works in Germany.   The linking of the petroleum and aluminium industry through the chloride process is expected to provide large economies.

Other researches of industrial importance have been made on the preparation of plastic materials.   Bakelite is made from basic concentrates.   They have prepared a plastic, which they have named carbolite, from acid concentrates.

They have investigated the catalytic hydrogenation of petroleum, which is used for manufacturing fatty acids for the soap industry, and they have studied chemical properties of peat and of artificial silk.

CHAPTER 12

THE INSTITUTE OF CHEMICAL PHYSICS, LENINGRAD

THE aims of the institute have been described by its director, Professor N. N. Semenov, and his description will be followed closely.

The modern advances in the physics of atomic and molecular structure were bound to have a lively influence on the development of chemistry. They could be expected to have particular influence on the theory of chemical dynamics, which, in contrast with the theory of chemical equilibria, could not be expected to develop on the lines of classical physics. Van't Hoff and Arrhenius obtained extremely important results in the theory of equilibria, but were unable to obtain comprehensive results in the theory of kinetics. Their kinematical researches show signs of the thermodynamical mode of thought, in spite of their immense importance for the development of chemical dynamics. The conception of the equilibrium of temperature has a very important part in them. But a self-developing chemical process unavoidably contains deviations from the temperature equilibrium, and deviations from Maxwell's distribution, which can reach very high values in chain reactions.

The line of the pure chemical development of the theory of chemical dynamics could not bring comprehensive results for the following reasons. Firstly, the intermediate products very often appear to be nothing but saturated chemical compounds. Radicals, atoms with free valencies, and excited molecules, are the types of intermediate links that appear most often in almost every reaction. The ordinary methods of chemical investigation provide little information about these reactions because their life is too short. Only the newest methods of theoretical and experimental physics provide some knowledge of these links of intermediate reactions. Secondly, the intermediate forms of the molecules in each reaction are distinguished not only by their composition and structure but also by their kinetic and oscillatory energy.

These energy factors are very often of decisive influence, and in this case purely chemical methods of analysis are helpless. The velocity of reactions may be formulated only through studies of the transference of energy from one particle to another, and investigating the times of relaxation.

The insufficiency of theoretical conceptions in the field of kinetics is also reflected in the material collected by the experimental researches on the velocity of reactions, and in catalysis. The material is insufficient and unsystematic. Only a few dozen reactions of the most simple type have been more or less thoroughly investigated, especially by Bodenstein. Even in these cases the mechanism is not exactly known. The chemical combination of hydrogen and chlorine is a classical example. It has been studied for a hundred years, and in spite of hundreds of researches its mechanism remains unclear.

The following proposals may therefore be made. Firstly, the comparative examination of the velocities of different reactions should be extended, so that they may be classified accurately, and provide the material for the deduction of general kinetical laws, which will have the same degree of importance as the second law of conditions of equilibria. Secondly, a new theory of chemical kinetics may be made only through the application of wave-mechanics and other principles of modern physics to the problem of the transference of energy, activation, and other fundamental elementary processes.

These questions present an immense task, of far more importance than the problem of chemical equilibrium. The connecting science of physical chemistry was founded to solve the problems of equilibrium, and now a new branch of science is required for the formulation of chemical dynamics, which will apply the new results of physics to chemistry, and produce many fruitful results.

The constitution of physical chemistry as a special science necessitates the organization of institutes, journals and seminars. The independent development of this branch of science is a fundamental condition for the growth of knowledge of chemical changes.

The leading rôle in establishing the independence of physical chemistry was taken by Germany, where the necessity for formulating the new branch of science was first recognized.

The first successes in the new field were gained by Bodenstein and by Franck, and section B of the *Zeitschrift für Physikalische Chemie* was formed for the publication of suitable papers.

In the U.S.S.R. the plans for industrialization, which included socialist economy and planned management of industry on scientific principles, required an enormous extension of the chemical industry, and created favourable conditions for the growth of the new science.

As a result of these circumstances, the first institute devoted entirely to the development of this new branch of science was established in the U.S.S.R., as the Institute for Chemical Physics, at Leningrad.

It was hoped that the organization of this institute would interest colleagues in other countries, and that some would come to work and lecture in Leningrad, from time to time.

The institute was opened in September, 1931, under the direction of Professor N. N. Semenov. There are six experimental departments. One is for the study of the fundamental elements of chemical reactions, under the direction of Semenov, Frenkel and Kondratiev. The second is for catalysis and is under the direction of Roginsky. The third is for combustion and gas explosions, directed by Sagulin, Chariton, Kovalsky, and Neumann. The fourth is for polymerization processes, under the direction of Shalnikov, and the fifth for surface phenomena, which has recently been extended into a separate institute, was directed by Talmud, who is now the director of the new institute.

The sixth department is for electro-chemistry and is under the direction of Shtshukarev, Nikolsky and Müller.

In addition to these departments there is a theoretical group directed by Frenkel.

The subjects of the first department's researches are the processes of energy-transference and activation, the mechanism of chains and their development, and the reactions in electric discharges.

The department for catalysis is intended to investigate the more recondite aspects of problems studied in many industrial institutes in the U.S.S.R., such as the Nitrogen Institute, the Sulphuric Acid Institute, the Petroleum Institute, and the Fats Institute. It is to be a theoretical centre worked in collaboration with these industrial institutes. All laboratories in the U.S.S.R. concerned with catalytical researches belong to an association which outlines the general plan of catalytical research in the U.S.S.R. and the catalysis department of the Leningrad institute is expected to attack the most difficult problems raised by the members of this association.

The scheme of catalytical research includes the examination of processes for making catalysts, theoretical and experimental research on the phenomena of adsorption, and the study of the simpler hydrogen reactions with the simpler catalysts.

The department for the study of combustion and gas explosions aims at a thorough examination of the effect of different admixtures on these processes, and is conducted in close contact with industrial institutes, with the object of providing a rational account and control of combustion, in, for example, internal combustion engines. The kinetics of oxidation, the mechanism of inflammation and detonation, and the transmission of combustion are the main problems of the department.

The department for the investigation of polymerization studies the theoretical aspects of the direct technical questions solved in the laboratories of synthetic rubber factories, and electro-chemical factories, where polymerization processes are used.

The department for electro-chemistry was established at the request of the association of institutes concerned with electro-chemistry. The electro-chemical industry develops rapidly owing to the electrification of the country. The aim of the department is to introduce new physical methods into electro-chemical practice.

In particular, the department applies the methods of wave-mechanics to the processes of over-voltage and the problems of electrolysis, including the properties of electrodes, electrode potentials, and the state of ions in solutions.

The department for the study of surface phenomena, which has now been established as an independent institute under the direction of Professor Talmud, is concerned with the general problems of colloid chemistry and their numerous relations to industrial processes.

Semenov was trained as a physicist, and was led to the study of chemical reactions through investigations of the mechanism of the breakdown of insulators under electric discharges. In 1927, when he was still specializing on these problems, he suggested the possibility of reducing the size of dynamos by running them in a vacuum. The possibilities of vacuum machinery have since been explored by van der Graaf in America. Bodenstein had begun the theory of chain reactions in 1913 in his study of the reactions between hydrogen and chlorine. The interest of Soviet physicists was attracted to the theory in 1926, by researches of Chariton and Walta on the phenomena of the oxidation of phosphorus. This is an intense reaction and is accompanied by a flame. But in spite of this, the reaction does not occur at all if the pressure of the oxygen exceeds a certain higher limit, or falls below a certain lower limit. The first fact had been noticed by Berthollet in 1797, and the second by Joubert in 1874. Chariton and Walta noticed that if argon was introduced into a vessel containing phosphorus and oxygen, it could, under certain conditions, provoke inflammation of the oxygen and phosphorus, as if it could lower the higher limit of pressure governing the reaction. In 1928 Semenov and Ryabinin proved in addition that the oxidation of phosphorus was suddenly stopped when the quantity of oxygen reaches a certain value.

Commenting on these experiments in 1928, Bodenstein wrote that: "the oxides of phosphorus and sulphur cannot practically decompose under the conditions of Semenov's experiment.   But here we have an example of pseudo-equilibrium . . . observations of the same sort, but referring to normal pressure, were published towards the end of the last century . . . I proved these observations to be fallacious . . . But although in my scientific youth I showed that the old pseudo-equilibria do not really exist, now we have ourselves found an example of pseudo-equilibrium in a new sense."

Semenov and his colleagues made a thorough investigation of whether oxygen really does not react with phosphorus at pressures below the lower limit, which is at some hundredths or thousandths of a millimetre of mercury, and whether the reaction starts suddenly after the pressure has risen above the lower limit.   In one series of experiments in which oxygen was introduced by a capillary tube into a vessel containing phosphorus they found that about the same limiting pressure of oxygen is required both to start and to terminate the reaction, but a slightly lower pressure, less than 1 per cent, is needed for extinction.   At a slightly lower pressure the oxygen could remain in contact with the phosphorus for many hours without reacting with it.   A slight increase after twenty-four hours' contact immediately produced the reaction, which is marked by a glow in the vessel.   In another series of experiments the volume of the space containing the oxygen and the phosphorus was suddenly reduced by running mercury into the vessel.   A sudden flash occurs at the moment when the pressure reaches the lower limit.

Shalnikov found that if the reaction is conducted in very large bulbs the critical pressure falls far below the usual one, and is found to be inversely proportional to the square of the diameter.   These experiments gave the first demonstration that the walls of the containing vessel could retard a homogeneous chemical reaction.

If the pressure of the phosphorus is kept constant, and the temperature is increased from $17°$ to $50°$ C., the limiting pressure remains virtually constant.

Kovalsky investigated the upper pressure limit by immersing the vessel containing the phosphorus in liquid air. It was thoroughly exhausted. A definite quantity of oxygen was introduced, and the vessel was heated until the pressure of the phosphorus vapour had reached the desired value. The oxygen was then pumped away, until the pressure dropped to the limiting point and violent combustion occurred. The pressure was registered with a manometer.

Kovalsky has recently shown that the addition of minute quantities of ozone raises the upper limit. This may explain the increased explosiveness if two successive experiments are made in the same vessel. The phenomenon has repeatedly been observed, especially by Haber in reactions between oxygen and hydrogen. Baker's observation that thoroughly dried oxygen and phosphorus will not react is probably due to a similar phenomenon. The absence of moisture may reduce the upper pressure limit, and the combustion occurs at pressures below those investigated by Baker.

Semenov is inclined to believe that Baker's experiments on the combination of sodium and oxygen may be incorrect for space reactions, but correct for surface reactions. Atomic sodium may have stable properties, or the reaction may not develop on a surface. They have often tried the distillation of sodium in dry oxygen. On one occasion they obtained layers on the bulb surface and observed the Fraunhofer lines, but they have not been able to repeat this experiment.

When the pressure of a phosphorus-oxygen mixture is slightly above the lower pressure limit, the flame of combination is of the cold type. This is demonstrated by the almost complete absence of rise of pressure through heating from the flame. It is unable to warm its surroundings. The explanation is due to the very small quantities of material undergoing combustion, and the thermal conductivity does not decrease much with the decrease of pressure.

The existence of these apparently cold flames confirms the explanation of the chain mechanism of combustion, which will presently be roughly described. At room temperatures oxygen and hydrogen can combine with the production of heat but without an increase of temperature. The extraordinary character of the oxygen-phosphorus reaction may be illustrated by comparison with ordinary chemical reactions. An increase of temperature, or pressure, or both together, usually increases the rate of chemical reactions. This is the reason why reagents are boiled together in test-tubes, and why the mixture of oil and petrol vapour in the engine of a motor-car is compressed. The violence of the explosion in the engine cylinder increases with the increase of the compression, so that racing motor-car engines have very high compressions.

Explosions occur when a reaction produces much heat that cannot escape quickly. The heat increases the temperature of the reactive gases, and hence the speed of the reaction. This in turn produces still more heat, and further increase of reaction speed, until an explosion wave of reaction rushes through the mixture.

The contrast of this behaviour with that of the phosphorus-oxygen mixture, that stops burning if the pressure is increased above a certain limit, is striking.

The explanation of the profound difference between the two types of explosion is due to the difference in the nature of their respective mechanisms. The first is due to a uniform type of reaction which occurs between adjacent reacting molecules throughout the gas. The reactions are going at approximately the same speed in all parts of the mixture in the same conditions.

The second type of explosion is not due to a uniform reaction that occurs at all points of the mixture irrespective of what is happening elsewhere. It is due to the spreading of a reaction that starts from a number of isolated nuclei. At some point, often on the surface of the containing vessel, a reaction starts. It affects a pair of molecules in its neighbourhood, and this pair in its turn affects another, and so on, so that a string of reacting molecules is formed. The spread of the reaction throughout the chamber depends on the extension and branching of these chains, and may therefore, for example, be affected by the breaking of the chains. If the pressure of the mixture is increased, the flying molecules of gas may become more crowded, and they may break the chains by bumping into their constituent members too frequently.

The existence of the low-pressure limit is due to the failure of the reaction that has started at the walls of the vessel to grow a chain into the body of the gas. There are not enough molecules about for the chain to grow, so it collapses immediately after it has started, and the phosphorus and the oxygen do not combine.

The depression of the upper pressure limit by the introduction of argon, discovered by Chariton and Walta, is due to capture of some of the energy of the reacting molecules in the chains, so that the branching mechanism is altered.

Kovalsky's discovery that the lower pressure limit is depressed if the size of the containing vessel is increased is explained by the breaking of the chains by collision with the walls. If the size of the vessel is increased the chains can grow farther before they break against the walls. Thus collision with the walls will be less frequent, and combination with the phosphorus and oxygen can still occur effectively at pressures below the ordinary lower limit.

The growth of the chains can be retarded far more effectively by substances that react with the reacting molecules, than with inert substances such as argon. This phenomenon is of great practical importance, for it provides the mechanism by which anti-knock substances prevent premature explosions in internal combustion engines. The compressed mixture of petrol vapour and air in the cylinder of the engine should not explode before the piston has reached the top of its stroke. The addition of a small quantity of lead tetraethyl prevents the premature formation of reaction chains in the compressed mixture, so that it does not explode until fired by the spark at the proper moment in the right part of the stroke. An addition of 1 part of lead tetraethyl to 1500 parts of petrol increases the efficiency of the engine by 10 per cent, through the elimination of premature explosions which act as a brake on the engine.

Semenov supposes that the development of the reaction chains in the phosphorus-oxygen mixture starts from the few free oxygen atoms that always exist among the molecules of oxygen gas. The free oxygen atom captures four atoms of phosphorus. Then this combination reacts with a molecule of oxygen and produces a combination containing two atoms of oxygen and four of phosphorus, leaving an atom of oxygen again free. This free atom then initiates a similar series of reactions. This is how the reaction chains branch out. The rupture of the chains is due to the adsorption and capture of the oxygen atoms by the walls of the vessel.

It is evident that chemical reactions that work according to a chain mechanism will obey the mathematical laws that describe the growth of such chains. Given the properties of the reacting particles, some of these laws may be deduced by the application of statistical and geometrical principles. The shapes of the curves relating pressure and temperature changes may be calculated. The chains of reacting molecules are of two types, non-branching and branching. The first are due to initiating centres, or free atoms, that can produce one more centre only ; whereas the branching type is due to centres that can produce two new centres. The power of a centre, or free atom, to produce one or two new centres depends, of course, on the chemical properties of the reacting substances.

The development of the theory of non-branching chains was chiefly worked out by Bodenstein and his school, and partly by the Oxford and Leningrad schools. The theory of branching chains has chiefly been worked out by the Leningrad school and partly by the Oxford school. Semenov is of the opinion that nearly all chemical reactions are analysable into chain reactions, and that the mechanism of their reactions is one of the foundations of chemistry. Semenov's colleagues have included Kovalsky, Roginsky, Bursian, Sorokin, Chariton, Frost, Shalnikov, Kondratiev, Nalbandyan, Gortchakov, Dubovitsky, Sagulin, Tchirkov,

Walta, Ryabinin, Leipunsky, and many others, including Eltenton, the English chemist.

Those who want a more detailed account of their researches may consult the English version of Semenov's treatise on *Chemical Kinetics and Chain Reactions*.

The remainder of this chapter will be given to a short description of the laboratory, and conversations with Semenov and some of his colleagues.

The building consists of an old secondary school. Semenov is pleased with it, as it is very solidly built, though old. Part of the ground floor is occupied by Walter of the Electro-Physical Institute, who is engaged in research on insulators. Another part was occupied by D. L. Talmud until recently, who directed the Laboratory for Surface Chemistry. This has now been established in the city of Leningrad in its own building, as an independent institute. The upper floors are occupied by the chemical physicists.

Chariton is working on the kinetic properties of explosives. He is searching for the microscopic explanation of the aerodynamical and hydrodynamical properties of the gas disturbances associated with detonation. How does the abrupt sound-wave front pass through a substance? How is the propagation of an explosion initiated?

They have examined experimentally the effect of bombarding the surfaces of high explosives with ions, electrons, etc., and by particles obtained in the process of explosions. Atoms with a certain amount of energy have also been used. The energies of particles that could produce detonation were much smaller than expected. For instance, crystals of lead azide could be exploded in a large exhausted sphere. The products of combustion are lead and nitrogen. It appears that these can pass through 50 centimetres of the vacuum and detonate a crystal at the other end. The energy that falls on the crystal may be calculated, and is very small: it is several hundred ergs per centimetre.

Particles whose energy can be controlled are obtainable by exploding a wire with a discharge from a condenser.

One active atom is needed to make one passive atom react in a unimolecular layer. The reaction takes one ten thousandth of an atom, but the atom is active for only one-ten-million-millionth of a second, hence the number of active centres is relatively few.   How do they spread?

Time intervals in the progress of explosions may be measured by fine wires near the crystal.   When the first wire is broken, a current goes through a valve, and when the second wire is broken, the current stops.   The amount of electricity that passes through in the interval is measured by a ballistic galvanometer, and the quantity is proportional to the time interval.

The effect of hydrostatic pressure is being studied. There is difficulty in getting good material for high-pressure experiments.   The behaviour of crystal and liquid explosives is different, though both are sensitive to mechanical shock.

They use cathode-ray oscillographs for rapid measurements, and piezo-electric methods for pressure measurements.

Kondratiev is working on photo-chemical reactions, and the exchange of energy between atoms and molecules.   He oxidizes carbon monoxide in order to obtain carbon dioxide molecules of high vibrational energy.   These are used to excite nitrogen molecules and make them react with oxygen, so that the oxidation reactions of nitrogen may be investigated.   He is also working on the oxidation of carbon monoxide.

Semenov is investigating the formation of silicon hydride. The reaction between silicon and hydrogen occurs very quickly or very slowly.   Very delicate manometers have to be used to detect the exact pressure, and the size of the slight changes of pressure, that governs the reaction.

They use a glass manometer invented by Shalnikov.   It consists essentially of a bulb containing a very thin glass diaphram.   The manufacture of these glass manometers requires great skill.   Experimental work of the Leningrad school has depended in a considerable degree on the use of this manometer, so they owe much to the exceptional skill of the Leningrad glass-blowers, who are excellent.   The Shalnikov manometer is more effective than Bodenstein's form of the Bourdon gauge. The manometer used in the silicon-hydrogen experiments registers pressures of one-hundredth of a millimeter of mercury, and gives a graph of the pressure changes during one-tenth of a second. The period of the manometer membrane is two-thousandths of a second. As the instrument is made entirely of glass the products of the reaction do not react with the materials of construction.

One of their manometers has a capacity of half a cubic centimetre. They hope to make glass manometers with a mirror system that will be sensitive enough to detect pressure changes of one-millionth of a millimetre.

They can follow reactions in a vessel of a few cubic millimetres volume.

The glass manometers are very simple. They are made by producing a diaphram across a bulb in a glass tube, by a glass-blower's trick. They also have a special method of blowing large glass vessels so that they have smaller internal stresses.

They have examined the passage of detonation waves down very long tubes. A lead tube had been coiled down a vertical drum. It was 30 metres long. The reaction fades away when the tube is long enough, and the explosion degenerates.

In their experiments on the oxidation of methane, they have arranged special tubes for collecting small quantities of various products of the reaction at different stages, so that they can be analysed, and the stages of the reactions followed in more detail.

Semenov believes that the phenomena of polymerization are governed by chain reaction processes, but Hinshelwood is not inclined to agree with this opinion. He believes, too, that the cracking of petroleum may be an endothermic, heat-absorbing, chain reaction.

The department of catalysis is directed by S. Roginsky. His approach to the problem of catalysis is more physical than usual. He remarks that the pure chemist thinks only in terms of reactions. But one has to deal with materials in different states, as solids, and in different conditions of

solidity.   A chemical formula states which atoms are concerned in a reaction, but does not indicate their individual
conditions and positions.   The deformation of the molecule,
or the surface, are the chief factors in catalysis.   The
investigation of catalytic processes must be done with pure
materials.   For instance, pure platinum is not a catalyst.
When one works with materials containing impurities,
then Taylor's theory is correct.   But pure nickel cannot be
activated.   They have found that nitrogen, hydrogen and
oxygen may be catalysed by simple arrangements.

Roginsky considers that molecular deformation is more
important than chains in the mechanism of catalysis, and
that the catalytical effect cannot be mechanically deduced
from steps.

It is very necessary to differentiate between the rôle of the
macroscopic structure of the solid body and its surface, and
the effects of the intrinsic properties of the atoms that form
the surface of the catalyst.   Experiments on the adsorption
and catalytic reactions at liquid surfaces, in which the factors
connected with macroscopic structure have no part, should
provide interesting information.   Magid and Roginsky
have pointed out that the researches of Bonhoeffer and
Farkas on the heterogeneous catalytic exchanges of the two
modifications of hydrogen show how such experiments
might be done.   This reaction is also a sensitive indication
for a more or less profound exchange effect of hydrogen
with the solid body, which has a part in other catalytical
hydrogen reactions.   They have extended Farkas's researches on the hydrogen exchanges on typical hydrogen
catalysts, such as copper, nickel, and cobalt.

Leipunsky and Roginsky have been investigating the
nature of activated adsorption and its connection with
catalysis.   It has been known for a long time that surfaces
have an important part in the catalysis of gas reactions.
Recent research indicates that this might depend on a sort
of exchange process connected with activated adsorption.
But it is not certain that activated adsorption is a factor in
catalysis.

The experimental facts are qualitative.   The effects of

the solution are not eliminated, and the nature of the re active adsorbed gases, as well as its connection with the surface, is not yet clear. The great influence of heat on adsorption and the considerable heat of activation indicate that there should be changes in the qualities of the surface.

They are making experiments to investigate the difference between the activated and the Van der Waals adsorption, besides the condition of molecules on the surface, in the case of activated adsorption. The photo-effect of a catalyst in a hydrogen atmosphere is being measured simultaneously with the adsorption.

The data of the photoelectrical properties of the alkali and earth metals suggest that the photoelectrical qualities of the surfaces at the two sorts of adsorption may be considerably different.

In another series of experiments the kinetics of activated adsorption on real metal and oxide catalysts were investigated, in order to test quantitatively the parallel between activated adsorption and catalysis.

Roginsky also works on the chemical mechanism of explosives. He has made important studies of the decomposition of nitro-glycerine and trotyl, and with Rosenkyevitch has given a quantum mechanical theory of the development of the process of explosive decomposition, which is started by fluctuations of energy inside the molecule.

Roginsky and his colleagues have shown that the addition of small quantities of oxides of nitrogen, water, or nitric acid catalyse the decomposition of nitroglycerine at 40° C., whereas it is normally very stable at this temperature, and does not explode until heated at 200° C. If the experiments are made in small vessels the process of decomposition resembles that of chlorine oxide, and ozone sensitized by bromine.

Roginsky has shown that if nitro-glycerine, and trotyl, are heated in small closed tubes, the explosion occurs at 100° C., or some hundred degrees below the explosion temperature in open vessels. The low-temperature explosions do not occur immediately, but after a considerable induction period. Semenov is of the opinion that the nitrous oxide and water vapour that participate in the mechanism of decomposition operate not as direct catalysts but as indirect developers of chain reactions.

Semenov is about thirty-nine years old. His personality is one of the most fascinating in the contemporary scientific world. He possesses a combination of theoretical knowledge with experimental skill and artistic feeling. His gift of imagination is particularly notable among the qualities of the other world-masters in the science of chemical physics. Besides, or because of, his high gifts he has the power of human management that has enabled him to create a large school of research, and enlist the enthusiasm of the post-revolutionary youth.

The former department of surface chemistry, which has recently become an independent institute, is directed by D. L. Talmud. The numerous experimental researches on surface phenomena have led to interesting industrial applications, and suggestions for new industrial processes.

Talmud and his colleagues have investigated the hardening effect of layers of adsorbed substances on sands, and other powders. They have examined the effects of paraffin, fatty acids, amines, alcohols, and other substances on quartz powders and sands. The compression strength of sand was found to be 12 kilograms per square centimetre. When treated with fatty acids it decreased a little, the amines increased it, and amyl-alcohol increased it to 28 kg. per sq. cm.

Quartz powder consisting of particles 0·08 centimetres in average diameter was treated with p-toluidine. Its compression strength increased from 27 to 40 kg. per sq. cm.

This process of hardening powders by covering their surfaces with layers of adsorbed materials which hold the particles together is described by Talmud as molecular soldering. He foresees important applications of the process for the strengthening of materials for house-building, for strengthening the foundations of roads, of rubber, plastics, and adhesives. It should also be of value for modifying the properties of soil for plant cultivation.

He hopes it will be possible to prepare fluids that may be sprayed on the earth in order to harden it. This would contribute towards a simple method of preparing good foundations for new roads, and would be especially important in the Soviet Union, where many new roads are needed, and where in many districts there is a paucity of the conventional materials for making roads.

He has devised a remarkable method of purifying crude sugar solutions by surface-chemical processes. Quantities of air are blown through the unpurified sugar solution. The bubbles produce a froth. The adsorption forces in the surfaces of the bubbles of froth attract foreign polar substances from the solution, so that the impurities are collected in the froth over the solution, and can easily be removed. The process has already been adopted in one sugar refinery, and should eventually lead to economies of millions of roubles a year in the sugar-refining industry. The general introduction of the process will take time, as it demands some technical skill in operation, and the majority of refinery staffs are not yet able to operate it satisfactorily. Bubbling with blasts of air is not an easy technical process. The process leads to the elimination of the production of molasses in sugar-refining.

Talmud has devised a new flotation method based on the principle that the hydrophobic, or water-repelling, particles from the mixture being separated by flotation, do not cleave to the surfaces of the froth-bubbles, but to the water-repelling strip.

In non-aqueous liquids the water-attracting, or hydrophilic, particles cleave to the water-attracting strip, where the water serves as a reagent. The forces that keep the particles on the surfaces of the froth are partly due to the mechanical solidity of the surface layers, and partly to the cleaving of the water-repelling particles to one another. The surface-active materials are adsorbed from the water. The measure of the cleaving strength may be obtained from the gliding speed of the particles relative to the surface of the froth (or gliding speed of the froth relative to the solid surface).

Talmud has made very interesting investigations of unimolecular fibres. These are produced along the line

joining the phases of substances of suitable properties, just
as unimolecular layers are produced between two phases of
substances, such as water and air.   A water surface may be
covered with a layer of fatty-acid molecules one molecule
thick.   If a sheet of glass or other material, is thrust into the
water, it is possible to get a single line of molecules arranged
along the line joining the water, glass and air.

With suitable choice of materials Talmud has succeeded in
preparing unimolecular fibres of cellulose.   This is equivalent to producing unimolecular fibres of artificial silk.   It is
well known that artificial silk is much weaker than natural
silk.   This defect could be obviated if artificial silk could be
spun from a multitude of very fine fibres, as strength partly
depends on the number of strands in the yarn.

If Talmud's unimolecular fibres of cellulose could be
spun, they would produce an artificial silk far stronger than
natural silk.   This idea will probably lead to a revolution
of the textile industry in the future.   The new Institute of
Surface Chemistry will have a staff of sixty persons, including
fifteen research chemists.   The work will be pure, but with
a view to application.   They will study organic compounds
in which ordinary hydrogen has been replaced by heavy
hydrogen.   Heavy hydrogen is prepared at Dniepropetrovsk, as electricity is very cheap there.   They will col-
laborate with physiologists at the Institute of Experimental
Medicine on the properties of nerve and muscle.

They will use electron diffraction methods for the determination of molecular structure.

The English chemist G. C. Eltenton is a member of the
staff of the Institute of Chemical Physics.   He is studying
the production of hydrogen carbons by ion guns, and streams
of atomic hydrogen.

He enjoys his work, as he finds the opportunities for pure
research wider than in England, where the researches of
the majority of chemists are too much restricted to immediate
problems.   He finds the chemist in the Soviet Union is
much more free to choose the sort of problem he would like
to investigate.   If he wishes to undertake fundamental
research, he is encouraged.   In England there is far too

much control by authority: the chemist is too frequently expected to attack problems chosen for him by his superiors. Eltenton enjoys the Soviet social life and the attraction of having a part, with all the other workers, in the discussions on the government of the institute. The innumerable committee meetings are attractive to those interested in the social problems of conducting scientific institutes, and relating their work to the life of the community. The youth of the staff is also very stimulating. One feels that one is collaborating in the construction of a new civilization.

The number and cheapness of entertainments is attractive. There are staff clubs for flying, ski-ing, chess, etc., and everyone can join these for virtually nothing. If a young chemist wishes to learn to fly, he need not spend anything. The institute's ski-ing club has stocks of skis at the disposal of the members.

Finally, there is deep satisfaction in joining the processes and mass celebrations of important social events. Through these the chemist feels that he has a significant part in the society of which he is a member.

CHAPTER 13

THE INSTITUTE OF PHYSICAL CHEMISTRY, DNIEPROPETROVSK

THE institute was founded in 1927, and grew out of the department of chemistry in the Mining Institute. It is directed by Pissaryevsky, and has a handsome building with many rooms, which like other institutes in Dniepropetrovsk, is clean and well kept. It is organized in four departments.

The staff includes 93 persons, 60 of whom are scientifically qualified. One of the most active members of the staff is A. Brodsky. He is pursuing several lines of research. The refraction of electrolytes is being investigated in order to collect data bearing on the work of Fajans.

He has studied the Raman spectra of solutions of acetylene chloride in relation to the theory of dipole moments.

Formerly he worked on electro-chemical potentials, and has experimentally confirmed part of Nernst's theory.

As electricity is cheap, owing to the proximity of the Dnieproges Hydroelectric Power Station, they have begun researches on heavy water, and were the original source of supply in the Soviet Union. They have prepared several grams of pure heavy water and large quantities of dilute solutions. They have worked out several small technical improvements in methods of preparation. Brodsky, Alexandrovitch, Slutzkaya and Sheludsky have used an electrolytic process in which a 3 or 4 per cent solution of potassium hydroxide is electrolyzed with iron electrodes, or a 2 to 4 per cent solution of sulphuric acid is electrolyzed with lead or platinum electrodes. The process gives a five to sixfold

194

concentration of heavy water for a reduction of tenfold in volume.

The optical properties of heavy-water solutions have been examined with interferometers.

They have found that the water condensed from the steam produced by the combustion of paraffin oil (naphtha) contains an unusually high percentage of heavy water. They consider this may be evidence that petroleum is produced from the decay of plants, and that the plants originally separated an extra amount of heavy water from the water of their environment, through the agency of their physiological processes.

They propose to measure the speed of heavy hydrogen ions, in order to see how the experimental data compare with the theory of R. H. Fowler and J. D. Bernal. They propose to study the absorption spectra of copper, salts and other substances in heavy water, as they believe there might be a change in colour.

The effects of electron emission, light, magnetic fields and other agents on the kinetics of chemical change, and catalysis, are being investigated.

The catalysis of ammonia is being studied from several aspects.

The photochemical reactions in solutions are another subject of investigation, and the general theory of chain reactions in solutions.

They have studied the part of the electron in chemical processes, by classical, X-ray and Raman spectral methods. They have found that the movements of the electrons are related to the Langmuir adsorption.

Brodsky has shown how the electrode potential may be divided into two factors by the application of the Debye-Hückel thermodynamical theory. One factor is determined by the nature of the electrode, and the other by the properties of the solution. A substitute for the second term is obtained with the assistance of the theory, which agrees completely with the earlier approximate calculations, and leads to a linear relationship with the dielectric constant of the solvent.

Brodsky has studied the electro-chemistry of the mercurous ion. He has examined the activity coefficients of aqueous mercurous nitrate solutions at four different temperatures by means of electro-motive force measurements. These show the dependence of these coefficients on concentration and temperature follows Debye's law in so far as the logarithm of the coefficient is proportional to the square root of the concentration. But the logarithm of the concentration proves to be larger than the value given by Debye's theory. He has calculated more accurately the solubility products previously obtained for the mercurous halides, and those of a number of other mercurous salts.

With J. M. Shershever he has examined the refractive indices of dilute solutions of potassium chloride and of potassium nitrate with a Zeiss interferometer. The solutions varied from one-tenth to four thousandths of the normal, and the measurements were made for three wavelengths and two temperatures. The interferometer gives more exact results than a refractometer.

He has improved this method, and with N. S. Filippova he has examined the refraction and refractive indices of dilute solutions of thallium chloride and thallium nitrate. The order of the accuracy of the method has been increased, and the error in the determination of the null-point has been removed. The refractive indices, dispersive power and temperature coefficients have been found for solutions of one-thousandth to one-tenth of the normal. It has been found that the ration of the difference of the refractive index between the solution and water, to the concentration, varies linearly with the concentration.

With J. M. Shershever he has extended the investigation to dilute solutions of potassium chloride, potassium bromide, sodium chloride, and sodium nitrate. The refractive indices of solutions of strengths one-thousandth to one-tenth of the normal were measured under atmospheric conditions at different times of the year. The refraction per gram-molecule has been calculated, and it is found that the relation to the degree of the concentration is non-linear, unlike that in concentrated solutions, where it is linear. The results agree with the theory of Debye and Hückel for strong electrolytes.

K. Fajans and W. Geffcken have criticized the results of Brodsky and Shershever for solutions of sodium chloride. They have pointed out that these results conflict with others found by Geffcken and Kruis. They have suggested that some systematic error, due possibly to the formation of association products, may have upset the measurements from which the relation between refractive index and concentration has been calculated. This difference of opinion has led to a lengthy controversy between Brodsky and his collaborators and Fajans and his collaborators.

Brodsky, Sock and Besugli have investigated the Raman spectra of arsenic trichloride, and benzene, and of solutions of arsenic trichloride in the other two substances, which are liquids. They have found that the Raman frequencies of the non-polar solvents remain unchanged in the solutions, but that the frequencies of arsenic trichloride are slightly changed.

Pissaryevsky's recent researches on catalysis have included studies of the mechanism of the catalytic action of metals and oxide of metals. He supposes that their catalytic action in heterogeneous systems is partly due to adsorption, and partly to what he names "electronic isomerism". A dynamic equilibrium is supposed to exist on the surface of the catalyst between passive and active atoms, which differ in their content of labile electrons. Catalytic power is supposed to be due to the possession of a labile electron.

Pissaryevsky has proposed an osmotic theory of the origin of the electric current. He supposes that in solid metals there is an equilibrium between atoms, ions and electrons. This is analogous to the electrolytic dissociation of salts, and the dissociated state of the constituents provides an explanation of the electrical properties of metals.

He has discussed the mechanism of the catalytic decomposition of the absorbed gases by the impact of the electrons from the catalyst. When the gases have been ionized they attack the salt.

He considers that adsorption has an important part in the mechanism of heterogeneous catalysis. A transition of what he names electronic isomerides occurs on the surface of the catalyst. The catalytic surface is supposed to contain groups of unactivated electrons, and the electronic isomerides are transferred from active to passive electrons. This produces an equilibrium between the isomerides. An active isomeride is one that has dissociated into ions and electrons.

He supposes that the action of metallic catalysts is due to the facilities with which their free electrons react with those of the substrate. For instance, platinum may catalyse hydrogenation by dissociating hydrogen into protons and electrons.

Pissaryevsky has recently discussed the energetics of oxides of nitrogen, and the structure of nitrous oxide, and the peroxides and per-acids of halogens.

M. Polyakov has discussed the mechanism of the oxidation of sulphur dioxide in the presence of vanadium catalysts. This is a contribution towards the introduction of vanadium catalysts into the Soviet sulphuric acid industry, in place of platinum, as has been done in other countries.

G. Korshun and C. Roll have investigated the absorption spectra of various organic compounds.

W. A. Roiter has studied the catalysis of hydrogen peroxide by platinum.

The activity of the institute is an illustration of the interest in modern physical chemistry in one of the newer centres in the Soviet Union.

PART IV

APPLIED SCIENCE

CHAPTER 14

THE STATE OPTICAL
INSTITUTE, LENINGRAD

THE State Optical Institute is directed by Professor
S. I. Vavilov. It was founded in 1918 by the
Commissariat of Education, and has now come
under the control of the Scientific Research Sector
of the Department of Heavy Industry. It was founded in
order to prosecute research in all branches of pure and
applied optics, and to assist the development of the optical
industry.

It contains seven departments: for spectroscopy; applied
physical optics; construction and testing of optical instruments; the calculation and computation of optical systems;
optical chemistry, especially the chemistry of optical glass;
photometry; and photography.

The institute possesses three large buildings, part
entirely new, and part the reconstructed palace of a former
multiple-foodshop proprietor and millionaire.

The annual budget is about 2 million roubles. The staff
includes about 250 scientists, and an appropriate number
of assistants. They have published about 100 volumes of
researches, and over 500 papers in the physical journals
of various countries. The present output of papers is about
50 a year.

Optical science and the optical industry were exceptionally
backward in pre-revolutionary Russia, and the creation of

this institute, which is absolutely one of the best in the Soviet Union, and is capable of superlative work, is one of the best achievements of Soviet physics.

The department of spectroscopy is directed by D. S. Roshdestvensky, who was the first director of the institute. He is the inventor of the hook-method for research on anomalous dispersion, which has been applied by him, and his colleagues Prokoviev and Filippov, to the spectra of many compounds of elements in the first and second group of Mendeleev's table. Prokoviev and Filippov have also published a number of papers on the intensity of spectral lines. Roshdestvensky and his colleagues have recently collaborated with the eminent American geneticist H. J. Muller on a search for the biological genes with an ultramicroscope. They have discovered important new data about the structure of the giant chromosomes of the salivary glands of insects, and appear to be approaching the identification of individual genes.

A. N. Terenin is director of the photochemical laboratory. He has published many papers on the spectra of excited atoms and molecules.

S. E. Frisch is working on the superfine structure of atomic spectra.

W. Tchulanovsky has published much on the spectra of the extreme ultra-violet region.

E. Gross has contributed to the literature of the Raman effect, and has observed a new effect whose existence was predicted by Brillouin and Mandelstamm.

V. Fock devotes part of his time to the institute, and works on quantum theory.

The director, S. I. Vavilov, has introduced the study of fluorescence, and has published important papers on the fluctuation of light at extremely feeble intensities.

The chemical laboratory directed by Grebentchikov has done much work on the chemistry of silicates and optical glass equal in quality to any that is obtainable.

Roshdestvensky, Lebedev, Katchalov and others have collaborated in this problem, and as a result optical glass of all qualities is now being manufactured in the Soviet

Union. This is one of the institute's most important achievements. The highest quality in scientific instruments is necessary for first-class research, and also for modern warfare.

It is well known that the British Government had considerable difficulty in the war of 1914–18 in creating an optical industry of the highest class. The German superiority in the optical industry left the British industry backward, and there was a severe shortage of knowledge and ability in applied optics. This deficiency cost many British lives. For instance, the battle of Jutland revealed the superiority of the German optical range-finders.

An optical industry of the highest class is essential for a first-class military power.

The condition and quality of the State Optical Institute at Leningrad are facts of first-class military importance, and worth serious consideration by all who wish to increase their understanding of international affairs, and the relative strengths of the great powers.

Attention has been given to the technique of glass-working. New methods of grinding and polishing have been worked out, and quicker methods for obtaining the finest precision in the manufacture of parallel plates for interferometers.

The condition of the surface of glass has been thoroughly studied, and methods of reducing the reflection-coefficient.

As a result of years of strenuous work, the computing department has worked out methods for computing optical systems. A. Tudorovsky and G. E. Yakontov have made original improvements in methods. Various new designs have been supplied to the industry, such as improved wide-angle photographic lenses and microscope lenses, and are now being manufactured.

The director of the department of physical optics is the able physicist W. P. Linnik. He is the inventor of many ingenious apparatuses and experimental techniques, such as the microscopical interferometer for the examination of surfaces, the interferometer with semi-diaphanous slit for the determination of wave-aberrations, the swinging microscopic object lens system for observing the lines on greatly enlarged spectrograms, and new methods for centring microscope lenses. Two of the practical tasks of the laboratory are the improvement of practical microscope design, and the construction by D. Maksutov of an 80-centimetre photographic lens for the Pulkova Observatory.

In the department of applied physical optics M. Romanova is engaged in a determination of the metre in terms of wave-lengths of light. The work has given valuable data on the fine structure of the lines of the spectrum of cadmium ; and J. Ossipov has prepared interferometer plates for the research plane to within one-hundredth of a wave-length.

The director of the department, A. Lebedev, has devised a polarization interferometer that has proved to be very useful in optical chemistry. Samarchev has done interesting research on electrolysis in the neighbourhood of electrodes.

The department of photometry is also concerned with the study of colour, artificial and natural lighting, physiological optics, and other subjects. Its publications include papers on the causes of colouring in optical glass, the construction of photometers, lux-meters, and colorimeters.

The department of photography is divided into physical and chemical sections. It studies problems such as the preparation of gelatine of high quality, light-filters and wedges, and precision cameras.

W. Linnik, the director of the department of applied optics, is one of the most talented physicists in the Soviet Union. Formerly he made experimental researches with X-rays, but he has now turned to applied optics, partly owing to the demands for improved optical instruments for practical purposes. It seems rather a pity that he has dropped X-ray research completely.

Linnik's method of producing X-ray interference fringes by the Lloyd's mirror method is well-known. The apparatus is designed very ingeniously, so that the necessary very precise adjustments may easily be made. The X-rays, from copper or iron, are passed through a slit between two polished plates one ten-thousandth of an inch wide. The slit is made parallel with the Lloyd's mirror by observing optical interference fringes in the film of air between the mirror and one of the plates. Part of the beam issuing from the slit is intercepted and reflected by the mirror, and interference fringes are produced at the plane where this beam crosses the path of that part of the original beam which has escaped reflection.

Linnik has published an interesting paper on the experiments of Kikuchi on the diffraction of electrons by very thin sheets of mica. He argues that the results could be explained, to a first approximation, by diffraction through a two-dimensional crystal grating parallel to the surface of the sheets. The same explanation was applicable to the results of his researches on the diffraction of X-rays by split mica and other crystals. But a closer examination showed that the effect could not be explained by the two-dimensional grating alone. It is strange that the little sheets, 100 molecules thick, do not show any space effect, and careful examination has shown that the X-ray spots did not exactly correspond to a simple two-dimensional grating. He considers that the following explanation appears to be able to account for both the electron-wave and the X-ray effects. Thin mica sheets split by heating are very much distorted and the waves fall on to a large number of thin sheets at different angles. The disorder destroys the arrangement of the Laue spots. If the specimen is rotated the Bragg reflections of the first order must be very near to those due to the first order two-dimensional grating. Thus the diffraction picture of a number of thin sheets bundled together at random angles must apparently be identical with the diffraction picture obtained from the rotation of a plate whose thickness is equal to the sum of the thickness of all the little sheets. An experiment with a mica sheet 0·15 millimetres thick showed that the pictures obtained in this way were very little different from those obtained by diffraction from split mica. He thinks that Kikuchi's results may be explained in this way. It is very difficult to fix thin mica sheets a ten-thousandth of an inch thick without deformation. Very small deformations are sufficient to destroy the Laue picture, because different parts of the electron bundle fall on to differently orientated parts of the sheet. Thicker sheets are less deformed, and these show the Laue pictures more clearly.

He has devised a modification of the rotating crystal method for the examination of crystal structures. The crystal is rotated on two axes giving diagrams that show the symmetry of the crystal and provide information on the structure.

Linnik's swinging microscope objective for studying photographs of spectral lines is extremely ingenious. The details of lines are often magnified by enlarging the photograph, or examining it under a microscope. But there is a limit to the value of magnification owing to the coarseness of the grains in the photographic plates. When the magnification is too great, the lines are resolved into disorderly arrays of black dots.

The general features of arrays of black dots on a plane surface are sometimes seen by looking at the plane from a very fine angle. The effect is sometimes employed in advertisements, whose letters cannot be read when seen from the front, but become recognizable when seen through the foreshortening caused by looking at them from an acute angle. Linnik produces a similar effect by having the microscope objective hung on two hinges. As it swings backwards and forwards the individual dots of the resolved spectral lines blur together, and the general features of the lines become beautifully evident.

He has devised a method of examining the spherical aberrations of photographic lenses. It consists of a collimator and two slits, the first of which is placed in front of the lens being examined, and the second across the focal plane.

In his department experiments are made with fluorite lenses as objectives. They have special simple methods of centring lenses by rotating them and observing the reflections of an incident beam.

Small objectives are held during tests by a layer of electrolytically deposited copper. Besides making the lens easier to handle, this method has the advantage of preventing the immersion liquid from penetrating the lens.

The department has a staff of fifty persons.

W. Tchulanovsky has made spectroscopic researches in the extreme ultra-violet with a vacuum spectrograph of his own design. It contains a concave diffraction grating arranged according to Eagle's system, and is about 1 metre long. It is considerably simpler than the usual models.

He has investigated the fine structure of the lines of the spectrum given by the singly ionized helium atom, and has collected experimental data bearing on Hund's theory of molecular rotations, especially in connection with the nitrogen molecule. He has also investigated the energy of valency binding between atoms, and quantum absorption spectra due to discontinuous light.

Vingerov is working on infra-red spectroscopy. His spectroscope is of the type used by Abbott. He is studying the spectrum of methane.

W. K. Prokoviev extends the work of Roshdestvensky on anomalous dispersion in the spectra of sodium and the alkaline earth. They have confirmed experimentally for calcium the type of curve calculated theoretically for lithium by Trumpe. Ladenburg has adopted their design of interferometer.

He has shown that the number of dispersion centres for the first and second lines of calcium, strontium and barium increases greatly with the increase of atomic number.

In collaboration with the late W. N. Soloviev, he has shown that the relation of the number of dispersion centres for two lines in the thallium vapour spectrum changes according to Boltzmann's law.

With A. Fillipov the anomalous dispersion near the twenty-five lines of the main series of sodium has been observed, and measured at line sixteen. The observed values for the four first doublets agree well with those calculated by wave-mechanics.

He has repeated the calculations of Sugiura for the two first doublets of sodium. The calculations have been considerably simplified by using Störmer's method of calculating the Schrödinger eigenfunctions. They could easily be extended to the third and fourth doublet of the main series and some first doublets of the parallel and combination series.

With A. Filippov he has examined the anomalous dispersion of thallium vapour, and determined the transition probabilities for the first and second parallel series.

With G. Gamov he has examined the relation of the dispersion constants of the red and violet doublets of potassium. They have found that this relation is independent of change in the density of the vapour.

Maksulov is making an 85-centimetre telescope objective for the Pukova Observatory, a new observatory in the Crimea. It is made of crown and flint glass, and will be accurate to one-twentieth of a wave-length.

He is making also a 150-centimetre reflecting telescope, and a 35-centimetre mirror correct to one-hundredth of a wave-length.

Pyrex glass with very small heat expansion coefficient is being used.

The polishing machine resembles that used by Ritchie in America.

The laboratory of photo-chemistry is directed by the well-known physicist A. N. Terenin. He is engaged in extensive researches on the radiations emitted during photo-chemical reactions. The mechanism of photo-chemical reactions is most satisfactorily investigated by examining emission rather than absorption spectra. Emission spectra are much more sensitive ; for this reason Terenin makes special use of them, but unfortunately they cannot often be used, as there are relatively few reactions during which light is emitted. In 1924–5 he determined the energy of dissociation of sodium chloride by emission methods. If the vapour is illuminated with ultra-violet rays, a very intense efflorescence of the D-line of sodium may be observed. Hence a dissociation occurs, and the required energy can be measured.

At present they are working with halides that can be vapourized at 300° C.

PLATE 6

Photo. Planet News Ltd.
Testing a large telescope objective at the State Optical Institute, Leningrad

[*face p.* 206

They are trying to extend this method to organic molecules. Ultra-violet rays of very short wave-length must be used for producing the dissociation. They use a vacuum spectrograph, and work in the Schumann region of the spectrum.

It is possible to dissociate the molecule of water, and also those of alcohols, by this method.

It is very neat. No discharge tube is necessary, and the notorious "Walpurgis night" conditions in such tubes are avoided.

The department for practical illumination is directed by Zelinkov. He studies the lighting of models of buildings under an artificial sky. The intensity of the light in various places is measured with a photoelectric cell. If the interior walls of the model are painted black it is found that twice as much light is necessary to produce the suitable illumination for comfortable working conditions.

The effect of flood lighting on the appearance and ornaments of buildings is studied, and the influence of lighting on the ease of reading and writing.

M. Romanova is comparing the metre with wave-lengths of light. The delicacy of the measurements is shown by the influence of air pressure, which may make a difference of 10 wave-lengths in result.

She makes aluminium mirrors for ultra-violet work. These are produced by a 1000-volt cathode sputtering on a glass plate in a hydrogen atmosphere.

Mirrors are being prepared for the observation of the 1936 eclipse. She is also engaged in the study of the hyperfine structure of cadmium and krypton.

The director of the institute, S. I. Vavilov, is engaged in various studies in the more refined types of optical observation. With E. M. Brumberg he has studied the interference produced by a cone of light of wide aperture. When two beams of light are sent in different directions from one source their ability to interfere when brought together by a suitable optical system can only be analysed by resolving the vibration of each beam into two polarized planes. This allows each beam to be examined separately.

Under certain circumstances the two beams will be exactly neutralized when they come in opposite directions from the source.

Vavilov has given much attention to the classification of luminescence phenomena. He divides them into three types: the spontaneous, the forced, and that due to recombination. He has given formula describing the varieties of these three types, so that the identification of the type of any particular example of luminescence may be facilitated. With A. A. Shishlovsky he has examined the decay of rhodamine orange N in very viscous solutions, with a special phosphoroscope that will measure decay periods of 0·01 to 2 seconds. The decay is strictly exponential and is interpreted according to the principles of his system of classification.

With E. Brumberg he has investigated the sensitivity of the human eye. This is of basic importance in all physical observations that depend on the eye's capacity for distinguishing between light and darkness. If an optical measurement depends on the production of darkness by the interference of two beams of light, its accuracy will depend on the accuracy with which the eye can decide whether darkness exists or not.

The limit of accuracy of visual extinction methods depends on the sensitivity of the eye adapted to darkness.

They have found that in the green part of the spectrum 50-100 photons are sufficient to stimulate the eye. This limit is beyond that of the ordinary photoelectric cell, and a photographic exposure of several hours would be necessary to register such a weak beam. The human eye adapted to darkness is therefore an instrument of extreme sensitivity.

CHAPTER 15

TSAGI, THE AERO- AND HYDRODYNAMICAL LABORATORY, MOSCOW

THE growth and changes in this laboratory between 1929 and 1935 are impressive. Six years ago the Soviet engineers were cautiously approaching the task of creating a first-class Soviet aviation industry. At that time six wind-tunnels had been built and a Froude tank had been erected. The design of non-aeronautical machines was absorbing a much larger part of the staff's attention than now.

The hydrodynamical model of the Osborne Reynolds type for the great dam on the Dnieper had been constructed, and data for the design had been collected. They have investigated the strengths of dams of various profiles, and the efficiency of different designs of water turbines.

There was considerable experimenting with windmills. A large model had been erected on the top of a tower. The wings had been carefully designed according to modern aerodynamical theory, and they were fitted with extra vanes that tended to make them revolve at a constant speed. The extreme variability of the speed of windmills is one of the difficulties which prevent them from being used more frequently for driving small dynamos for producing electricity.

Windmills are important sources of power in arid districts, where other sources of power are scarce. Some have been used for pumping oil near Baku. Meteorologists have been studying the winds in Turkestan in order to see whether they might conveniently be harnessed by windmills, and experiments have been made in the Crimea with windmills whose wings sweep a circle 100 feet in diameter, and develop about 100 horse-power.

The laboratory designed an aero-sledge for the delivery of mail over the frozen steppe. The postman steered himself in a small cabin carried on three skates, and pro-pelled by a small air-screw driven by a motor-engine.

Researches of these sorts occupy a less prominent part in the laboratory's activity to-day. The purely aeronautical work has become much greater in volume, and the smaller applications occupy a less noticeable place. The spirit of the organization of the laboratory has changed. In 1929, the staff gave the impression of attacking the problems of aerodynamics and aeroplane construction tentatively. Now they give the impression of being masters in the process of accomplishing great programmes. There is an atmosphere of competent enthusiasm, and a brightness and confidence not so noticeable in 1929. The visitor has no difficulty in perceiving that this laboratory is one of the chief centres of the contemporary Soviet State. It is the brain of the vast Soviet air force that is having such a decisive rôle in international affairs.

The laboratory is controlled by the Soviet War Depart-ment, in collaboration with the Department of Heavy Industry. Its director is a colonel, a short, dark-haired soldier of proletarian origin, and smart attractive person-ality.

The laboratory is very carefully guarded. Visitors are followed at a distance of two paces, even through wind-tunnels, by a pair of armed guards. The Soviet authorities allow more visitors to this very important institution than one might have expected. It is possible for two air attachés from the American Embassy, and an English scientific journalist to visit the laboratory on the same morning. It would be difficult to imagine two American naval attachés and a Soviet journalist visiting the British Admiralty's Research Laboratory at Teddington on the same morning.

But the Soviet authorities for obvious reasons are not too communicative about the details of their aeronautical re-

PLATE 7

Wind tunnel building, and experimental tower, Tsagi

searches, so only a very rough idea of the laboratory can be given here.

In the structures laboratory there are many researches on the strengths of parts of aeroplane structures. The behaviour of full-sized aeroplane structure under strain is compared with experimental tests on structures of simpler form whose stresses can easily be calculated. In this way, the designer learns what allowances to make for deducing the behaviour of complicated actual structures by analogy from the behaviour of simpler structures.

Much work is done on welded metal frames, and experimental frames with interchangeable parts. Bulkheads for large seaplanes had been constructed by spot welding, out of rustless steel, and there were full-scale models for the chassis of the giant aeroplane, the Maxim Gorky, with special tyre fittings. The main tubes of this were oval, and constructed of molybdenum-chromium steel. They were designed and tested for strains of 100 tons. These tubes looked more like parts of a steel bridge than parts of an aeroplane.

Deflection tests for the tail plane of very large seaplanes were in progress, and dynamic testing for engine-frames. The vibration of spars was registered by automatic recorders.

In the optical laboratory the methods of Brewster, Maxwell and Coker for investigating stresses in frames by polarized light were in use. The stresses in plates with an orifice were being investigated, and the secondary stresses in models of ribs of aeroplane wings. These were made of cellonite. Cellonite and glass are generally used in these investigations. They are using the method for examining the stresses on valves in aeroplane engines, and the stresses produced in seaplane bulkheads by side-landing. They have a rough method of estimating stresses by comparison with a colorimetric scale.

In the experimental aerodynamical department they have four big wind tunnels, and a variety of smaller ones. The 50-metre tunnel is 6 metres wide at the big end, and 3 metres at the small end. The fan is 6 metres in diameter,

and is driven by an engine of 650 horse-power. The
maximum air speed is 60–70 metres per second.

They have an open-jet wind-tunnel of Prandtl's type.
It gives a wind speed of 70 metres per second and its fan
is driven by a 250 horse-power motor. Before the Prandtl
slots were put into this tunnel, the vibration from it nearly
shook down the walls of the building. This was an interesting demonstration of the efficiency of the slots in preventing eddies leading to vibration. These remarkable
tunnels consist of one big funnel emptying air into another
funnel directly opposite, a few feet away. When the design
is correct the air rushes across the gap almost like a solid
bar. If an object is placed near the line connecting the
rims of the opposing funnels it is not displaced until it is
pushed right into the stream of air. The edge of the
stream is precise almost to a fraction of an inch. Inside
the stream the motion of the air is extremely uniform.
The advantage of this type of tunnel is due to the direct
access of the experimenter to the model suspended in the
stream. He can observe it directly, without even the inter-
vention of a glass window.

The models are carried by a truck that may be run in and
out of the tunnel along rails.

Side-stresses are investigated by mounting models on
rotating tables.

An apparatus for studying the behaviour of propellers in
wind-tunnels has been constructed. The torque, thrust,
etc., may be measured. There is a combination of a propeller with a fuselage, and propellers in tandem.

Their experimental investigations of spin with models
have given good results. The angular velocity and two
other moments are observed, which give the complete
spinning properties of the machine. The apparatus
measures the steady spin and shows whether the aeroplane
would recover, or not. The comparisons of the results with
full-scale experiments are very good.

They have an air-tunnel for working with air-streams
travelling at 1000 feet per second. This is nearly equal
to the velocity of sound in air, and comparable with the

PLATE 8

A large wind tunnel, Tsagi

[*face p.* 212

PLATE 9

Testing aeroplane wings to destruction, Tsagi

The Froude tank, Tsagi

speed of a rifle-bullet. Experiments with models in very swift air-streams are useful for analysing the forces that act on the tips of high-speed propeller blades, and for designing machines that fly at extremely high speeds. The forces acting on models in this tunnel are self-registered.

There is a novel sort of wind-tunnel consisting of a barrel containing air and a model aeroplane. The barrel was rotated about the model, and dragged the air round, so that the conditions of an aeroplane in a spin are simulated.

The organization of the aerodynamical equipment is highly centralized. The air-stream in the wind-tunnels is controlled from a central power station. The observer at the tunnel instructs the power station engineer to vary the stream, and does not do this himself by manipulation of switches beside him.

The Froude tank is 200 metres long, 6 metres deep, and 12 metres broad. The travelling carriage, which is of German construction, will run at 15 metres per second, or about 30 miles an hour. It is driven by four 25-horse-power motors. It was being used very industriously for the investigation of the properties of models of hulls for seaplane floats, large river ships, and the characteristics of screws. The models are made of wood and paraffin.

Small instruments registering deformation and vibration during alighting were attached to the seaplane floats.

The mathematical department is directed by A. I. Nekrassov. Besides organizing the solution of practical mathematical problems, he continues research on classical hydrodynamics. His recent papers include analyses of the diffusion of vortices in viscous fluids, and the analysis of classes of integro-differential equations. About 200 memoirs of researches have been published for the laboratory, and at the present time about 1000 research problems are being investigated.

The institute's laboratory for the study of the physics of metals is one of the finest of its sort in Europe. The X-ray investigations of the structure of metals are exceptionally good.

It is noticeable that many of the scientists who work in

the institute and speak English have an American accent. This is noticeable in the structures department. Many of the young Soviet aeronautical engineers have had one or two years' experience in America.

The work of the aeronautical instrument department was also noticeably good. Many of the recording instruments for routine use in flying were of original and neat design.

The institute has a vivacious air, and much of the scientific research is of first-class world standard. It is one of the best disproofs of the idea that Russians are not mechanically minded. This is a mistake. They are not lacking in insight into mechanics and machinery, and often are inclined to be too ingenious. This institute seems to show that the Russians possess mechanical talent of the same quality as that of Western Europeans. It is not so completely developed, through lack of experience, but in a decade or so it should be equal in every respect to the degree seen in the most advanced Western countries.

At present, it is as good in many points, and the Russians make up for the weaker points by their great enthusiasm.

They follow foreign researches with the utmost industry, and they speak with high admiration of authorities such as E. G. Coker and H. Glauert. They were upset by Glauert's premature death.

The condition of the institute is of much significance to those interested in international affairs.

CHAPTER 16

THE EXPERIMENTAL ELECTRO-TECHNICAL INSTITUTE, MOSCOW

THIS vast institute was opened in 1930. It has large new buildings on a site of several acres in the outskirts of Moscow. When the institute was visited during construction in 1929 the beautifully designed new buildings were rising like huge white modernistic mushrooms out of the bright brown earth. They looked as if they had been pushed up from underneath the earth, and the soil had fallen back in piles along the edges. In that year the buildings contrasted remarkably with the neighbouring decayed appearance with the former Tsarist academy for cadets, and other dirty ramshackle buildings. The appearance and atmosphere of the district had been transformed by 1934. The vast laboratories of the institute had been enclosed in a park which had been laid out with paths and flower-beds, and planted with trees. They looked smaller than before, as equally vast new buildings, such as the Telephone Laboratory, had been erected on the other side of the road.

Many Soviet citizens are no longer pleased with the beautiful lines of the institute's buildings. The unfortunate revulsion against modern architecture in the Soviet Union at the present time is partly due to the misfortune that many of the modernist buildings were erected during the period of greatest difficulty, at the beginning of the first Five Years' Plan. The large area of windows, and the insufficiently thick walls due to shortage of building materials, have made many of the new buildings cold and draughty, and hence very expensive to heat. In many cases the heating apparatus is unable to warm the rooms and corridors to a comfortable temperature during the coldest periods of the winter. In addition, the materials on the outside walls frequently have not withstood the severe frosts. This has made the walls peel and become unsightly. Those who have never liked the modern style can find plenty of arguments against it.

The institute is at present directed by I. Speelerin. Its scientific department has laboratories for electro-physics, ceramics, vacuum technique, arc carbons and graphite, rare gases, etc. They manufacture in these laboratories such things as tantalum carbide, sodium vapour lamps, cæsium photoelectric cells, etc. The engineering research department includes a section on high tension. They have a 1-million-volt testing plant, and have made a number of researches on overcharges on transmission lines and insulators. They research on cables, transformers, protection apparatuses and lightning arresters.

The laboratory for electrical measurements has done much work on cathode-ray oscillographs and manufactures them for other institutes.

The stability of networks is investigated according to the methods of Steinmetz and Fortescue.

Research on mercury rectifiers has shown how automatic control may be devised.

There is a section for the study of the problems of railway electrification.

They have produced thyratron units for controlling electric welding plants, and have investigated the electrical driving of coal-cutters, and the ventilation of turbines.

They have designed and tested regulators for driving electric tramcars.

The electric light department studies the theory and practice of electric lighting. They worked out the lighting system for the new Moscow Metro, or underground railway.

In the metallurgical and magnetic laboratories they are studying magnetic steels, and elements for electro-chemical installations.

The institute does not work on problems of radio communication. These are now studied in other institutes.

PLATE 10

Photo. *Planet News Ltd.*

One of the six blocks of buildings of the Experimental Electro-Technical Institute, Moscow

[*face p.* 216

The staff includes 1700 persons. About 200 of these are qualified scientists. There are 15 to 20 aspirants (corresponding to students working for a degree as doctor of philosophy, under direction) and about 10 to 20 students taking practical courses.

The heads of the departments lecture in the Moscow universities and technical high schools.

The high-tension department is directed by Bernkov. Its equipment includes a 1,000,000-volt cascade transformer, and a 1,500,000-volt impulse generator. It is chiefly concerned with research on transformers and insulators, and does not do much routine testing. They have been working on Soviet substitutes for the American Tyrite material for insulators.

A magnetic machine has been constructed for examining and testing parts of machinery and registering internal defects.

The research on insulators has included the study of the influence of climatic conditions. They have found that conditions in the Soviet Union require heavy types of insulator for transmission lines. One large cable is preferred to several small ones, as in American practice. They have designed insulators that will carry a mechanical load of 12 tons, and a range of designs from 2 tons, up to the 12-ton size.

The institute has designed an inexpensive form of non-resonating transformer.

In the vacuum department they have made sodium-vapour lamps with an efficiency of 40-50 lumens per watt. They have obtained 140 lumens per watt from their best lamp. They have improved the insulation of the vacuum.

They have made mercury lamps working at a pressure of three atmospheres, and 220-volt neon lamps giving 40 lumens per watt.

The special glass for the sodium-vapour lamps has been made in the Leningrad and Moscow optical glass factories.

Tager, who made original contributions to the development of sound-recording for films in 1930, is now working with Shoring at related cinematographical problems at

Leningrad.   Their designs of photoelectric cells for sound-films are already in use.

They prepare their own lubricating oil for their vacuum pumps.

The illumination department has done much research on street, interior, and flood-lighting.   They have designed reflectors that distribute the light evenly, and increase the practical illumination by 100 per cent.   They find that 40-watt lamps supplied with these reflectors are effective path illuminators when spaced at distances of 30 metres.

They have made models for studying the lighting and flood-lighting of the stations of the Moscow Metro underground railway, the proposed Red Army Theatre, the Moscow Big Theatre, and other buildings.

This department was particularly well-run.   A collection of photographs of the flood-lighting and interior lighting of many of the world's most famous buildings had been made, and designs of every sort of electric light fittings. For example, there were models of the fittings in the underground station at Piccadilly Circus.   It is not surprising that the lighting and furnishing of the Moscow underground has received universal praise, as the preliminary experimental work with small-scale models had been done in an excellent manner by the institute.

The model for the proposed new Red Army Theatre looked hideous.   The plan is in the form of a five-pointed Soviet star.   The outline of the star is marked by hundreds of concave-fluted columns.   The theatre auditorium covers a relatively small area of the plan within the enormous surrounding porticos of columns.   Though at least one person has found the design repellent, the problems of flood-lighting are being solved by thorough preliminary study.

In the laboratory for research on insulators, the English electrical engineer C. G. Garton is working on the electrical constants of resins, benzamylon, and chlorinated starch. He left England after being victimized in connection with a strike.

Research on the thermal conductivity of dielectrics is being done in this laboratory.

The department for magnetic investigations has been studying magnetic steels, and the construction of copper bus bars with iron cores.

They have been studying the possibilities of using iron rails as substitutes for copper wires, and improved forms of iron-molybdenum alloys.

In the machine-testing shop they have been working out methods of applying electrical drives to various sorts of machinery.

They have been studying rectifiers with grid-control; and the elimination of sparking at the brushes of machinery.

They are investigating the division of electrical drive on small machines, so that several small motors are used for the smaller actions. The object is to increase the flexibility of the machines. For instance, they are designing coal-cutters driven by two motors instead of one.

They act as consultants to factories and power stations, in order to solve difficult problems that have arisen during operation.

They also test Soviet and foreign electrical machinery before it is accepted for installation.

CHAPTER 17

THE ELECTRO-PHYSICAL
INSTITUTE, LENINGRAD

THIS large institute is directed by Professor
Tchernitchov. It has a vast and beautiful
building in a modern style, and very large additional buildings for high-tension research.

It is organized in five departments: high-voltage; radio-
technique; acoustics; electrical measurements; dielectrics;
and specialities such as photo-cells, thyratrons, instruments
for stratosphere ascents, lightning protectors and electric
arcs.

The staff includes about 450 persons, of whom 200 are
qualified engineers. The high-voltage and radio departments are the largest.

Their work is concerned with the theoretical problems
underlying electrical engineering practice.

They have a 500,000-volt experimental transmission
line 1½ kilometres long. Its construction cost 300,000
roubles. It is supported by twenty-four insulators of
special design, which allows the distance between each
cable to be varied. The towers are of welded materials.
The conductor is 5 centimetres in diameter and consists of
a steel core with an aluminium cover. The voltage limit of
efficiency for bare transmission lines is about 500,000, as
the corona discharges and leakage at that voltage produce
losses greater than the economy in other directions.

These very high-voltage lines are of special interest in
connection with the electrification of Siberia.

They have a 2-million-volt impulse generator.

The effect of lightning discharges on transmission lines
is investigated with cathode-ray oscillographs.

The American engineer Newman is engaged in high-voltage research.

The photo electric cell department works out methods of construction that can be adopted by industry. The cells are designed so that vibration of parts shall be avoided, and disturbing noises eliminated.

Valves for protecting low-tension lines from surges in adjacent high-tension lines have been designed successfully by Tchernitchov, and have proved of much value on the Soviet electrical transmission lines. One electrode is connected to the low-tension line and the other to earth. When there is an excessive voltage, there is an arc in the valve, which contains argon. The gas is kept permanently ionized by the presence of a small quantity of potassium. The valve has no inertia. It may be arranged to switch off the line for a variation of 5 per cent on a working voltage of 175–300.

A mixture of potassium bichromate and iron is used in their preparation. Small valves operating at 50–70 volts have been constructed for protecting instruments.

A variety of copper oxide, iron, and selenium cells are made for various purposes. On the basis of careful voltage-current characteristics, cells can be designed for any sensitivity, in series or parallel. They can obtain a two volts current from sunlight by using several cells in series.

A new type of electric dynamo has been constructed in the laboratories, according to principles suggested by Mandelstamm and Popalevsky, on the basis of researches by Rayleigh. Mandelstamm's researches on non-periodic vibrations have been discussed in Chapter 9. Mechanical energy is transformed directly into electrical energy by moving a system of plates in a condenser. If a circuit of suitable self-inductance and capacity is connected with the condenser, it can be thrown into a state of oscillation. It is possible to arrange that the energy of the oscillation losses is less than the amount of energy put into the circuit.

The small dynamo which has been constructed develops

power of the order of 1 kilowatt.   The system of moving
plates, which looks like a concertina, produces a considerable amount of vibration and noise.

Kovalenko, Rozansky and Sena have studied the properties of electric probes, or collectors, for investigating the
electrical conditions in discharge tubes and radio valves.
They have shown that the most probable causes of the
distortion of the current characteristics of the collector are
the incorrect determination of the ionic current, the current
of primary electrons, and the drift current.   The measurement of the velocities of ions has led them to conclude that
the temperature of positive ions does not exceed 3000° C.,
and is probably considerably less.   These results agree
with similar ones obtained by Langmuir.

Inge and Walter have investigated the ageing of insulation on high-tension cables.

The evaluation of high-voltage insulation is difficult,
because ageing has an important effect.   Tests lasting a
few minutes or hours generally do not give a proper idea
of how the insulator will behave after tens of thousands of
hours.   If the processes of ageing were exactly understood,
it might be possible to forecast the condition of an insulator
after a long period of use.   Inge and Walter have studied
the direct effect of the electric field on the insulation, and
attempted to estimate the maximum working tension for
the insulation of a high-tension oil-filled cable, whose
insulation consisted of oil-impregnated paper.

Two fundamental types of breakdown occur in solid insulators, the electrical and the thermal.   The first depends
on the release of ions or atoms in an electric field.   The
second is due to the heating of the dielectric.   It is
characterized by a sharp fall in the breakdown voltage with
increasing temperature, and the influence of time.

The breakdown in a non-uniform insulator begins in the
weakest part, and spreads into the undamaged parts until
complete.

It is well known that the breakdown voltage of liquid
dielectrics increases with external pressure.   Inge and
Walter have shown that an increase of pressure of one to

eight atmospheres on a cable insulated with oil-impregnated paper layers doubles the breakdown voltage.

They find that the breakdown begins in the layers of oil. It decomposes and produces gas bubbles, which leads to ionization and further destruction of the oil. At field intensities of 20,000 volts per millimetre of insulation the decomposition is swift enough to reduce the life of the cable to a few hours.

If the factory tests are made above that figure they may damage the cable. The working voltage should not be more than 7000 per millimetre for the design of oil and paper insulation which was investigated.

In the manufacture of cables it is desirable to wind the paper as tightly as possible. The conductor should be covered so that the metal surface, being smooth, will hinder the formation of a layer of oil near it. The paper should be as thin as possible, so that the thickness of the layer of oil should be as small as possible.

If possible, the cable should be worked under external pressure, and impregnators which break down at higher voltages than transformer oil should be used.

This research was subsidized by the Soviet cable industry, and assisted by the cable factory Sevkabel, which gave the necessary materials and apparatus.

I. Goldman and B. Wul have also investigated the ageing of insulators.

They have shown that the ageing of organic insulators such as cable vapour, varnished cloth, and acetyl-cellulose, is chiefly due to chemical reactions between the insulator and the products arising from discharges in its pores and air pockets. These reactions reduce the dielectric properties. When the ageing process has been started by a discharge it continues, even when the current is switched off.

Materials that resist attack by oxides of nitrogen and ozone age less quickly than less resistant materials.

As ageing depends so much on oxides of nitrogen and ozone, it can be reduced by removing oxygen from the neighbourhood of the insulation, by surrounding the cable with an atmosphere of nitrogen, argon, or hydrogen.

It is desirable that the pores of the material should be as small as possible, as the size of the breakdown voltage increases with the smallness of the pores.

Walter explains that the mathematical principles of insulation breakdown, and of chemical chain reactions are similar. In order to elucidate the fundamental facts, it is necessary to experiment with pure substances and liquids. When the breakdown occurs in pure substances it is electrical, and when it occurs in impure substances it is thermal.

Interesting work on solid insulators is being done at Tomsk.

A. Lazarev has investigated the effects of hydroscopy on liquid insulators and emulsions, in order to explain the effects of the adsorption and mixture of water in dielectrics such as transformer oils. He studied transformer oil, tetraline and hexane.

He showed that when water is added to hydrocarbons containing capillary active bodies, part of it goes into a molecular solution, and part forms a stabilized emulsion. The stabilizers are naphthenic acids.

The individual effects of the molecular and emulsified water on the insulating strength of transformer oil have been investigated. The emulsified water has the larger weakening effect.

If the proportions of molecular and emulsified water remain constant, the strength of the insulator passes through a maximum when the temperature is increased. This is not entirely due to the evaporation, but is partly due to an increase in the proportion of water in the emulsified state.

S. Gutin has investigated the electrical properties of the oxide layer on aluminium. He has shown that it is thermally stable, and retains a high resistance at $250°$ C., and does not lose its resistance until it is heated to $500°$ C. If the oxide layer is made several tenths of a millimetre thick, it can resist a voltage of several thousands. The brittleness of the layer increases with thickness.

The hygroscopical properties of the layer, and its porous structure, greatly reduce its resistance, if it is not dry.

The presence of water-vapour spoils the insulating properties of the layer.

Excellent results are to be expected from oxide layer insulators if they are used in a dry, compressed gas.

Research on the combination of aluminium oxide layers with organic and inorganic substances might give interesting results.

CHAPTER 18

THE THERMOTECHNICAL
INSTITUTE, MOSCOW

THIS very large and excellent institute was founded on the personal initiative of Lenin during the fuel crisis of 1921 for research on fuel and the application of heat as a source of power. A building that had been erected before the Revolution for the second Moscow Tramway depot was appropriated for it, and opened in 1925 with a staff of 100 persons. The institute belongs to the Energetics section of the Department of Heavy Industry. The present director is Professor Yurkin, who gave the following verbal sketch of the institute's chief researches and aims. Engineer Zhitomirsky acted as interpreter, and gave many interesting details during a tour of the laboratories and installations. It has done work of great importance on fuel-drying on the lines of Professor Rosen's methods in Germany. It has worked out methods of drying fuel in suspension that are now used in Tula, Lipitz, the Urals, Bobrika, and Moscow power stations.

It has perfected a new method of disintegrating coal. The coal is subjected to heating by steam under pressure, and the pressure is then suddenly released. The same principle was used by Fleischer in Austria to dry coal, but failed from his point of view because it also disintegrated the coal, whereas he wanted drying only. The method dries and disintegrates the coal in one operation, which is very convenient if dry pulverized fuel is required.

The institute conducts a survey of the distribution and qualities of coals in the U.S.S.R. The coalfields now produce five times as much coal as before the Revolution. Specimens of all of the coals are tested in the institute, and their firing prospects are directly tested by burning in the numerous experimental boiler-furnaces. They have given special attention to the low-grade coals of the types that occur in the Moscow basin, to the oil shales of the Volga district, and the brown coal of the Ukraine. Low-grade fuel is burned best in the pulverized form. In Germany the tendency to low-grade fuel research is in the direction of experiment with new types of automatic stokers. This is due to the medium size of the German boilers.

The institute studies the properties of boiler feed-waters. It has a laboratory for studying water-softening processes, such as the permutite process. In 1934 materials suitable for water-softening on the same principle as permutite were found in the Soviet Union, and water-softeners constructed of this material have been introduced into many power-stations. These water-softeners make the water less alkaline, and free it from organic matter. They are of particular value for supplying purified water to high-pressure boilers, of quality as good as condenser water.

The various laboratories include a boiler laboratory, where the burning of fuels can be studied in boiler tests, and the efficacy of fuel-drying processes, etc., may be tested. There is an analytical laboratory for studying the composition of coals. There is a combination of heat and power stations, in which back-pressure turbines are used, and electric power is produced by steam-turbine-driven dynamos, and heating is supplied both for power and warmth to neighbouring factories. There is a water laboratory. The laboratory for driers studies drying processes for coal, wood, cereals, textiles, etc., and anything that can be used as fuel.

The laboratory for internal combustion engines studies the use of liquid fuels, the burning of heavy fuels, and methods of increasing efficiency.

In addition to these, a laboratory group studies the properties of liquid fuel.

Until 1933 the institute had a gas laboratory for studying gas-producers, coke ovens, etc. This has now been organized as a separate institute.

One of the most extraordinary features of the institute is the experimental station for high-pressure boilers. Two Loeffler boilers working at a pressure of 130 atmospheres, or 1820 lb., or more than three quarters of a *ton* to the square inch, are being installed. One is of foreign construction by the Witkovsitsky Works in Czecho-Slovakia, and the other is being manufactured by Soviet engineers. The Loeffler boiler already in operation is the largest super-high-pressure boiler in the world and provides superheated steam at a temperature of 500° C., not very much below the temperature of red-heat. Each boiler is to produce 130 tons of steam per hour, and give 60,000 kilowatts of power to the turbines in the very large neighbouring factories.

One unique turbine is being erected in the station by Metropolitan-Vickers Ltd. It was made in Manchester, after extensive preliminary research on the strength of materials at high temperatures. It is to develop 24,000 kilowatts, and to work at 125 atmospheres, or three-quarters of a ton to the square inch, and at a temperature of 470° C.

The rotor for this turbine had been unpacked, and rested on supports beside the turbine bed. In spite of the enormous power it was to develop, its dimensions were quite small. It looked less than 2 feet in diameter, and several feet long. The engineers charged with the task of erecting and operating this turbine must bear a heavy responsibility. It is by far the largest super-high-pressure turbine in the world, and its performance will be awaited with universal interest. The installation of this superb and unique machine is an example of the courage of the Soviet authorities. In a country where there is still a severe shortage of skilled engineers a machine that might intimidate the best operating engineers of Western Europe and America is being put into service for the first time. This event is one of the best illustrations of the nature and strength of Soviet technical initiative.

The back-pressure, or exhaust pressure of the steam from the super-high-pressure turbine will be 25 atmospheres, or 350 lb. per square inch. The exhaust steam will operate two Siemens-Schröder turbines of 12,000 and 24,000 kilowatts capacity respectively. The 24,000-kilowatts machine is of conventional design. The steam from the 12,000-kilowatts machine discharges into a controlled vacuum of 0·05 to 1 atmosphere. The turbine efficiency is therefore low, but the condenser cooling water is heated considerably, and is supplied to the pipe-lines for the central heating systems for warming the neighbouring factories. Siemens did this as a special job.

When the turbines are not working, the heating systems may be fed with steam from the high-pressure boilers through reducing valves. At present, while the high-pressure turbine is being erected, steam is supplied from the 130-atmosphere boiler through a reducing valve to the 25-atmosphere pressure turbines.

Research is being conducted on high-pressure steam. The viscosity has been measured up to 100 atmospheres, and the measurements are being extended up to 225 atmospheres. It is hoped that the results will be of value to the International Steam Table Conference.

The rate of the burning of particles of coal is being investigated, and the radiation and absorption in boiler furnaces. Accurate knowledge of these is needed in order to burn low-grade fuels satisfactorily, as this depends on a good control of the temperature in the furnace. Temperature control is necessary also to keep the gases in the furnace relatively cool, so that they will not transport the highly fusible ash to the heating surfaces, and interfere with them. A rational construction of heat-absorbing surfaces produces sufficient absorption for radiation, so this point requires investigation.

Research is being conducted on heat conduction with very high gas velocities. Brown Boveri have constructed a boiler which operates with very high gas velocities, and have found that the standard formula for heat conduction at high velocities is not correct. The heat conduction is in fact more than that given in the formula. It is expected that the researches done here in 1935 will provide a new heat-conduction formula for very high velocities.

In the fuel-drying laboratory research is being done on the dynamics of drying. The statics is well known. Experiments are being made on the drying properties of materials in various structural forms.

Two new stations each of 300,000 kilowatts are to be built in Moscow for the production of electric power and of large-scale central heating. This combination of electric-power stations with enormous central-heating systems for whole districts is being developed in a unique manner in the U.S.S.R. It is expected that by 1947 Moscow will need stations producing 1,600,000 kilowatts to supply these combined systems.

The whole of Moscow is to be supplied with one grid for central heating. Central-heating mains are to be laid throughout the city, and each building will be able to draw its heating from these mains. The laying of these central-heating mains will be an immense constructive work, and the invention of economical methods of construction will lead to immense savings in costs. The system of mains for central heating is already used to some extent in America, and in the American practice the heating pipe-lines are usually laid in ducts built of concrete or other materials. If Moscow were to be supplied with a complete system of concrete ducts, the cost of construction would be immense. They have therefore experimented with cheaper forms of construction. They have found that suitably wadded and packed pipes can be laid in the subsoil without ducts. The heat losses to the soil are not greater than with the ducts, and the mechanical strength has proved to be sufficient. This research should enable very large sums of money to be saved on the construction of the Moscow central-heating grid.

Research is being made on gas-engines. Before the Revolution all gas-engines used in Russia were imported. They require to cultivate the technique of gas-engine manufacture, and to design engines specially suited to conditions in the Soviet Union. For instance, the natural gases issuing from the ground in various parts of the country should be used for feeding gas-engines. The survey of

Russian natural gas resources before the Revolution was not very thorough, and not much was known about them.

They are studying subsoil gasification. In this process, the coal in seams too thin or twisted to be mined in the usual way is converted into gas underground by fires made under seams. The coal-seam is roasted in a gas retort whose walls consist of the neighbouring strata of the earth. In the Kuzbas producer gas is led off with a heat-value of 1200 calories per cubic metre, or about 150 B.T.U. per cubic foot.

The low-grade fuels used in the Moscow power stations contain 2 to 3 per cent of sulphur. Much research on the removal of sulphur from furnace gases has been made. The gases have been washed or scrubbed with water, and sulphuric acid produced from the solution by catalysis. At the Battersea Power Station sulphur is removed from the furnace gases by water scrubbing and neutralization, and the sulphur products and water are thrown away. At the Kashierei station 100 kilometres from Moscow the same method of sulphur removal is used, but the water is repurified and the sulphur recovered. The sulphur dioxide is converted into sulphur trioxide by an electric discharge method, and sulphuric acid is prepared from the trioxide.

The institute is consulted by industrial trusts and factories for the testing of turbine and boiler equipment.

They have a staff of about 750 persons. About 220 of these are qualified engineers, and of these 120 have higher engineering qualifications. Seventeen of these have the same scientific standing as university professors, and lecture on their subjects in the universities and technical high schools. About 50 lecture as assistant professors in the higher academical institutes.

The budget of the institute in 1934 was 4,500,000 roubles. About 3,000,000 roubles were paid in salaries, and about 1,000,000 was spent on experimental research. The estimated budget for 1935 is 5,200,000 roubles.

The work of the institute is planned in the manner usual in Soviet organizations. The planning department has a staff of sixteen. It devises a skeleton plan for the next

year's work on the general lines indicated by the State
Planning Commission, for the satisfaction of the needs of
the State.   Copies of the skeleton plan are given to the
various laboratories, who devise a detailed plan on the
lines of the skeleton.   The detailed plans are returned to
the planning department and then to the director of the
institute.   A five-year plan is devised first, and then one-
year plans.   These are subdivided into plans for each
quarter of the year, and schedules are drawn up for the
monthly expenditure of each laboratory.

The plan for 1934 contained about one hundred problems
for investigation, including those on high pressure, burning
of low-grade fuels, problems of plant operation, and design
of new types of plant.

The planning department acts as a consulting body to
the director.   The final decision on features of the plan
rests with the director of the institute.

Twelve per cent of the staff are Communists.   The
Communists as a cell discuss the plans and the results
of the laboratory in which they work.   They stimulate the
enthusiasm of the laboratory brigade, and help especially
to strengthen its weak points.

Examples of agitation by Communist members of the
staff are on the policy concerning research on low-grade
fuel, and on equipment.   Some of the engineers wanted
to reduce the amount of money and attention given to
research on the well-known low-grade fuels, and give more
to the study of new fuels.   This would have been a mistake,
as an improvement in the efficiency of widely used fuels is
generally more important than the introduction of new
fuels of uncertain possibilities.   The tendency to become
bored with the old fuels and pursue the entertaining novel-
ties of the new fuels is natural, but it is usually uneconomic,
and disadvantageous to the State.   Similar difficulties have
arisen over the problem of scientific apparatus and equipment.   The Communists have done much to encourage the
production of better Soviet-made instruments, so that
engineers need not continue to look abroad for special
apparatus.   The enthusiasm of skilled mechanics has led

to the improvement of the quality of machines, and has helped the movement for independence for special equipment.

The institute has a scientific council, or governing body, of leading men in industry.   There are 105 members, and all major reports have to receive its approval.   The routine management is conducted by the director with the advice of a council with fifteen members.

In the technical physics department a method of sampling the sulphur content of gases with lime has been worked out. The sulphur gases are dissolved and gypsum is precipitated and some sulphuric acid is formed.   In the electrical department experiments on dust precipitation are made with precipitating plates charged at 80,000 volts.   Experiments are also made with 100-metre radio waves.

The Johnstone method of scrubbing gases with water and manganese catalysts is being studied.   They are investigating the possibility of preventing the catalysts from being poisoned by treating them with ozone.

The laws governing the elimination and transport of dust apply also to the manipulation of pulverized fuel.

The phenomena of the loss of pressure in tubes and pipes are being studied, and the viscosity of water and steam at high temperatures.   In these researches mercury or tin is used to force steam or water through a capillary tube fixed so that it can swing on supports.   The time taken by the tube to return to its original position is a function of the viscosity of the water.   The capillary tube may be made of steel or platinum.   The apparatus gives the viscosity of water up to 450° C. and 240 atmospheres pressure.

In another apparatus two capillary tubes are joined in a circuit.   Drops of mercury drive steam through the narrower tube, and the speed of fall is connected with the viscosity.   The coefficient is independent of pressure up to 90 atmospheres.

The dielectric constant of steam is being measured by filling an electric condenser and finding the change in its capacity.   The change is of the order of some parts in a million.   The experiment has a bearing on a general research on the study of the stability of the water molecule.

The velocity of the burning of fuel is investigated by burning specimens in a molybdenum-steel tube. The velocity is measured by recording the decrease of the weight of the specimen by the deflection of a glass suspension.

It has been shown by experiment that the relation between the change of area with the time of a burning carbon sphere is linear

The rate of burning of liquid fuel in the vapour phase was calculated from the shape of the cone in a bunsen flame of the burning vapour. The shape of the cone is determined by photography, which gives very fine pictures.

In experiments on the combustibility of coal, which have a bearing on mine explosions, and Galloway's method of destroying the combustibility of coal-dust by mixture with stone-dust, powdered activated coal is placed in a glass tube with a mixture of air and carbon monoxide. The combustion flame is photographed by the rotating drum method. The concentration of the coal-dust is shown by an electric filter. A first series of experiments was made on inert powder, and a second with pulverized coal. It is found that the larger the particles of inert dust the smaller their influence on decreasing the rate of propagation of flame.

The behaviour of mixtures of air and coal-powder is compared with that of mixtures of air and sham coal.

The interesting investigations on pipe-lines for district central heating have been made by Shubin. The metal pipes are 6 inches in diameter, and laid in trenches about 1 metre deep. The pipes are laid on blocks and planking is built round them so as to shape a filling of foam concrete into a wadding.

The pipe is circulated with water that passes through a close circuit. The loss of heat from the pipe is first measured before any wadding or heat insulation has been put on, and then with various forms of insulation. Segments of various materials are fixed around the pipe, and then surrounded with foam concrete. Other pipes were surrounded with castings, and some had an air-place between the pipe and the foam concrete.

The temperature of the neighbouring soil was measured by buried thermocouples. These registered the temperature gradient, or fall with distance, from the pipe, and the time taken by the soil to reach steady temperatures after the hot water had been turned into the pipe. The variation of soil temperatures with changes in climatic conditions are also recorded. In Moscow the air temperatures often fall to $-30°$ C., (54 Fahrenheit degrees of frost, or $-22°$ F.), so the loss through the metre of earth from the pipe to the surface may be considerably more in severe winter than in autumn weather.

It is found that segment insulation gives the best results. The segments are made of special plaster insulating materials.

The fall of temperature from the pipe, which is at about $90°$ C., is $75°$ C. through a distance of 2 metres. Thus the temperature of the soil 2 metres from the pipe is about $15°$ C.

After two years the pipe was dug up. None of the segments was deformed or cracked, though five-ton motor trucks frequently ran over the ground above the pipe.

The institute supplies the neighbouring large Stalin Motor Factory with heat and power. They supply 650 tons of water to the Stalin heating system.

The feed-water for the high-pressure boilers is treated in a large soda-lime plant. The make-up water is 35 per cent; that is, only 65 per cent of the water passing through the turbines is returned to the boilers, and 35 per cent has to be made up with fresh softened and purified water.

The feed-water for the 125-atmosphere Loeffler boiler is pumped up to a pressure of 33 atmospheres in the first stage. In the second stage the pump water is raised to a temperature of $210°$ C.

Considerable difficulty was experienced at first with the deaeration of the feed-water. If all the dissolved air is not removed, the dissolved oxygen in the water attacks the boiler pipes and seriously corrodes them.

Two small breakdowns with the boiler have occurred in six months. Owing to a fall of pressure, tubes in the furnace became overheated and buckled at a temperature of 800° C. These have been repaired, and the installation now works well.

There has been trouble with the corrosion of tubes in the evaporation drum, particularly in the nozzles. This was due to dissolved oxygen. Cast-steel nozzles were first used, but they have found that cast-iron nozzles resist corrosion better.

They have experimented with a low-temperature carbonization plant. An industrial plant has been erected in Siberia for the production of oil from sapropelite coals. These give a large yield of volatile products, and provide oil for Siberian districts remote from petroleum fields. The process has been worked out by Karaviev, and Brailo in New York.

The boiler department contains a splendid range of equipment. A special Cornish boiler has been erected in eight water sections so that the temperatures in each section may be measured exactly.

The research on shredded peat in this department is one of the most interesting and important engineering investigations done by Soviet scientists. The peat is dried and shredded and then blown through a nozzle into the boiler furnace. It has been practically investigated in ten different styles of experimental boiler furnace in this department. The peat is broken into shreds by a fan, and then blown into the furnace. This method of firing is now being used in industry.

Zhitomirsky is engaged in researches on vibrations of the types that occur in the shafts of Diesel engines. He has devised a machine in which a geared shaft is exposed to three forces producing vibrations. He gives a theoretical analysis of his experimental results. This work, which is very technical, is mentioned here because an interest in vibration problems is a mark of the most advanced outlook in contemporary engineering. The condition of any research institute connected with mechanical engineering

PLATE II

Photo. Planet News Ltd.

A Laboratory of the Peat Institute, Moscow

[face p. 236

may usually be judged by the attitude and degree of interest in vibrational problems. With the increase in size and speed of revolutions in modern engines, the importance of vibration increases, so the best engineering minds tend to devote more and more attention to it.

The institute is affiliated to similar institutes in the Leningrad, Siberia, and Volga districts. It has sheds for specimens of fuel from all parts of the Union.

Much research has been done on the drying of fuels. The Sub-Moscow coal is very wet, so it is dried and powdered. The Moscow Kashierei Station, the Bobrikov and Moscow Thermo-Electric Central Station use mainly powdered coal. The furnaces are designed to work with hard, fluid or gas fuel.

The Sub-Moscow coal contains 35 per cent of water. If the water is reduced to 25 per cent by drying, this coal can be burnt. The process which has been adopted for drying and powdering it by hot gases consumes little extra electric power.

In winter the Sub-Moscow coal is frozen into plates. It is thawed by pipe driers. It contains much ash and sulphur.

There have been great developments in the use of Frazer turf. This is a form of peat. The top dry layer is dug up by tractors. Within two or three days the exposed layer is dry enough to be skimmed off again. Forty layers can be taken off in one season. The expenditure of labour power per unit of fuel is six roubles compared with twelve to sixteen roubles to machine-made peat.

Frazer peat may be burnt only when mixed with lump peat. The institute has devised methods for doing this. Frazer peat contains 45–55 per cent of water. When lying in bunkers it disintegrates rapidly. They have designed a machine for avoiding the difficulties presented by disintegration. The Frazer peat is dropped through a sieve and falls into a funnel-shaped elevator, and then through a ventilator which sucks in hot air and breaks up the peat, and blows the mixture through four long pipes into the boiler furnace. The torch of burning peat is directed towards the boiler tubes. The large unburnt pieces are burnt on the grate. Most of the peat is burnt in the torch. This system works successfully with peat containing up to 50 per cent of water.

Frazer peat, like Moscow coal, is also dried with pipe-driers.

Much research has been done on fuels for the Ural-Kuznetz Combine. In 1931 30 per cent of the institute's income was spent on this work.

Research on water-tube boilers has shown the importance of smooth interior surfaces of tubes, and that inlet and outlet pipes should not be arranged opposite each other in the stream drum.

The suitable speeds of air for conveying powdered coal have been investigated.

By 1931 thirty water-cleansing plants had been erected on the institute's advice for power stations.

At the Kashierei Station the Sterling boilers have a superficial heating area of 3134 square metres. They work at 30 atmospheres and a temperature of 400° C., and drive a 44,000-kilowatt Siemens turbine. There was trouble with acid in the supply water, which was cured by making the water alkaline.

At Poltava Power Station water was taken from wells. It was hard, and led to trouble. On the institute's advice they took water from the river, and the difficulties were overcome.

Difficulties with the water at the Central Station in Moscow, and at Bereznikovsky Station, have been successfully overcome. At the latter, a permutite plant was erected.

Experiments on steam wagons have been made. In the northern regions of the Union, petroleum is expensive, so the steam wagon may have special value there. They have been studying British practice.

The institute's experience as a supplier of heat to a complete city district is being used as a basis for large-scale centralized heating. The institute supplies the Amo factory, the Dynamo factory, the Locomotive works and the Ball-Bearing factory with heat and power. It also heats the adjacent swimming baths of the Moscow trade unions, dining-rooms and clubs, up to distances of 3 and 4 kilometres.

Some of the research on central-heating insulation has already been described. The Munich method of heat insulation has been studied, and the Junkers systems of heating. They have found there is no great difficulty in converting steam into hot-water heating systems.

They have an experimental 6-inch heating pipe 80 metres long buried in the ground. It is divided in six sections, each of which has a different method of insulating, with various sorts of brick, asbestos and slag wool.

They have tested non-metallic pipes, and wooden and cement pipes, with various types of joints. Large quantities of metal can be saved by using other materials.

They have worked out methods of calculating the cost price of hot water and steam. The problem is quite complicated.

They have also investigated lagging for boilers and steam-pipes.

Several of the new power plants operate at 60 atmospheres steam pressure. The institute's 130-atmosphere Loeffler boilers are to provide experience for the introduction of still higher pressures into practice.

The Loeffler boiler uses Donetz coal at present. Later on it will use the Sub-Moscow coal, which is damp and has a high ash-content. It is proposed to dry the coal with air-equipment and a gas drum from a water-content of 35 per cent down to 18 per cent. It is expected that 120 wagons of Moscow coal will be used daily. This would produce 20 wagons of ash. If emitted from chimneys it would cover a circle 2 kilometres in diameter to a depth of 5 centimetres in one year. One boiler will use a dry cleaner, and the other a damp filter with indirect drawing.

The processes of drying in industry and fuel usage are very important. The amount of fuel consumed in the industrial drying processes in the Soviet Union is equal to that used for firing the whole of the electric power stations in the Union, and is estimated at 9,000,000 tons per annum.

The sugar, paper, grain, and timber trusts use drying processes on an immense scale. The institute advises them on their processes. Attention to drier design in the timber industry gives an economy of 30 per cent in heat, 50 per cent in metal, and 30–50 per cent in time of drying. Grain driers have been designed with an economy of 20–30 per cent in heat, and 20 per cent in metal, compared with Randolph driers.

The drying of agricultural produce absorbs 900,000 tons of fuel yearly, 80 per cent of which is high grade. This presents a field for economy.

The institute has designed driers for cuprous ammonium artificial silk plants.

The design of driers for the Sub-Moscow and Ukrainian brown coal has saved 40 per cent on the capital investment, and 15 per cent in fuel consumption.

The water content of 160 tons of Sub-Moscow coal is reduced from 35 per cent to 18 per cent every hour.

Driers for mineral phosphate, bauxite and other crushed minerals have been designed. The introduction of drying increases the productivity of disintegration equipment, in some cases as much as 100 per cent.

With all this experience in design and testing, the institute has accumulated a vast amount of data for large-scale design and operation of power plants. It has detailed records of several hundred large-scale tests of power plants.

CHAPTER 19

THE INSTITUTE OF APPLIED MINERALOGY, MOSCOW

THIS fine institute is directed by Professor Fedorov-sky. It is concerned with every scientific aspect of minerals, from the deposits to the factories. Special attention is given to the co-ordination of its work with industrial requirements. The institute does research on the uses and industrial properties of minerals. It has geological, mechanical, chemical, and physical departments, and deals with non-metallic minerals and complex ores. Sixty-eight per cent of its varieties of non-metallic minerals found in the Soviet Union are studied here.

The institute has a splendid museum collection. Besides having a magnificent variety of specimens it is arranged in a simple and instructive way, so that groups of workers and students may learn from its exhibits. There are carefully written explanatory notes on the cases, and enthusiastic attendants and museum lecturers.

Museums are frequently well-run in the Soviet Union, and this is a good example.

Specimens of sulphur from new sulphur deposits are shown. These are of special importance in connection with the development of the Soviet rubber industry. There are specimens of fluorite from newly found deposits, and barite, graphite, chromium and titanium ores, and slate.

Talcum has been found. There was no talc industry before the Revolution.

They have found abrasive materials, and can now make their own grinding-wheels. They have discovered deposits of andesite, and acid-resistant stone. The stones for crushing paper pulp were imported before 1932. They are now made in Leningrad, and natural stones are found in the Ukraine and Caucasus. The hardening of artificial grind-stones with Portland cement was first investigated in Canada during the War. The known deposits of the best natural grinding-stones were in England (Yorkshire millstone grit, Yorkshire "grit"). The activities of the German sub-marines prevented their export to Canada, so research on artificial pulp-grinding stones was started, that they might be replaced.

Before the Revolution pigments were chiefly imported from France. The institute now has a vast range of speci-mens from newly discovered deposits of brown-pigment minerals, such as ochre and red ochre. Whole mountains of some of these have been discovered, and some are already being exported. There is a laboratory for studying pig-ments, and their preparation from minerals.

Before the Revolution the export of asbestos was small, and there was no asbestos-manufacturing industry. Huge new deposits have been found. Three factories are now making asbestos-cement tubing.

Insulating materials are being made from dolomite, which is cheaper than the magnesite used in foreign countries.

Hornblende asbestos is found in the Soviet Union. The South African variety is blue, whereas the Soviet is white and acid-resistant. Physico-chemical and mechani-cal studies show asbestos is a colloidal system. Long-fibre asbestos is exported from the Urals to Canada and America.

They have interesting specimens of diatomite from Caucasus deposits. It contains 99 per cent of silica, and very large radiolaria.

Nonpareil bricks are now made here.

There are shell limestone deposits in the Crimea.

Volcanic lavas are now used for building and are exported. They have remarkable properties. Pieces may be nailed together, and nails may be driven into walls built of them. They may be stuck together with glue. They have excellent heat-insulating properties, and a 40-centimetre (16 inches) wall is sufficient even in the climate of the Soviet Union.

The stone is made from lava by the natural gases. Owing to the distribution of the pores it is very strong, and is resistant to bullets. It takes enamel excellently. This lava stone is also found in America.

Before the Revolution slate was not used in Russia. Many deposits have been found, and methods for using waste slate for roofing, insulation and other purposes have been worked out. Slate powder is used for dusting coal-mines in order to prevent coal dust explosions.

When heated to 1200° C. it swells to eight times its original volume. This puffed slate may be used for heat insulation.

The methods of slate-mining have been mechanized. In foreign countries they remain peculiarly backward, and slate workers often live under semi-feudal conditions; modern methods have not been introduced because of the existence of cheap labour.

They propose to use more slate for roofing instead of metal, which is generally used for roofs in the Soviet Union. There are large slate deposits in Nova Zemlya.

The marble industry is being developed. They have interesting deposits of onyx marbles, valuable for architectural and electrical uses. Near Moscow they have some excellent brown marbles.

Agates have been found. They are required for the bearings of the axles of watch wheels, the knives of chemical balance supports, radio-sets, etc.

Beautiful bird's-eye marble is found on the banks of the River Okka. These deposits were formerly used for lime-burning, and the æsthetic qualities of the material visible after polishing were not known. The museum specimens had delicate grey figuring on a cream surface.

An optical method for analysing minerals has been devised. Sections of the mineral are examined under a microscope, and seen through a network of squares. The area of each constituent is measured by counting the number of squares occupied. This method may be used by unskilled workers, and for many purposes supersedes chemical analysis. An analysis may be made with it in about two or three hours, whereas the usual chemical method takes two days, and costs about 15 roubles, compared with 200 roubles for the chemical method.

The institute has devised methods of preparing silica gel and permutite from Ural minerals.

It has given special attention to fluorite. It is used also for the impregnation of railway sleepers and in the melting of steel. Before the Revolution there was no fluorite industry. A large part of the non-metallic industry, with a capital of hundreds of millions of roubles, has been created on the basis of work done by the institute. The deposits of fluorite occur in Siberia, Central Asia, and the North.

They have worked on artificial cryolite, enamel, etc.

In the Soviet Union large quantities of sulphur are obtained from copper-smelting furnaces, but large deposits have been found. In Central Asia there is an enormous deposit estimated to contain tens of millions of tons, and there are deposits in Saratov and other places. A deposit of pure rock sulphur has been found.

They have developed the kaolin deposits, which contain both primary and secondary types. In Western Europe there are no secondary kaolins, but the Soviet Union has these, and some of them contain no quartz. They may be taken straight from the deposit and used in industry without preliminary treatment. The Ukraine is particularly rich in these deposits. The output of China clay for the pottery, paper and rubber industry is expected in 1935 to reach 1,500,000 tons.

The mica-manufacturing industry is new in the Soviet Union. Large quantities of mica are required for electrotechnical and household purposes. Mechanite is made by glueing waste bits together. There are great deposits in the Trans-Baikal district, and especially above the Arctic circle.

The development of the northern sea route from Leningrad to Vladivostock will enable these northern mica deposits to be worked. The potassium mica from Mamor is specially interesting because of the perfection of its crystals.

They have a magnificent and unique specimen of optical

fluor-spar. It is in the form of a thick slab 2 feet square. Some of the crystals have edges 4 inches long. They are of value for optical research in the infra-red region. The specimen was found in Tajik, and they have altogether 6 tons of crystals.

They have found new barytes deposits. The mineral is used as a basis for paint, and the transparent variety for optical purposes.

In their studies of the utilizations of chalk they have devised a new flotation method for purifying it.

Iceland spar and calcite has been found in the Tunguska and Yakout districts.

Arshinov has designed a new optical apparatus for investigating colours. A small sphere of paint is spread between two plates, and can be examined with a hemisphere without using a Federov stage. The instrument has been exported for use abroad.

The institute has studied beryllium, tungsten, and other rare ores. Vanadium ores containing 12 per cent of the metal have been found, and zirconium ores also. The methods of working complex ores have been investigated experimentally in the institute, including the salt-cake process. The introduction of salt assists smelting. The recovery of titanium, vanadium, and manganese from slag has been studied.

The institute has developed the graphite industry, and it is no longer necessary to import graphite from Madagascar. Some of the Soviet graphites have larger grains than Madagascar graphite. The manufacture of carborundum from slag has been started.

In the research laboratories admirable work on the physics and chemistry of surfaces is being done by Rehbinder and his colleagues. The Bradley-Thomson theory of the collisions of glass-spheres has been developed, and the peculiarities of liquid films on solid surfaces. The work of W. B. Hardy is regarded as the basis of their researches. When water is confined between glass plates close together its viscosity increases. They do not differ from Bastow and Bowden, as they work with thinner films.

They have been investigating the lubrication of mica surfaces with mercury, and use a method of measuring the friction which is much more sensitive than Hardy's.

The hardness of material in thin films whose thickness is of the order 50 millimicrons is often greater than in the solid block.

They have found that if thin films of lead are put on glass, their hardness measured by resistance to mechanical work is twice that of glass itself, though the hardness of block lead is only one-thirtieth that of block glass.

Rehbinder also has a laboratory in the Physical Institute of the Academy of Sciences. Some account of the results of his numerous researches on surface chemistry are described in Chapter 3.

Tolstoi has investigated the viscosity of rocks, and the connection between fluidity and electrical conductivity. Kurnakov's work has shown that the viscosity at low temperatures gives information on the chemical composition of binary systems.

With Volarovitch he has determined the viscosity of the system borax-boric oxide by the rotating cylinder method. The comparison of the viscosity composition curves and the fusion curve shows a striking coincidence between their maxima. The latter correspond to integral ratios of the components.

Tolstoi has investigated the plastic flow of concentrated suspensions with a coaxial cylinder apparatus in which the axial translation of the inner cylinder is produced by a suspended load. Below a velocity of four ten-thousandths of a second, the behaviour of the concentrated clay suspensions departed considerably from Bingham's law of plastic flow.

I. D. Gotman, A. A. Glagolev and others have worked on the improvement of methods of sampling: sections of minerals are placed under microscopes and the areas of the constituents measured by the method of counting squares, which has already been mentioned. This technique has been greatly defined with the assistance of integrators for measuring the areas of the curves exactly. The slides are illuminated and the light reflected on to a photo-element connected with a galvanometer. The index of reflection of the mineral is used in the quantitative and qualitative analysis. All of these methods are being combined in one automatic machine that makes them without an operator. The mineral section has merely to be put into the machine, and its composition is then automatically found and registered.

A. A. Glagolev and I. D. Gotman have used these methods of analysis for examining the sample taken at intervals of 1 metre from boreholes for Kourad copper ore. They have compared the results with those obtained by chemical analysis, and found them very satisfactory. They were able to draw from them definite conclusions on the processes of mineralization, oxidation, leaching and concentration occurring in the ore body, and to provide technologists with guiding information for concentration and smelting processes.

N. Vedeneyeva has described a modification of Wright's microrefractometer which allows the graduation of the ocular micrometer without the use of liquids as recommended by Wright. This consists of a glass plate with a given refractive index and polished face. It gives measurements correct to 0·002 units and to 0·001 with care, which is quite sufficient for petrographical routine.

N. Melanholin has shown how Emmon's double variation method can be used without complicated devices with the heating stage and a Wright's microrefractometer. He is able to measure the refractive indices of minerals in the range 1·46 to 1·75 with an accuracy of 0·02.

N. Vedeneyeva and A. Kolotuskin have devised a method of determining the main refractive indices of crystal grains by means of a rotated needle. A minute grain is placed on the point of a needle, parallel to the microscope stage and immersed in a liquid; the needle can be rotated about its axis, as in the Bertrand microgoniometer. When the grain is rotated, its indicatrix is also rotated about the same axis. Each of the three axes of the indicatrix describes a cone, whose axis is the needle. As the axis of the cone is parallel

R

to the stage of the microscope, each of the slant heights of
the cone may also be made parallel to the stage.   In other
words, the rotation of the needle enables optical sections of
the grain to be investigated, for which one of the waves pro-
pagated in it has a main velocity.   In such a section it is
therefore possible to measure one of the three refractive
indices, and the others can be obtained by suitable
manipulations.

S. Grum-Grimailo has examined the refractive indices of
mixtures of piperine and the iodides of arsenic and antimony
with a Fuess goniometer.   These were prepared in Tchichi-
babin's laboratory in 1929.   Their indices were different
from those published by Larsen.

Besides applying dispersion variation methods to materials
of high refractive indices they have studied light absorption
in the visible and ultra-violet parts of the spectrum, and
pleochroism, or the rings produced in minerals by the decay
of radioactive substances.

They have examined the colouring of tourmaline.   They
find it is not due to impurities, and experiments on bombardment with electrons gave no change.   It appears to be
due to peculiarities in internal structure.

They have 110,000-volt X-ray apparatus for researches
of this sort.

The physical chemists are studying the equilibria of iron
oxides, and the dissociation of carbonates.   They have an
adiabatic calorimeter for low temperature measurements,
and measure specific heats and heats of formation.

The fast electron beams for investigating mineral structures are obtained from a 50,000-volt tube.

The chemical physicists work with atomic hydrogen.   Inorganic compounds in the solid state have been reduced,
and the recombination of atoms at high temperatures has
been studied.

The total staff of this institute includes 1100 workers.

CHAPTER 20

THE INSTITUTE OF
FERTILIZERS, MOSCOW

THE Institute of Fertilizers is at present directed by Academician E. V. Britzke. There are three heads of departments : (1) Professor Volfkonitch, the head of the technological department; (2) Professor Dubov, who is head of the department of scientific information, and (3) Professor Gogitidze, who is the administrative manager.

The head of the agricultural department is Academician Pryanishnikov, and of the geological department Professor Kasakov.

Research is conducted in four directions, in mineralogy, technology, agricultural chemistry, and field testing.

The aims of the institute resemble those of the American Bureau of Soils. It has a staff of 550, the largest section being engaged in prospecting for minerals which provide the raw material of fertilizers. About 90 persons work in the technical department, and are engaged on the study of the technological processes of the preparation of fertilizers from minerals. The agricultural section has a staff of 80, the insecticides section one of 90, and the mineralogical section has one of 150. This section works in collaboration with the Institute of Applied Mineralogy in Moscow. There is also close collaboration with the Nitrogen Institute.

The institute has three field stations for testing the qualities of fertilizers.

During the first period of the institute, from 1919 until 1929, which will be described presently, the main line of research was in agricultural biology. The investigators were chiefly interested in the investigation of how fertilizers affected plants. This aspect of research is still held in regard, but the technological problems of fertilizer manufacture now receive the first consideration. The purer problems of geological research in connection with fertilizers have given place to the study of such processes as that of ore-dressing.

The agricultural department is organized in three groups: soil, microbiology, and plant physiology. The influence of nitrogen, phosphorus and potassium and manganese, boron, etc., on crop production is studied.

With their field experiments they study the influence of fertilizers in different climates. Their conservatories for plants under glass contain 12,000 pots.

A special group works on concentrated fertilizers, and another on the production of fertilizers from coal and peat by colloidal treatment.

In the geological department there is a fine collection of new specimens and newly prepared maps. In its chemical laboratory the potassium, phosphorus, and other constituents of rocks, such as apatite, are determined.

Methods of granulating fertilizers have been worked out. This gives them valuable physical properties. The fertilizer is whirled in a centrifuge, and granulation occurs at high speeds. Fertilizers are prepared in a spaghetti-like form by melting them and forcing them through a perforated pipe, according to an American process.

Methods of colouring fertilizers are studied, so that agricultural workers shall have no difficulty in distinguishing between different sorts.

Attempts are being made to manufacture borax from tourmaline and other minerals, because the usual types of borax deposits are not common in the U.S.S.R.

Mustard, flax, and other crops benefit from fertilizers containing boron, especially in soils rich in calcium.

They are also interested in the preparation of boron for medicines.

The minerals being investigated as raw material contain about 5 per cent of boron.

In their study of the extraction of phosphates they are

PLATE 12

Testing fertilisers in a glass house of the Institute of Fertilisers, Moscow

Photo. Planet News Ltd.

Apparatus invented by Meerov for prospecting for minerals by high-frequency currents

Apatite Mines at Khibinogorsk

PLATE 13

trying to work out a method of preparing calcium phosphate pure enough to be fed to cattle. The difficulty is to get rid of fluorine.

The phosphoric acid is prepared from apatite as raw material, and is fairly free from iron and aluminium. They attempted to avoid dissolving the iron and aluminium salts by cold digestion of the phosphate. Sulphuric acid was not used in the digestion, but the extract was afterwards heated with it.

The calcium phosphate is to be mixed directly with the cattle fodder. If it is not free from fluorine, the animals' bones will thicken, and the teeth will fall out.

The institute has published 125 papers on the various researches made by its staff. They issue a monthly bulletin on their work. Everyone connected with the institute receives this, on the field stations, and in the geological expeditions in distant places. It is found to be very useful for keeping everyone generally informed, even when they are working in distant isolation.

The geological department is particularly active. Its archive contains 2500 papers and surveys. It works in groups, arranged according to the bases of the chief minerals studied. There is a boron group, an arsenic group, and others for potassium, etc.

In one of their laboratories they produce urea artificially from ammonia and carbon dioxide. The process is secret.

The palæontological section has discovered new forms of ammonites, not described in the literature, useful for determining geological levels.

Near Moscow the institute has a semi-industrial experimental plant for studying ore-dressing, heat-treatment, flotation processes for phosphates and apatite, etc.

The institute has had much to do with the development of the vast apatite deposits at Khibinogorsk in the Karelian peninsula. The factory there produces 1 million tons of phosphate per annum by flotation processes. Another is to be built. Phosphoric acid is prepared by heat treatment.

This new city already has a station of the Academy of Sciences and other interesting institutes.

At Selikamsk, two days from Moscow, there are colossal potassium deposits, several times as large as those at Strasbourg.   They are very clean and pure.   An industrial plant for producing 1,500,000 tons of sylvin, or potassium chloride, has been erected.   This town now has a population of 24,000.

At Berezinkovsky, about 30 kilometres from Selikamsk, there are large deposits of carnallite, a compound of potassium and magnesium chlorides.

The institute's main building is in Moscow, and is about five years old.   Its size is immense, and it is designed in an attractive modern style.   The institute was founded in 1919 with the object of advising the fertilizer industry. The scheme of co-operative research was conceived clearly at the beginning, and a complex programme of research work involving the study of raw materials, the technological methods of manufacture, and the methods of applying the fertilizers in conditions peculiar to the U.S.S.R. was prepared.   The experience gathered since 1919 has shown that this system of collaboration saves much time and labour.

The founder of the institute was Professor J. Samoylov, who, with Professor D. Pryanishnikov, had done much work on the commission for geological research on phosphate rock deposits, which had been organized by the old Moscow Agricultural Institute.   The work of the present institute is in some respects a continuation on a much larger scale of the old work.

The mineralogical section has three groups, for exploration, mining, and ore concentration.

The exploration involves topographical and geological survey, determination of the type and size of deposits and chemical composition.   The field work is done by groups of workers during summer and autumn, who return to the institute during the winter and spring to study the material they have collected.   The material is examined from the aspects of petrography, chemical analysis, palæontology, and crystal analysis, in order that more detailed geological maps may be drawn, and plans for drilling and excavating. A whole cycle of field, laboratory, and semi-industrial scale

PLATE 14

The Institute of Fertilisers, Moscow

[face p. 252

experimental work, including flotation, is carried out in order to discover the modes of work most suitable to the economic and industrial conditions.

The phosphate deposits that have been thoroughly explored by the institute and transferred to industry for exploration include the upper Kama deposit (Vyatka gub), the Bryansk-Yisdrinsk and Tchigrov (Kursk gub), and the smaller deposits at Tchuvash, Podolsk, Dmitryevsk, Bytchkovo, Setchensk, and others. Besides these there are the vast Khibin apatite deposits already mentioned. These were discovered some years ago by workers of the Soviet Academy of Science, under the direction of Professor A. Fersman. The known deposits of phosphate rocks in the U.S.S.R. contain at least 1000 million tons.

The mineralogical section has in recent years done much research on methods of mining phosphate deposits. The best methods of planning the mining, and of making underground shafts and galleries, and open cuts, have been worked out. Experimental work of this sort was done on the deposits at Tchrifgrovsk, Dmitryevsk, Tchuvash, Krolevetz, and Polpinsk.

From 1925 the institute has worked at methods of mechanical ore-concentration in order to improve the efficiency of the exploitation of phosphate rock deposits. The processes of mechanical concentration and ore-dressing have been investigated, and the designs of milling and ore-dressing plants have been improved.

The members of the staff who have done this work are consulted by managers of factories and industrial organizations for advice.

Beside phosphate, apatite, and potassium deposits, the mineralogical section investigates limestone, gypsum, barite and phosphoric iron ore deposits.

The experience of the technological section concerned with the conversion of raw materials into fertilizers is always drawn upon when new fertilizer plants are being designed. Besides advising on processes, the section can prepare drawings of plant in its drawing offices. The processes worked out in the laboratory are always tested on a semi-industrial scale in various factories.   For instance, research on processes for producing concentrated phosphate fertilizers has been done for the Tchernovyetchensky factory at Gorky.   The thermal volatilization method of Britzke for producing phosphoric acid from low-grade phosphate rock has been adopted at the Constantinovsky factory in the Donbas.   This process produces from low-grade rock treble superphosphate containing up to 50 per cent of available phosphoric acid.   A method of manufacturing ammonium phosphate has been worked out for a semi-industrial unit belonging to the Industry of Applied Mineralogy.

The institute has been provided with its own semi-industrial plant at Ugresk, as experience has shown that experiments conducted in industrial factories are often hindered by practical difficulties.

The institute has also worked out processes for producing ammonium phosphate, potassium phosphate and double superphosphate from low-grade phosphate rocks.   These have been tested at the Tchernoryetchensk chemical factory.

A new cycle of acid treatment of phosphate rock for producing phosphates, ammonium sulphate and calcium nitrate has been worked out, and also new thermal and wet methods of producing ammonium phosphate.

A method of recovering ammonium sulphate directly from sulphur dioxide, ammonia and water-vapour has been found, and also a method of treating the Solikamsk potassium salts for the manufacture of potassium phosphate.

The five-years plans of industrial construction have contained schemes for a series of large-scale fertilizers factories, each with a capacity of 200,000 tons per annum.   The planning and construction is based on information provided by the institute.

In connection with nitrogen fertilizers new methods of preparing urea salts have been found.   Ammonium nitrate is prepared from gaseous oxides of nitrogen and ammonia.

Methods of manufacturing phosphate, nitrate and sulphate of potassium from the Solikamsk potassium deposits have been worked out.

They aim at working out a series of concentrated phosphate, potash, organic and combined fertilizers. The latter are of chief importance, owing to the long distances of transportation in the U.S.S.R.

Quick methods of analysing fertilizers are studied.

The fertilizer factories are expected to have detailed knowledge of markets for their products, and the prospects of being able to dispose of their products. This depends on the nature of the agricultural district, transport facilities, etc.

The factories can receive help on these points from the institute's section of agricultural chemistry. This section conducts research on the most effective methods of applying various fertilizers to various crops under the economic, soil, and climatic conditions existing in the U.S.S.R. It has the use of test-fields besides the usual laboratories for analysis, etc.

The section for microbiology and pedology studies the effects of fertilizers on the dynamics of the soil and microbiological process.

The experimental field of the agricultural chemistry section is near the Dolgoprudny station on the Sovyelov railway, about 18 kilometres from Moscow. Other experimental fields are at Luberzy and Kryukovo, on sandy soil and heavy clayey soil respectively.

There are large vegetation sheds and glasshouses for studying the fertilizer requirements of various soils by the Mitcherlikh method.

The section of agricultural chemistry has an information group which checks all information in the Russian literature of fertilizer research. In Russia, this began about 1840.

Besides using the experimental fields near Moscow, the institute collaborates with the Commissariat of Agriculture in the use of test plots in various parts of the U.S.S.R. Over 300 test plots in White Russia, the Ukraine, the Transcaucasus, Middle Asia, Siberia and the Far East, enable the behaviour of fertilizers to be tested in all the different conditions of those regions. The results of the work of all these stations are correlated and discussed at a yearly conference, and plans for the next year are prepared.

Among the more important problems studied by the section for agricultural chemistry are the liming of podzol soil, and the effects on its chemical, physical and microbiological properties.

The availability of the phosphorus in the various phosphorus rocks has been studied, and the effect of particle-size on fertilizing capacity.

Their results have been used by the All-Union Chemical Trust (Vsechimprom) in the planning and prospecting for the phosphate fertilizer industry.

The geographical boundaries and districts in European Russia where the use of lime and phosphate is valuable have been investigated.

As a result of the institute's work, the liming of soil and treatment with pulverized phosphate rock has been made compulsory in the agriculture of the non-black earth regions of the Union.

Experiments on the use of peat as a nitrogen fertilizer have been made in the northern agricultural districts of the U.S.S.R.

The results of the institute's researches are seen first in the technical crops such as cotton, sugar, flax, hemp, tobacco, starch, etc.

It is expected also to organize courses on the technology of mineral fertilizers in the Moscow technical high schools, and to provide opportunities in its laboratories for the specialist training of a considerable number of students and capable workmen.

In 1933 the institute issued a comprehensive *Handbook on Fertilizers*, edited by E. V. Britzke and L. L. Balasheva. This volume of nine hundred pages and about half a million words gives detailed information and instruction of the manufacture, use, and properties, of mineral fertilizers.

CHAPTER 21

THE CERAMIC INSTITUTE, KHARKOV

THIS institute for the investigation and testing of glass and refractory materials is much bigger and better equipped than any similar institute in Britain. The refractories problem is very important in the U.S.S.R., as the technique of the production of the linings for the vast new smelting-plants was unknown in the U.S.S.R. As the local raw materials for refractories are rather different from those in foreign countries, foreign practice is not a complete guide for the Soviet refractory industry. Thorough researches on refractories became essential and pressing. A large factory laboratory, which will be unique in Europe, is being built. It will have an a nual production of 1200 tons of refractory materials. Methods of manufacture will be tested on the full factory scale of production in this laboratory. Its equipment includes a 15-metre rotary kiln, and a variety of mixers and presses. The large experimental furnaces range from a capacity of 24 tons to 1½ tons.

The Ceramic Laboratory was visited at an interval of eighteen months, and provided a good example of Soviet development in such a period. It was internally tidier, and externally beautified by the planting of a number of trees and flower-beds. The scientific staff had been strengthened by the appointment of Dr. Pines, who has done some very interesting new research. It is well known that the brick linings in Bessemer furnaces for converting iron into steel are consumed much more quickly than the lining in Martin furnaces. In the Bessemer furnace the impurities in the iron are removed by blowing air through

the molten metal, whereas in the Martin furnace no such
blast is used.   The rapid wearing of the linings in the
Bessemer furnaces might therefore be connected with the
turbulence caused by the air-blast.   Dr. Pines, who is a
physicist by training and familiar with the theory of hydrodynamics, decided to attempt to investigate the turbulence
in the Bessemer furnace, with the technique which has been
developed particularly for the investigation of turbulence
produced by aeroplanes in air and ships in water.   Previous
investigators had approached the problem of Bessemer
furnace behaviour from the view of the metallurgical or
ceramic chemist.   The influence of the violent fluid movements produced by the blast had been studied empirically,
as the scientific staffs of steel factories were too close to the
chemical and routine work to be able to apply to blast
furnaces the refined methods of modern hydrodynamics,
the applications of which have produced Schneider Cup
winners and the *Bremen*.   Pines has made glass models of
Bessemer furnaces and photographed the turbulence produced in them when filled with liquids of various viscosities,
such as alcohol and glycerine, and subjected to air blast.
He has also investigated the effect of blowing gases such as
hydrogen chloride (hydrochloric acid gas) into liquids such
as solutions of ammonia.   The gas and liquid react chemi-
cally and produce phenomena similar to those of the
chemical reactions that occur between the blast of air and
the impurities in the Bessemer furnace.   Pines succeeded
in photographing the effects of changes in the shape of the
model furnace, and of the number and position of the holes
through which the air is blown.   Further, and even more
excellent, he has succeeded in giving an approximately
accurate mathematical theory of the rate at which brick
linings will be consumed in furnaces of various shapes and
specified working conditions.   He accomplishes this by
the application of the modern theory of vortex motion.
This intrusion of mathematics, especially the abstract
mathematics of Göttingen, into the steel-manufacturing
industry, is unexpected but welcome.   Where mathematics
appears, the soil is fertile for science.   Experiment and

calculation shows that the wastage of brick is related to the velocity of the fluids in the vortex with which it is in contact. In furnaces of various designs Pines finds experimentally that the bricks in the wall lining are wasted respectively 300, 30, and 4 times as quickly as the bricks in the floor lining. His mathematical analyses give the respective figures of 106, 14, and 8 for the ratio of the velocities of the fluids scouring the walls to those of the fluids scouring the floor. The results are of the correct order and show he has found a promising line of research for the smelting industry. His experimental work was done in the Dzerzhinsky Steel Works, which is the largest steel works in the Ukraine.

In the Ceramic Institute, Pines is making an interesting series of researches on the application of X-ray analysis to the atomic structure of refractory materials. He has discovered the composition of a well-known refractory material which is manufactured by a secret process, and appears, according to X-ray analysis, to consist of the minerals spinel, fosterite and periglass. Minerals of very similar constitution often provide refractory materials with markedly different technological properties. X-ray analysis provides a powerful method for discovering the explanation of these slight constitutional differences. The differences in a series of closely related minerals may be due, for example, to the replacement of some silicon atoms by aluminium atoms in a standard silicon compound. The way in which the aluminium atoms are introduced might be impossible to decide by chemical methods, but might be easily determined by X-ray photographs. The explanation of the difference between the minerals sillimanite and mullite may be deduced from their photographs. Small rotating chromium anti-cathode X-ray tubes are used for the production of the X-rays.

In the physical chemistry department the properties of chromite and magnesite are being investigated. They will not bind together to form strong bricks so they must be mixed with binding materials.

The heat of solution of silicon oxide is being measured

as this is necessary in the calculation of the speed of the chemical reactions in refractory materials at high temperatures. The measurements are made in a diphenylmethane calorimeter designed by Szukharev. The measurement of the internal pressure produced in lime when wetted is another subject of measurement. Satisfactory types of refractory bricks have been prepared from coal-shales, and from minerals not used in other countries. The Russian raw materials are different, and the technology of their use has to be worked out.

In one of the rooms there is a scale model of the Pantele-monovka Silicate Factory in the Donbas. This factory is designed for an annual production of 88,000 tons of refractory materials. The object of the Ceramic Institute is to assist the birth of these vast factories, and, for the Soviet Union, of a new industry.

CHAPTER 22

THE LENIN ACADEMY OF AGRICULTURAL SCIENCE

I

THE President of the Lenin Academy of Agricultural Science is Professor N. I. Vavilov, one of the most remarkable men in the Soviet Union, and in the whole world. His charm, and gifts of leadership, energy, and intellectual power make everyone his friend, and his great achievements have secured universal admiration. He is not yet fifty years old. In spite of the enormous number of persons and the amount of business that pass under his consideration, he remembers almost everyone and their needs, and always has sympathetic and encouraging advice for them. He habitually sleeps very little, and yet is without nerves or exhaustion.

A short time ago Vavilov took a group of friends on a visit to Transcaucasia and Baku. In order to save time, a journey of 300 miles over desert to Baku was undertaken by aeroplane. As they approached Baku they ran into a terrific gale, of the type that is common at that city. The word Baku comes from the Turkish name for the City of Winds. The aeroplane was tossed about wildly, and when the aerodrome at Baku was approached, the pilot was informed by signals that the gale blew at 90 miles an hour, and landing was impossible, and he was to return to his starting-place.   This would have been quite an acceptable instruction, if he had not known that his supply of petrol was nearly exhausted.   He had been fuelled for Baku, and the rough flight had consumed most of his reserves.   He turned off, and decided to fly to some neighbouring hills and try to land in their shelter.   All through this time the machine had been thrown about like a leaf.   The majority of the party were thinking of their last wills and testaments, but this was the solitary occasion on which Vavilov has been seen to fall asleep in public.   The circumstances were such that no other useful activity was possible; no observation could be made from, no discussion could be held inside, the tumbling machine, so finding for once no opportunity for the advancement of science, he slept.   The pilot succeeded in landing behind the hills before the petrol was exhausted.

Vavilov's office is in the building which used to be the Stroganoff Palace, on the October Prospect (Nevsky) in Leningrad.   In dining-rooms decorated with tiles and paintings of innumerable varieties of fish and food, one now finds the world's largest collection of specimens of domesticated plants.   The maps of Vavilov's expeditions in search of the origin of domesticated plants and animals hang over the scarlet and gilt of the old drawing-room which is now his study.   His desk is a very long table, covered with specimens of plants, and papers, with a small area cleared for serving tea.   Glasses of tea are served at intervals of a few minutes, and the old ones replaced by new, even though the contents may not have been drunk, so that there is a continuous supply of hot tea.   Cakes of a unique Russian size are provided and eaten during the reception of the latest news of plant research in the Soviet Union.

The old Stroganoff Palace as the head of the world's greatest organization of plant research presents one of the most remarkable contrasts of the old régime and the new culture in the Soviet Union.   In the future, when the institutes have all been housed in more suitable new buildings, visitors will not have the opportunity of seeing this pictorial illustration of historical change, and they will miss one of the most dramatic sights that the world still offers. It is to be hoped that the Soviet Authorities will make a documentary film of this institute and its director and his colleagues, before the inevitable time for the demolition of the old building, or the removal of its staff and contents to more suitable premises.

The organization of agricultural research has been considerably changed recently. Hitherto about 400 institutes were operated in one system. The Lenin Academy now has about ten research institutes, with a looser connection with the rest.

The Soviet Academy of Sciences has about 80 academicians. About 30 of these are also members of the Lenin Academy of Agricultural Science. The chief institutes attached to the Lenin Academy include the Institute of Plant Industry, the Institute for Agricultural Physics, for Agricultural Electrotechnics, etc.

Over 300 institutes of various sizes do part of their work in their various places in the Soviet Union under the direction of the Lenin Academy. The Academy is able to direct the whole or part of the work of 10,000 scientists scattered among its own and related institutes. In addition to these, there are about 8000 general assistants, field and laboratory workers, on the staff of the institutes. The Lenin Academy has more or less directive control over 18,000 persons, on whom it can call for assistance in the accomplishment of its research objects.

The administration and the planning of the scientific work of this system are conducted separately. Vavilov is the director of the scientific planning. He organizes this work according to several principles. In plant research they aim at mobilizing the plant resources of the world for human uses. All the plants of the world are to be examined and investigated as one system of material for human social and intellectual interests. This is a grand and original conception of the social rôle of the botanist. The Soviet philosophy in no way regards the botanist primarily as an amateur of plants, but as a person whose work is concerned with one of the bases of civilization, that particular part of the foundation, which consists of plants and plant products. With the support of his Government Vavilov has succeeded in beginning this vast organization of the resources of plant life for the material and intellectual benefit of humanity. This is the first time that the science of botany has been approached in such a comprehensive manner.

He explained that the most interesting botanical parts of the world have not yet been adequately developed. For instance, methods of utilizing the plant life and energy of Brazil and other tropical and sub-tropical countries have not yet been worked out.

His department has sent over sixty botanical expeditions to various parts of the world during the last ten years. These have included about 300 botanists. They have collected 300,000 specimens of plants. The scope of botanical field work may be illustrated by the varieties of wheat, of which there are at least 1 million. Five hundred separate genetical characters have been identified in natural wheat.

Extraordinary data concerning potatoes have been collected. The Soviet expeditions in South America have found thirty wild species, and it appears that the Indians have produced at least eight new species through domestic cultivation.

The second sector of their work is concerned with varietal tests. One thousand workers are investigating 2000 varieties of plants as possible sources of new crops. The Government introduces new agricultural crops on the basis of their results. They have 250 testing stations each with 100 acres of fields for doing this work.

The third sector is concerned with the organization of laboratories, libraries, etc. Five hundred scientists are on its staff.

The fourth sector is concerned with the bases and testing stations in various districts. These investigate the agricultural properties of local soil, its iodine content, etc.

The fifth sector provides scientific advice to agricultural and other organizations.

Vavilov has been particularly interested in research on the

origin of domesticated plants and animals. Some remarks made by him in conversation will be recorded here, and further information will be given later in this chapter.

There are about 700 or 800 plants of industrial importance. According to Vavilov's investigations about 150 of these arose in China, 130 in India, 60 in Indo-China, 40 in Afghanistan, including peas and lentils, 80 in Persia, including apples, pears, and millions of varieties of plums. (The Persian jungle largely consists of wild species of trees related to the domesticated fruit-trees, and is the source of the myth of the Garden of Eden. Vavilov and the Bolsheviks have discovered the material basis of the old story in Genesis.) Seventy of the industrial plants found in the Mediterranean region probably arose in Abyssinia.

The plant life of America is much better known than that of many parts of the Ancient World. Potatoes arose in Peru, and were taken to Chile.

Concerning domesticated animals, there are forty important species. Vavilov's latest researches indicate that they arose in five regions. Pigs and three species of hens arose in China. Cattle, buffaloes, etc., arose in India. Sheep and goats arose in Asia Minor and the Near East. Rabbits arose in the Mediterranean region. Guinea-pigs, llamas and alpacas arose in the Andes. The ass arose in Abyssinia. The turkey arose in Central America. The reindeers arose in the Altai region.

The yaks, zebus, etc., of the Himalaya are differentiated by environment from buffaloes of India.

The origins of agriculture are as yet little understood, but Vavilov considers that the researches of himself and his colleagues indicate there are fundamental relations between the origins of domesticated plants and animals and the sites of the human invention of agriculture. The origin of human civilization is intimately connected with the invention of agriculture and its relation to the sources of the wild parents of the domesticated plants and animals.

Vavilov expects these researches will be significant in connection with the discoveries of the sites of fossilized ancestors of man. He considers, for example, that the recent discovery of the fossilized remains of early men in Mongolia would not be surprising in the light of his own results with plants and animals.

The researches on plant-breeding conducted by Vavilov and his collaborators in the U.S.S.R. have been summarized in the fifteenth Anniversary Number of the Soviet journal *Plant Industry in the U.S.S.R.* This has been translated into English and published by the Imperial Bureaux of Plant Genetics. The information in the following pages is mainly drawn from this publication. The editors of the translation remark that Vavilov's results, and plans for further work, are of inestimable value to any breeder about to prepare or revise his breeding programme. They write that since 1917 Vavilov has succeeded in organizing the greatest experiment in plant breeding that the world has yet witnessed.

The general line of Vavilov's researches has grown out of his discovery of homologous mutations. In his studies of cereals and other plants he noticed there was a parallelism between the mutations that arose in entirely distinct species of plants. If a mutation of a certain sort appeared in one species, then it was possible to forecast its appearance in another species.

This comparative motive is seen through all of the extensions of Vavilov's researches. Wider and wider collections of plants were made in order to collect data for the study of homologous variations. These collections began to be wide enough to provide information on the comparative frequency of different sorts of plants in different parts of the world. In some regions far more varieties of a species occurred than in others. This may be reasonably explained by the supposition that this species has existed longer in that region than in others. Thus the origin of a species is indicated by the number of varieties in the neighbourhood. In this way it is possible to deduce that soft wheats, rice, small-seeded flax, peas, lentils, broad beans, poppies, apricots, almonds, and other plants arose in south-west Asia, because they exist in the maximum variety in that region.

Naked oats, barleys, millet, soya bean arose in south-east Asia. Cultivated onions, peach, olive, fig arose in the Mediterranean region. Hard wheats and oats arose in Abyssinia, and potatoes, maize, tobacco and sunflowers arose in South America and Mexico.

The collections of specimens from the expeditions in various parts of the world and the Soviet Union are larger in some of the chief crops, such as wheat, than those in the United States Department of Agriculture. A large part of the Soviet specimens are kept in the live state. They have 31,000 wheat specimens. Many of these remain alive for two years in closed boxes, and for five or six years in special boxes designed by Maximov.

The world collection of wheats enables the plant breeders to discover which may be of use in the Soviet Union. Thousands of specimens are sown, observed, harvested and threshed in various parts of the country each year. A few hundred of the specimens which prove to be the best suited to the various environments are selected for further study and experiment.

The director of these field studies, A. K. Flaksberger, and his colleagues, have shown the varieties of wheat are highly specialized in their adaptation to the various district environments. For this reason, foreign wheats cannot be directly introduced.

As the best Russian wheats have various excellent qualities, such as the highest known content of protein, or extreme resistance to cold, or maturity earlier than the earliest Australian varieties, they do not aim at replacing them with foreign varieties chosen from the world collection, but try to improve defects such as shedding, lodging, small grain, low yield, and susceptibility to fungus attack, by crossing them with suitable foreign wheats.

Various new wheats have been discovered. Vavilov discovered a wheat in 1918, in Transcaucasia, which grows in regions up to an altitude of nearly 3000 feet, and is very resistant to rust and mildew. Zhukovsky discovered a wheat, resembling spelt wheat, which is completely immune to rust. The Abyssinian wheats are remarkably early.

Wheats hitherto found in Syria and Palestine, which are resistant, and tolerant of bad conditions, have been found also in Armenia and Kakhicevan. The Egyptian wheats are very early, have very short grains and are susceptible to rust. The Dutch and Scandinavian wheats have good straw, do not shed, give high yields and large grains, but are late, moisture-loving, and of poor quality. The wheats of Afghanistan are early, drought-resisting, do not shed, and have some resistance to cold.

On the basis of these experimental classifications, the plant-breeders work at the production of suitable new types.

Vavilov himself has led many of the expeditions for the collection of this material. He has visited more than forty countries, and has pressed every sort of transport into his service, including aeroplanes. Samples from many parts of the country can be quickly collected by aeroplane.

Pissarev has made interesting experiments with Novinka wheat. It is early, with fairly large grains, a larger yield than early Northern wheats, but sheds its grain badly. Its ancestry contains Onegin, Siberian, Galician and Indian wheats. When crossed with the Scandinavian winter wheats such as Grenadier and Thule, it gave a spring wheat which did not shed, with large ears, and yields about 15 to 20 per cent higher than that of Novinka.

The wheats typical of each country have been divided into 300 spring and 200 winter varieties. Complete sets of specimen grains of these have been sent to forty stations in different parts of the Soviet Union for breeding. Each station concentrates on one or two dozen types, and the material from all stations is returned to the Leningrad office for collection and study.

Five thousand specimens of world wheats have been sown after vernalization at Odessa, Saratov, Omsk, North Kasakstan, the Giant Collective Farm, and Detskoe Selo. The Saratov Institute of Irrigated Grain Culture breeds with the 5000 world specimens, and the crossing of wild and cultivated wheats.

In the work on oats, A. J. Mordvinkina has produced forms hardy enough to be winter-sown in Transcaucasia.

She has produced varieties more resistant to drought, excessive salts, and fungus diseases, such as leaf-rust and bunt, than European oats. These forms are to be crossed with Russian oats and introduced into Transcaucasia. A Mediterranean oat crossed with the American White Tartar gave a new form of superior yield, drought resistance and immunity. It ripened nine days earlier, and yielded 18 per cent more than the standard form.

Under the direction of A. A. Orlov, the world collection of barleys, which contains over 13,000 specimens, has been examined. It has been concluded that all barleys, wild and cultivated, are a single species with three sub-species; those with six rows, those with two rows, and intermediates. The two world centres around which they are found in greatest diversity are Afghanistan and Abyssinia, and China and Japan.

The most interesting cultivated barleys are from Arabia, which provides the earliest ripener, the most resistant to drought, with very large grain and relatively high yield; from Asia Minor, which gives strong straw, large grain, relatively large resistance to drought and relatively large yield; from Abyssinia, which gives large grain, strong straw, relatively large yields, even in very northern latitudes, and good malting grain in White Russia; from the Mediterranean region, which gives large grain and is drought-resistant; from Syria and Palestine, which give large grain, resistant to drought and fungous disease; from China, which gives early ripeners, with naked grains and strong straw, and is adapted to Northern conditions; from India, which gives early ripeners, with strong straw and almost round grains; and from Afghanistan, which gives early ripeners resistant to drought, with grain of good shape.

Three hundred and fifteen types have been selected from those of all countries, and are being grown and bred at a station in the North Caucasus.

The barley of China, Abyssinia and Arabia provide the most suitable types for the extension of barley cultivation to the North of the Soviet Union, and those of Abyssinia and Asia Minor are most suitable for malting, while those of Arabia are most suitable for dry regions. Barleys of high yield, such as the naked barleys of Asia Minor and Italy, and the two-rowed Armenian barleys, have been isolated and already distributed for adoption in agriculture.

The work on maize has been directed by N. N. Kuleshov. He has selected from the world collection forms of special interest, such as an extremely early ripener, that becomes mature in seventy days. This allows the cultivation of maize in much higher latitudes than is usual. Forms that remain green until maturity have also been found. They are of importance for silage: the method of harvesting fodder while it is still green, so that losses due to bad ripening and harvesting weather are avoided, and storing it in silos or towers.

The best sweet maizes, for use as table vegetables and for canning, have been selected from the varieties that grow in various parts of the U.S.S.R. Experiments with a large collection of American and Western European varieties have been made in the North Caucasus. White dent was studied for industrial use, and yellow dent for fodder. It was found that certain varieties were relatively resistant to the European corn-borer.

During a visit to America in 1931, Kuleshov obtained 150 specimens of aboriginal Indian varieties, and 120 specimens of new inbred hybrids. Starchy types excelling Ivory King in quality and with much higher insertion of cob were selected from the Indian material.

E. A. Stoletova has selected specimens from the buck-wheat collection which possess early ripening qualities, and yield about 40 per cent above the usual.

The work on rye has shown that persistent inbreeding will isolate recessive characters that cannot be obtained by ordinary selection. It has been found that forms with long and strong straw, with augmented leaf production, which are of interest in the production of rye for hay, may be obtained by this method. Forms immune to mildew and rust have also been obtained.

The methods of close breeding have been applied to turnips and rape. Crosses between forms of Krasnozel

Swede, whose dry content has been raised by selection, with Swedish forms, in order to obtain new forms with increased yield, and to study the inheritance of individual characters.

The researches on grasses, herbage and forage plants have been directed by P. P. Zvorykin and V. A. Kuznetzov.

The various biological qualities of Sudan Grass have been comprehensively studied by T. N. Erkina and A. V. Talanova. This grass has recently been introduced into the U.S.S.R. for cultivation.

L. P. Bordakov has collected more than 2000 specimens of lucerne. Some new forms of blue lucerne of great agricultural value have been bred, such as more tender Provence types, and relatively productive and winter resistant Central Asiatic types. Lucerne hybrids have been extensively compared with races of blue lucerne, and it has been found that though they are less productive, they are more resistant to winter conditions, and are of increased importance in regions with severe winters.

Forms of yellow lucerne which are more erect, leafy and with a higher seed yield, have been bred in the North Caucasus; and the explanation of the generally low seed yield of yellow lucerne is being pursued.

In the Ukraine, a study of sainfoin has been made, and A. G. Khinchuk has published a synopsis of the literature.

A. Y. Tupikova has analysed a world collection of 3000 specimens of spring vetch. Certain Soviet, Bulgarian, Swedish, Czechoslovakian and German varieties appear to be particularly suitable for cultivation in the U.S.S.R.

A collection of 150 specimens of Teff grass has been studied, and forms for use in various parts in the U.S.S.R. have been selected. This grass is of value when sown with lucerne mixtures in cotton-crop rotations.

P. P. Zvorykin and his colleagues have published a handbook on the distribution of agricultural plants in the U.S.S.R. It includes explanations of their suitability for hay or silage in the conditions of the various districts in the U.S.S.R.

Inbreeding has been found of great value in isolating

very valuable recessive characters in herbage plants such as legumes, and certain grasses. For instance. *Trifolium pratense* have been bred with a short corolla. This facilitates pollination by honey bees, which increases the yield of seed.

Forms of field peas for replacing vetch as hay have been bred. Some of these surpass the hay yield of local peas by 85 per cent, and surpass local vetch by 40 per cent. Field peas with small seed have been selected for competition with vetch.

The research on vegetables includes studies of the cabbage, tomato, carrot, pepper, egg-plant, onion and beet.

The Pimento Pepper, which has very regular smooth fleshy fruits, has been introduced for canning, and more piquant varieties than the standard have been selected for cultivation.

About 2000 specimens of vegetables are sent to the various experimental stations every year.

Other vegetables newly introduced are Chinese onions, a Boston cucumber relatively resistant to drought and uniform in shape, Egyptian beets of flattened shape and intense pigmentation, and Nantes carrots which retain the root form, keep well, and resist drought.

The group working on Cucurbits, or melons, under K. I. Pangalo, has selected a number of entirely new varieties from the world collection. About twenty varieties of melons, water-melons and pumpkins have been adopted for immediate cultivation, as they are superior to those already cultivated in the U.S.S.R.

The luffa plant has been subjected to breeding, especially those types which produce tow suitable for padding, as used in the railway industry.

The research on potatoes has been of exceptional interest and importance. It was started in 1921 by making a very large collection from foreign institutes, private persons, and seed firms in all parts of the world.

In 1923 Bukasov published a revision of the systematic botany of potatoes, and included a guide to the description of varieties, based on characters such as dissection of the leaf.

The study of the chief commercial varieties of the potato showed their narrow limits and possibilities. "Potato breeding was stewing in its own juice, using for the introduction of new varieties always the same old parents in innumerable combinations. A cul-de-sac had been reached, with many problems still unsolved, such as phytophthora and virus diseases." The Soviet investigators decided a break with the customs of the potato specialists was required, and the subject should be approached in a more fundamental manner.

An expedition led by Bukasov and Yuzepczuk was sent to South and Central America, the original home of the potato, in order to discover more about the origins and relations of the plants. During the years 1925–8 this potato expedition, the first of its sort, explored Mexico, Guatemala, Colombia, Peru, Bolivia, Chile and the Argentine. The expedition returned with no less than 1000 specimens of potatoes, including those from inaccessible mountain regions, and other places where none had previously been known to exist.

Some of the native potatoes proved to be very similar to the commercial varieties, and others were quite different and were found to belong to distinct species.

When these potatoes were planted in the U.S.S.R. they gave very varied crops. Some gave no tubers at all, and others, hitherto unknown, had excellent qualities; in particular the drought-resistant species "akhaniurti", "chokepitu", and "orko-malko".

The collection of wild species of potatoes was larger, and even more varied and interesting. A stemless potato was discovered in the mountains of Peru and Bolivia growing near the snow-line, at a height of 15,000 feet. Many wild Mexican species resistant to phytophthora were found, and one was resistant also to frost.

Altogether, several dozen wild species and varieties were collected, and fourteen cultivated varieties.

The species most nearly related to the European potato were chosen for cross-breeding. It was found that the species *Solanum audigenum* crossed most satisfactorily with the early European varieties. The species is highly resistant to frost.

American potatoes immune to phytophthora diseases have been crossed with European potatoes.

Polyploid series with somatic chromosome numbers 24, 36, 48, 60 and 72 were found by cytological examination in potatoes, including the wild species from the Andes, and 24, 36, and 60 chromosome species were found amongst cultivated potatoes for the first time. This showed that the cultivated potatoes belong to several species, and stimulated the study of their physiological properties.

V. I. Rasumov and A. V. Doroshenko have investigated the effect of light on the different species. It was discovered that many species develop tubers only when growing in days with short periods of light. It is expected that the study of the period of rest, length of vegetative period, reaction to virus diseases and to unfavourable environmental conditions will provide important new knowledge.

At the Krasny Pakhar 10,000 infloresences were hybridized in 1932. Methods of mass hybridization were worked out, so that hundreds of plants could be pollinated. This technique, and the favourable conditions of soil, climate and long summer days near Leningrad, rendered the most difficult interspecific crosses successful.

Nesterovitch has obtained hybrids with exceptionally high yields, and Vesselovsky has obtained hybrids combining high yield with early maturity.

Among the large number of related botanical researches, those of Voskressenskaya on the induction of flowering on shoots from tubers, and Yurkov's budding of a number of wild and cultivated species on to nightshades and related plants, are of particular interest.

The researches of Soviet botanists on the potato are one of the most original and important contributions to agricultural botany made in the twentieth century. They are an interesting example of the value in scientific research of freedom from narrow commercial motives, as the organizations interested in potato culture could easily have found

PLATE 15

Photo. Planet News Ltd.

A lemon grove hot-house built in tiers on the shores of the Black Sea near Batum

[face p. 275

the philosophical and pecuniary courage to make a world-collection of material, and to send scientific expeditions for long periods to remote regions. The seed merchant is far more inclined to breed and select the potatoes already in his fields than to send botanist explorers to the Andes in search of entirely new stock.

One hundred valuable varieties of fruit-trees have been collected by expeditions to the Caucasus and Central Asia. These include 15 varieties of apples, 6 of pears, 15 of apricots, 10 of peaches, 5 of plums, 5 of institia plums, 5 of hazel, 5 of walnut, 1 quince, 5 of pistachio, 5 of almond, 5 of fig, 2 of pomegranate, and a number of olives, chestnuts, willows and others. Some of these are resistant to disease, and some are suitable for immediate introduction into cultivation. Apples of particularly good keeping quality, size and colour, and immune to the woolly apple aphis or fly, have been found in Azerbaidjan. Excellent wild apples from Alma-Ata have been introduced into cultivation.

Interesting new varieties of pears with good keeping qualities, transportability and resistant to drought, have been found.

Hitherto unknown types of apricots which give excellent dried fruits, have been introduced from the Fergana valley. Those from East Fergana and Alma-Ata are resistant to frost and of value for breeding.

An enormous collection of varieties of peaches has been made by the expeditions to Fergana and Azerbaidjan. Many of them are unnamed. One variety resembling the Elberta peach, but of superior flavour, has been found, and another excellent table peach resembling the Elberta, but with a much smaller stone, has been found in Azerbaidjan.

A quince which makes jam with an excellent aroma has been found in Kubin.

Wild walnuts were found at Kopet-dhag with an oil content of 76 per cent, compared with the ordinary content of 50–66 per cent. The hazel nuts of Abkasia are as good as the best European varieties, and nearly immune to fungous diseases.

Wild pistachios resistant to frost, and with kernels

nearly an inch in diameter, were found in Turkmenia. First-class varieties were in local cultivation, and had found their way from Persia.

Thirty-one thousand cuttings from the best varieties of fig found by the expeditions were planted out at Apsheron in 1931.

Many valuable varieties of grapes have been discovered. These include black, red and white varieties, and are excellent for export and drying. The Nimrang clones of export grapes have been studied in order to produce one with the grapes closer together and of more uniform size. This has been done, and the variety is being multiplied for cultivation.

Much attention has been given to the study of drought-resistant fruit trees. It has been discovered that the bush almond, the Afghan almond, is the most drought-resistant of all fruit-trees, and with the exception of the pistachio is the only fruit-tree that can be cultivated in the non-irrigated territories of Central Asia and Transcaucasia. The expeditions have found another drought-resistant fruit plant named *Crataegus azarolus*. Its largest fruits are more than one inch in diameter, are very sweet, and resemble strawberries. It is also resistant to drought, and should be suitable as a raw material for alcohol.

The large fruits of the willow are also suitable for alcohol manufacture. The tree has the advantage of growing on the salty soils of river-banks.

In the work on small bush-fruits, 1000 specimens of varieties have been collected, and 2000 specimens of wild forms. The material includes interesting forms such as bisexual strawberries. The Caucasus, Siberia and Altai mountains have many gooseberries, and there are many raspberries and edible honeysuckle in the Far East.

The extension of berry cultivation to the northern regions is one of the chief problems of research. Attempts to obtain more varieties more resistant to cold and drought, with earlier ripening, are being made.

The research on the breeding of medicinal plants is being conducted on the same lines as that on agricultural plants. World collections and expeditions are being made.

G. K. Kreier and N. A. Adolf have isolated varieties of Valerian with yields three to four times more than the usual.

Camphor trees with a higher yield of camphor have been isolated, and 1300 standard plants have been multiplied for introduction to cultivation. Nesterenko has discovered a new camphor plant, the "camphor basil", which is being multiplied.

Dalmatian camomile is being multiplied for use as an insecticide.

Lobelia with a content of 0·39 per cent of lobelin has been grown in the Leningrad district, and it is expected that non-shedding forms of coriander and cummin will be bred successfully.

The poppy plant has been studied, and the introduction of the cinchona tree in Abkhasia and Adjaristan has been attempted.

Much study has been devoted to the difficult problems of flax breeding. Crosses of different types have given non-lodging forms that do not stick in reaping machines, and are suitable for mechanized harvesting.

Various experiments have been made in crossing hemps, and some new fibre plants have been studied. One of them, *Apocynum venetum*, can be cultivated in areas not occupied by cotton, ramie and other standard crops.

II

The two chief methods of improving the varieties of plants are selection and crossing. In wheat-breeding crossing is of the greater importance, as the old varieties are generally inclined to shed or lose their grain during harvesting, and to lodge or stick in the machinery.

These characters are not avoided by selection. The possibility of making the widest use of crossing has been provided by the world collection of specimens.

In studies of the main characters of practical value in wheat, an analysis of the characters associated with high yield has been made. It was found that the chief of these were the number of grains per ear, and the average weight of the grain. These were found to be much more important than the number of shoots, or tillering, from the original seed. The variation of the number of grains per ear is very different in different crops. For instance, the number of grains per ear is much more valuable in oats than in wheat and barley, but the size and weight of grain are relatively constant.

The combination of early maturity with high yield has been studied. In general, earliness and low yield go together, but it is possible to break this usual connection. In order to do this, the parents must be chosen with extreme care. The complex of characters is complicated, and a proper choice cannot be made without a thorough knowledge of the genetics of the material.

The creation of early forms for cultivation in subarctic regions has been specially studied. Various lines of oats from a cross between Ligowo and the Norwegian variety Nidar have been fully ripened in subarctic field stations. This enables seed to be obtained from fodder oats in regions such as the Kola Peninsula, and removes the necessity for importing seed from the South for each sowing.

The studies of the properties of seeds have provided methods of distinguishing standard varieties of wheat by the colour given to their grains by phenol. The characters that distinguish the red clovers from the East of the U.S.S.R. from those of the West, and the characteristic weeds associated with these clovers, have been determined. The eastern clovers usually contain 30–40 per cent of yellow seeds, while the majority of western clover seeds are purple. This helps to determine the origin of any particular sample.

It has been discovered that there is a correlation between the capacity of seeds to retain germinating power and their region of origin. Seeds from the continental regions of the U.S.S.R. are superior in this respect to those from Western Europe and North America.

The director of research in field genetics, G. D. Karpechenko, has demonstrated that the hereditary constitution of cereals from widely diverse geographical regions are very different. It is found that if specimens from such regions are crossed, they may produce offspring in the second and third generation with longer ears, height of plant and number of spicklets, than the parents. This does not occur when specimens from neighbouring countries are crossed. Similar phenomena have been observed by E. I. Barulina in vetches and lentils.

An extra large tetraploid cabbage has been produced by S. A. Shchavinkaya by decapitation and regeneration. As its constituent cells are larger than the normal size, the plant is exceptionally juicy. The new cabbage has been introduced for cultivation, and it is expected that new varieties of other plants will be successfully produced by the same technique.

Karpechenko has investigated the possibility of crossing entirely different species of plants whose cells contain the same number of chromosomes. The tetraploid cabbage, i.e. one whose cells contain four times the normal number of chromosomes, can easily be crossed with the Abyssinian mustard plant, though these are very different types of plant. On the other hand, it is extremely difficult to cross the diploid, or double-chromosomed cabbage with the mustard plant.

The possibilities of creating whole ranges of entirely new cultivated plants are immense. The hybrids between the tetraploid cabbage and mustard are very luxuriant, and should be of great value for silage, or storing as green fodder before ripening, if stable forms can be determined.

As this method of crossing between entirely different species depends mainly on the preservation of equal numbers of chromosomes in the cells of the respective parents, and depends in a lesser degree on the intrinsic nature of the individual chromosomes, many fertile strange mixtures of plants are possible. Karpechenko and his colleagues have obtained hybrids which consisted of a mixture of the radish, cabbage and mustard; and others which consisted of a mixture of radish, cabbage, rape and turnip. The cabbage-radish hybrid is sterile, and becomes fertile only when its chromosome number is doubled. The multiplication of the chromosome number is an important technique for converting sterile into fertile hybrids.

T

Senyaninova-Korczagina deduced from studies of the morphology or shape of the chromosomes of the wheat-plant *Ægilops persica* that it is of a composite nature. It appeared to be a combination of *Æ. caudata* and *Æ. umbellata*. *Ægilops persica* has now been synthesized out of these two plants by crossing.

O. N. Sorokina has synthesized the Persian wheat *Triticum persicum* by crossing *Æ. triuncialis* with *T. diccocoides*.

S. A. Eghis, D. Kostoff and Clausen have proved experimentally that the common tobacco plant can be bred synthetically by crossing different species.

The work of G. D. Karpechenko, D. Kostoff and other distinguished geneticists has brought the conquest of sterility in hybrids nearer. D. Kostoff and S. A. Eghis have shown how fertile hybrids may be obtained by crossing three species of tobacco with other plants. Kostoff uses a method of triple crossing between plants with different chromosome numbers. He crossed the wheat *T. monococcum*, which has seven chromosomes, with *T. durum*, which has fourteen. These give a sterile hybrid. He then crossed this sterile hybrid with *vulgare* wheat, which has twenty-one chromosomes. This last hybrid proved fertile. Thus Kostoff's work confirms the possibility of producing a fertile plant from three other plants of different species. Each of the three parents may have valuable characters, so it is conceivable that breeders will be able to synthesize a plant which combines the most valuable characters from all of the parent plants.

These researches demonstrate that crossing between distant species requires a deep knowledge of cytology. The breeder who wishes to enter this field must have the guidance of the cytologist whose microscopical analysis will indicate the number of chromosomes in the cells of the various parent plants, and the general behaviour of the chromosomes to be mated in the distant crossing.

The remarkable results of the potato investigations have already been mentioned. The study of the chromosome constitution has contributed towards the demonstration that the European cultivated potatoes constitute only a small part of the potato family. Many of the uncultivated forms have useful qualities. The determination of the number of chromosomes in the various forms, and the study of the conjugation of chromosomes between European and American forms has explained many of the past failures in potato breeding, and has indicated the directions in which successful new breeding is to be expected.

The practical qualities of plant products are investigated as thoroughly as the scientific characteristics. A palace at Detskoe Selo, which previously belonged to Prince Yussupov, who was connected with the murder of Rasputin, has been converted into an excellently equipped laboratory for testing the milling and baking properties of the various sorts and mixtures of flour. An expert can frequently tell, from an examination of a loaf of bread, the variety and origin of the wheat from which it has been made. Makers' assertions that the bread has been made from certain brands of flour can be checked.

Chingo-Chingas has invented a machine for registering the volume of dough during fermentation and baking. A little weight at one end of a string rests on the surface of the dough. The string passes over a pulley and has a balance-weight at the other end, which is connected with an electrical register. As the dough rises, the increase is registered. At the moment when expansion ceases and contraction begins, a bell and electric light give warning signals which indicate the end of the fermentation process. Different varieties of flour have different periods of fermentation.

The apparatus may also be employed for automatic baking ovens. When the loaf has risen enough, the pulley may be made to operate an arrangement for putting the loaf out of the oven automatically.

Sections of dough are preserved by the usual methods of biological preservation. A section 3 or 4 millimetres thick is placed between glass plates, one of which is covered with formalin. The plates are pressed together, the margins are stuffed with cotton-wool, and sealed with paraffin wax.

A new method of milling maize has been worked out.

The grain is steamed so that the centre remains dry while the seed-coat and embryo become soft. These are removed by a brushing machine, and the central portion is milled in two stages. The embryos are flattened out in the second stage, and can be separated from the flour with a sieve. This method gives a percentage of 60–70 per cent of flour which contains 0·70–1·67 per cent of oil, compared with percentages up to 3·5 by previous methods.

Similar laboratories have been organized for testing the technological properties of other products. A standard method of roughly analysing the technological quality of specimens of flax on the farms where they are grown has been worked out. The sample is subjected to hot maceration, and the pulp is washed, pressed and dried, and the fibre is extracted. The varieties giving the most constant yield of straw and fibre, and other good qualities, are selected for future planting. A similar method is being elaborated for hemp.

Biochemical investigations for improving the quality of plant products, and for finding new sources of biochemical products, are pursued extensively.

A method of titrating tannins with gelatine has led to a large saving of expense. Over 2000 analyses can be made with 1 kilogram of gelatine. The method is simpler than the standard method.

The possibility of extracting other products besides tannin from the tannin plants has been demonstrated. Hydroquinone may be prepared from *Saxifraga crassifolia*. Gallic acid and pyrogallol may be extracted from the roots. Tannins and dye may be extracted from larch roots, and cellulose from the xylem. Attempts are being made to obtain agarcin and saponin from *Polyporus*, tar and basket fibres from willow twigs, and cellulose paper from the xylem.

A micromethod for estimating the oil-content of single seeds, or portions of seeds, has been worked out. One worker can make 400 estimations in a month with it. This greatly facilitates the technique of increasing the oil-content of cultivated plants by breeding. The method is used in researches on the breeding of sunflower plants. Sunflower seeds are a very important source of oil in Russian diet.

The researches in plant physiology have provided a large number of interesting results. A method of growing cabbages without having to transplant them has been worked out successfully. The method does not cause any loss of yield.

The eminent plant physiologist Maximov has shown that the development of potato tubers may be accelerated before planting by treatment with ethylene chlorhydrin. The treatment is particularly effective on early potatoes, and enables two crops of the same variety to be sown in one year.

V. I. Rasumov has investigated the effect of artificially altering the length of daylight on the early stages of plant growth. In some cases the development of the plant is accelerated, and the ultimate yield and period of growth is changed. The method is being used in plant-breeding researches, in horticulture, and in the study of transplanted crops.

Studies of the water requirements of plants have shown that the time of supply is important. The amount of water required for application can be reduced by 15–25 per cent by correct choice of the time of application.

Wind-chambers are being used for the investigation of moisture, temperature, and air current on plants. The conditions of climate that occur in desert regions, and in other regions, can be simulated, and the reactions of the plant to these conditions can be examined thoroughly. The characters that enable a plant to withstand climatic rigours may be exactly determined. Similar experiments are made with frost chambers, in order to investigate resistance to frost and cold. The resistance of various species and varieties of plants may be measured exactly by this method.

The degree of resistance to frost can be determined by measuring the electrical conductivity of sap taken from the plant exposed to the frost. The electrical conductivity of the tissue of the plant is also significant. It is found that the conductivity increases with the degree of injury.

Investigation has shown that there exists a correlation between resistance to frost and the length of the day during the period of growth. For example, the apricot, Fergana rhubarb, walnut, yellow French raspberry and white acacia become resistant to frost in the neighbourhood of Leningrad if the length of daylight, to which they are exposed, is reduced to 14 hours. It is hoped that this discovery will assist the introduction of plants such as the cinchona tree, citrus trees, and sugar-cane, into the U.S.S.R. in regions where they are as yet unable to resist the cold.

The length of day during the growing season in the hottest parts in the Soviet Union is about 16 hours or more, so it is necessary to consider methods of shortening the day for all plants, in which the amount of vegetative tissue is important, as a reduction in the length of the day frequently produces an increased vegetative development.

In experimental work the shortening of the day may be accomplished by growing the plants in pots and wheeling them in trucks in and out of sheds. The blinds are drawn, as it were, from the plant in the morning, and it is put to bed, and the blinds drawn, in the evening. In the fields similar effects may be obtained by placing boxes over the plants from the late evening until the late morning, so that the length of daylight, to which the plants are exposed, is curtailed.

In addition to affecting the volume of tissue produced by a plant, an adjustment of the length of the day frequently accelerates the rate of reproduction in plants. This makes breeding work with perennial plants much easier.

The power of resistance of plants to drought is measured by wilting. The length of time for which a plant can withstand wilting without damage is used as a measure.

Vernalization, or the stimulation of development before planting, has been effected in corn-seeds by a short period of curtailed daylight, followed by the normal methods of cultivation. This method does not require a reduction of temperature. It has been found that spring grains may be distinguished from autumn grains by an examination of the shape of the growing point two weeks after germination.

III

In his introductory address on the Plant Breeding Programme for the Second Five-Year Plan (1933–7), Vavilov has discussed the recent changes in the nature of biological research, and the opportunities for new applications of biology in the revolution of Soviet agriculture and industry.

During the last ten years methods of producing artificial mutations have been discovered by H. J. Muller and others, and crosses between different species and genera have been made successfully. This type of experimental work is dissolving the lines of definition in classical biology. The biology of the nineteenth century was descriptive, but that of the twentieth is chiefly experimental, and aims at the experimental elucidation of the mechanism of the process of evolution. The steady advance towards this aim is giving knowledge that enables new forms of organisms to be produced by rational, consciously understood methods.

This tendency of biological science is seen in the genetical research institutes in England and America. Owing to the social organization in those countries, the pure and applied genetical research is not conducted according to any comprehensive plan, as each institute is, as a rule, conducted privately with its own system of endowments. Besides leading to absence of comprehensive planning, this system tends to contract the amount of research during periods of economic crisis. The income from private endowments decreases, and the size of the staff is diminished. Again, owing to the crisis, agriculturists are unable to sell a large part of their crops. The failure to profit from agriculture destroys the incentive to improve the technique, and the demand for improved varieties loses its force. Why improve crops if they cannot be sold? Vavilov remarks that the contraction of genetical work in capitalist countries is confirmed by the number of geneticists and breeders who apply for posts in the Soviet Union.

In contrast with this position, the profound changes in Soviet agriculture offer immeasurably vast opportunities for pure and applied work in genetics, and geneticists are enjoying the stimulation of working in an atmosphere where there is an immense thirst for results. The collectivization of the land has provided the possibility for introducing new methods of cultivation, and new crops, throughout the whole of the U.S.S.R. New varieties of plant and animal stocks have to be bred for all of the regions of the country. Cold-resistant forms are necessary for the North, and drought-resistant forms for Central Asia.

The five chief aims of the agricultural part of the Second Five-Year Plan are the transformation of agriculture in all moist regions to intensive systems based on the use of mineral fertilizers; the creation of new agricultural districts, especially in Siberia and the Far East; the creation of special wheat areas in the Volga Basin by vast irrigation works, the extension of the area under crops by 60 to 70 per cent, and a general improvement in the yield and quality of crops.

The contemplation of such plans immediately prompts the desire to review the whole of plant knowledge in order to see which parts could be of use, and in which directions new knowledge is required. A comprehensive examination shows that in the past breeding has been detached from genetics. The breeders have accumulated an enormous quantity of material, much of which has not been analysed from the genetical point of view. The material frequently remains unpublished in the archives of private breeders and seed firms, and often no written notes of the data exist. The work of Luther Burbank on plant breeding is a remarkable example. No written data of it are available. Nor are any available of the production of noted wheats such as Marquis. Breeders in Europe and America have often deliberately refused to analyse the genetics of their material. In some cases this attitude arises from the desire to preserve trade secrets about the seeds of food plants, and is an example of the interference of capitalist principles with the advancement of science.

The comprehensive mode of approach to the world's plant population inspired by Soviet philosophy has revealed the degree of fragmentariness in past breeding research. The choice of material was usually made at random; an investigator decided to study certain material or varieties because they happened to be available.

It is not usually possible to have a correct view of any species unless all of the members are known, and this requires comprehensive study of the systematics and the geographical distribution of all the varieties. In the past the geneticist has usually attempted to generalize on the basis of fragmentary material, and consequently has drawn false conclusions.

The history of the cultivated potato provides an extraordinary example. The whole of the breeding and genetics of potatoes has been done with one Linnæan species (*Solanum tuberosum*). This appears to be due to the accidental choice of this species for import into Europe by Sir Walter Raleigh, or the actual pioneer of the time. For nearly four hundred years farmers, and latterly plant breeders and geneticists, have tried all sorts of experiments with this single species, and the whole work on improving the potato has been confined within that single circle of biological characters.

The Soviet plant breeders smashed this four-hundred-year-old circle soon after they had begun their world collection of specimens of potatoes. Their expedition to South America, the home of the potato, returned with no less than thirteen new well-defined Linnæan species of cultivated potatoes found among the Indian population. Many of these have important practical characters, such as resistance to frost and disease. Wild forms of potatoes found in the mountains of Peru and Bolivia can tolerate — 10° C. without loss of leaves. It became evident that the labours of the nineteenth- and twentieth-century geneticists to improve the potato had been conducted with the fragments of one species, collected at random by the first travellers.

Vavilov considers the theory of the vegetative period is providing the most remarkable advances in plant physiology at present, and cites the work of T. D. Lyssenko as outstanding. The possible industrial application of vernalization has immense applications. Vernalization is the process of stimulating the early development or sprouting of the seed by various sorts of treatment. If it could be applied on a large scale to industrial crops, especially in regions with short summers, it would be of immense practical value.

Experiment has shown that the use of vernalization on a large scale should be practicable. Vernalization has, of course, long been used by gardeners in Western Europe. In England many gardeners sprout their potato seed before setting. But the Soviet scientists have been the first to convert it into a general agricultural method. The Soviet work on vernalization has received special praise from Sir John Russell, the director of the Rothamsted Agricultural Experimental Station in England.

The vernalization experiments with wheat have been particularly striking. The agricultural possibilities of the varieties in the world collection have been transformed. Winter varieties are converted into spring varieties, and late into early. The variety *Triticum turgidum* had never been seen in the south-eastern districts, as it died if sown in the autumn, and its ears did not develop if it was sown in the spring. When the seed was vernalized it grew perfectly normal large-eared specimens. The success with vernalization has transformed the crop possibilities in many regions. With irrigation and vernalization the Volga Basin will be able to grow the most productive varieties, including *T. turgidum* wheat.

Important advances in the breeding of fibre-plant for industrial use are to be expected. The knowledge of the inheritance of fibre characters of industrial importance is remarkably defective. For instance, the world literature of the genetics of the cotton plant is scanty. No adequate data on the genetics of lint length, that is, the length of the hair of cotton which is the basis of the cotton fibre, are known; yet a difference of a millimetre in the average length of the lint produces a difference of millions of dollars in the industrial value of the cotton crop. The genetics of boll size and quality of lint has also been neglected.

Cereal plants whose external characters exhibit no recognizable differences may have markedly different reactions to chemical manures, and these reactions are often hereditary. The productivity of two wheats that look exactly alike may differ as much as 15 to 20 per cent under chemical manuring. This work, which was developed in Denmark, Sweden and Germany, has provided the possibility of selecting and breeding the varieties which receive the maximum stimulation from chemical manures. Research on the same lines has been started in the Soviet Union.

It is expected that the development of crosses between widely different species will become of increasing importance in plant-breeding. Among wheats, for example, the species with a small number of chromosomes are genetically distinct from the common wheats, and have much immunity to disease and resistance to drought. The breeding of crosses between these wheats and the common wheats depends on the successful combination of plants with different numbers of chromosomes in their cells.

A similar problem is presented by oats, and by the vine. The vine-breeder aims at combining the resistance of the American vine to disease with the quality and yield of the European vine. The Soviet fruit-breeder I. V. Michurin was the first to cross the wild cold-resistant Eastern Asiatic vine, pear and apple, with the more delicate cultivated varieties.

The Soviet cotton-breeders aim at combining the lint of Egyptian cotton with the early ripening of Upland and Central Asiatic native cottons. The achievement of this would have great industrial importance. The crossing of Upland and Egyptian is usually regarded by the most eminent cotton-breeders as impracticable, owing to the wide differences of the species. Vavilov writes that the Soviet work shows this opinion is too pessimistic. Crosses of Upland and Egyptian cotton have been used in the Tashkent Institute, and the second and later generations have been obtained from crosses between New and Old World cottons.

He considers that the breeder should be able to obtain many plants with valuable combinations of characters by a more thorough investigation of crossing of varieties from different geographical regions. Under Karpechenko's direction work has begun on this line, and interesting new barleys, with smooth awns or grain-sheaths, and other characters, have already been obtained.

Among the various branches of the science of agricultural botany, Vavilov mentions the problem of sex in plants as requiring extended study. Recent work has shown there are often many types of sex within one species. The old terminology of self-pollination, cross-pollination, self-sterile, and self-fertile, requires revision. For example, self-pollination has been found in rye, which is a typical cross-pollination plant, and the vine has many varieties of sex.

Sex, fertility and sterility are of fundamental importance in plant cultivation and breeding, especially in connection with fruit-trees. The sex of plants is often affected by external influences. For instance, Lyssenko has shown experimentally that changes of temperature can change a bisexual wheat plant into a unisexual plant in which the anthers fail to mature. There is wide scope for experimental research on the change of sex in plants by chemical, physical and biological agents.

More is to be expected from inbreeding. Experiments with maize, rye and other plants have shown that inbreeding can bring out characters beyond the limit of species-differences. For instance, bisexual plants may appear among unisexual forms.

It has been found that the application of inbreeding to a small collection of tea-plants can bring out the whole of the varieties known to the tea-breeder.

IV

Readers who desire to follow in further detail the Soviet programme for research in plant-breeding may consult the translation of Vavilov's addresses published by the British Imperial Bureaux of Plant Genetics, which has already been mentioned.

The colossal activities of the Soviet agricultural botanists require innumerable buildings and fields. The chief experimental station near Leningrad is at Detskoe Selo. This village grew around the Tsar's summer palace, and contains a collection of mansions that belonged to the members of the court. After the Revolution the village Tsarkoe Selo, or Tsar's Village, was given its new name, which means Children's Village. Most of the mansions have been converted into children's hospitals and summer-holiday homes. Several have been converted into laboratories for the study of agricultural science. The Genetics Laboratory was built by Queen Victoria. The Grand Duke Boris gave her a present in memory of her jubilee, and in return she presented him with an English mansion. The design and the oak and all the materials of construction were sent from England, so Boris had a small baronial mansion done in the Victorian style. It is well made, though the style and stained glass are not to the modern taste. The geneticists find it comfortable.

The gardens contain a large number of plots for plant-breeding, and one may see Karpechenko's fertile crosses between cabbages and radishes, and many other interesting plants.

Some of the outhouses have a rather elaborate appearance. When the geneticists asked for additions to their buildings, the architect insisted on constructing them in the same Victorian baronial style as the mansion. The devotion to architectural uniformity cramped the space of the scientists, as so much money was spent on the preservation of the style that there was not enough to erect buildings of adequate size. This occurred soon after the Revolution, before the country had begun to recover from the devastation, and it is interesting to note that æsthetic considerations influenced the architects even at that difficult time.

Botany is studied with exceptional zest in the Soviet Union. This may be partly due to the severity of the climate. Plants often survive with difficulty, so they are cherished more than in places where they may grow more easily. Further, the Soviet Union is predominantly an agricultural land. There are still far more peasants than industrial workers. This increases the general, State, and scientific interest in plants and animals.

Details that reflect these tendencies are seen in daily life. There is a remarkable number of flower-shops in Leningrad.

In the most difficult days of the Revolution and collectivization, when shops were almost empty, it was still possible to buy fine cut flowers, bouquets and roses. At the present time large numbers of flowers in pots are seen in living-rooms, hotel rooms, restaurants, railway stations and other places.

The interest in botany is shown by the number of botanists. In the Leningrad district there are over 500 botanists. This must be very many more than in any district in England.

The developments of agricultural science are reflected in the improved vegetables obtainable in the towns in midwinter. During the winter of 1934–5 remarkably good green peas, carrots, cauliflowers and other vegetables were obtainable in many places. These peas were smaller, softer and sweeter than the fresh green peas usually available in England in the early summer. It appears that the Soviet experts have produced better varieties for preserving and canning, or they have worked out better methods of preservation and cooking, than those used in England.

Of all the many subjects discussed by a visitor recently returned to England from the Soviet Union, none has aroused more interest than the small, soft, luscious green peas. Many will listen with a greater or lesser polite attention to accounts of remarkable achievements in engineering, agriculture and science; of the latest tendencies and plays in the theatre, of the changes in the party line on political and philosophical questions, of the failures in various directions; but it appears that accounts of the green peas attract more than polite attention from the English: they secure their liveliest interest.

CHAPTER 23

THE MAXIM GORKY MEDICO-BIOLOGICAL RESEARCH INSTITUTE, MOSCOW

THIS institute is directed by Professor S. G. Levit. Until recently it was established in a building that had been specially designed for it. When the Academy of Sciences was transferred from Leningrad to Moscow during 1934 there was much difficulty in finding enough buildings for the various departments. The building of the Medico-Biological Institute was acquired by the Academy for its Department for Energetics and Technology. This involved much structural change, as the institute had special rooms and miniature architectural features for the children and twins which were part of the material of its studies. The Medico-Biological Institute is now in a much less suitable building, but it is hoped that another special building will be erected within a few years. The precedence of the requirements of technical science over medical science receives an interesting illustration in this occurrence. It is an example of the belief in the greater importance of physical science in a machine civilization, which is the basis of the common opinion that physics is a more fundamental science than biology. There is no logical ground for the opinion that physics is more fundamental than biology. The explanation is social. Physics is more immediately useful to a machine civilization, so men come to believe it is philosophically more fundamental. From the belief that physics is the more fundamental science, many Western European writers conclude that God is a physicist or a mathematician. This is a rationalization of the fact that physics and mathematics are the most important sciences for a machine civilization.

The department for the study of human heredity has a staff which includes twelve scientists with medical qualifications. Eight hundred pairs of twins living in the city are observed regularly. They come to the institute on special days to be examined from all points of view. The effects of differential agents of education and feeding are studied. The traits of character are correlated, and original experiments have been made on twins, such as the comparison of the electro-cardiograms of their heart movements.

The institute has a unique laboratory for investigating the cytology of human cells. They have devised a technique of investigating the chromosomes in human cells quickly. They find a big variation in somatic cells, but no variation in gonad cells. They prepare tissue cultures of leucocytes.

In their experiments on the treatment of children with ultra-violet rays, they find that in rickets the rays at first produce good results, but bad effects are found months later. In their research on identical twins of the ages of five to seven years suffering from rickets, they found that the twin treated with ultra-violet rays sometimes died.

In their experiments with the education of identical twins, they have obtained results which appear to be of great importance. In their former building they were able to keep several pairs of identical twins living in the laboratory, under excellent conditions. The conditions in the new quarters are not so good. With special furniture, kindergartens, toys, unique experiments have been made. In one series of experiments the twins were divided into two groups, one from each pair being in each group. One group was given a collection of bricks and a model castle to copy, and the other group a similar collection of bricks. But the model castle of the second group could be taken to pieces, whereas that of the first group could not. Thus the children working in the first group could not copy its castle without analysing its structure, whereas the second group had merely to repeat the positions of the bricks in their model. It was found that the group that could analyse its problems gradually improved in intelligence relative to the other group. The analytical method led to a relative increase in intelligence. But another still more important fact was discovered. The relative improvement in intelligence appeared to be permanent. At periods of three to six months after the differential system of education had ended, the difference in intelligence remained. These experiments could have been made only with identical twins, for human subjects of identical and equal quantity and quality of intelligence are provided by identical twins only.

The Institute has published several volumes of papers, from which the following are quoted. L. J. Bossik has published a paper on the Rôles of Heredity and Environment in the Physiology and Pathology of Childhood. He states that the Genetical Department of the Institute had investigated up to January 1st, 1933, 458 pairs of twins, and in his present paper data on 366 pairs under fifteen years of age are given. One hundred and thirty of these pairs were identical. The physiological characters, weight at birth, beginning of teething, sitting up, and walking are discussed, and pathological characters such as affections of the peripheral lymphatic system, tuberculosis and acute infectious diseases. The data have been analysed in order to determine the relative influences of heredity and environment in producing the effects. It is found that the hereditary factor has no significant influence on the variability of the weight of twins at birth, but the extension of this result to the general population has not yet been proved. There is evidence that genotypal factors have some influence on the beginning of teething, sitting and walking.

The affections of the lymphatic apparatus in children is chiefly due to environment, but genotypal factors have some influence.

The data on tuberculous intoxication and tuberculous broncho-adenitis in children point to the predominating rôle of environmental factors, and heredity appears to have an insignificant influence.

U

The material concerning infectious diseases does not present definite results, but there is evidence that heredity has some influence in susceptibility to infection.   This is derived from the observation that simultaneity of sickening occurs more frequently with identical twins than with fraternal twins.

N. N. Malkova has investigated the Rôles of Heredity and Environment in the Variability of Blood-pressure and of Pulse-rate.   Her material for examining the relations between hereditary and environmental factors on the variability of blood pressure consisted of a group of 142 pairs of twins between the ages of four and thirteen years. She found that the genotype plays the prevailing part in the variability of blood-pressure.   The pulse-rates and blood-pressures were determined simultaneously in 245 pairs of twins.   It was found that the genotype has a considerable part in the variability of the pulse-rate, being greater in girls than in boys.   But not too much weight is given to the conclusion, as the standard error of the figures is considerable.

J. G. Dillon and J. B. Gurevich have made a Twin Study of Pneumatization of the Nasal Accessory Sinuses, Mastoid Processes and the Form and Dimensions of the Sella Turcica.   They have found that in the difference in form and pneumatization of the nasal accessory sinuses and of the mastoid processes, the part played by paratypical factors is predominant.   The differences in form and dimensions of the sella turcica are chiefly influenced by genotypical factors.

In an investigation of the Electro-cardiogram in Twins, I. B. Kabakov and I. A. Ryvkin have studied the intrapair similarity and differences in the electro-cardiogram of identical and of fraternal twins.   Eighty-one pairs of identical, and 69 pairs of fraternal twins have been examined. The majority of pairs were between the ages of six and sixteen years, only 21 pairs being older than sixteen years. The electro-cardiograms of the identical twins showed similarities in 87·6 per cent of cases.   In 5 cases out of the 81 pairs of identical twins the similarities were slight, and in 5 cases there was dissimilarity. Six pairs of adult identical twins, between the ages of twenty and forty-six, had very similar electro-cardiograms, in spite of certain differences in the peaks, which may have reflected differences due to infectious diseases suffered by the twins, and to differences in the general state of their health.

Of the fraternal twins intrapair dissimilarities were evident in 76·8 per cent of the cases. In 7 of the 69 pairs the electro-cardiograms were identical, and in 9 cases partly similar. The authors conclude that the electro-cardiogram depends largely on genotypal factors, so that electro-cardiographic methods may be of value in the diagnosis of the identity of twins.

A. N. Mirenova has investigated the influence of psycho-motor education on the general development of children of pre-school age. She studied the degrees to which different psychomotor activity is conditioned genotypically and para-typically; the degrees and the nature of the influence of training upon the development of psychomotor functions of different complexities, and the effect of the training of psy-chomotor activity upon the general development of the pre-school child. The subjects of the first problem were four pairs of identical twins, and six pairs of fraternal twins, aged 4 to 4½ years. All of the children lived in the kinder-garten of the institute, and systematic records were made of observations by teachers, parents and experimenter. The psychological examinations were made by the methods of Binet and Terman, and the psychomotor functions were tested according to Oserersky's scale. The performances of each pair of identical twins showed very great resem-blances, but also substantial differences. The differences between the members of the pairs of fraternal twins were greater. It was found that intellectual and elementary psychomotor functions, i.e. actions controlled by the mind, were conditioned to a considerable degree by genotypal factors. The motor functions characterized by more complex psychological structure are in a far lesser degree conditioned by the genotypal, hereditary factors.

The second and third problems were investigated by

giving the inferior of each of the pairs of identical twins special psychomotor training for a period of $4\frac{1}{2}$ months. These children were trained to make special jumps, to hit a mark by throwing a ball, and to hit the mark by rolling a ball.

After the $4\frac{1}{2}$ months the trained and untrained identical twins were examined. It was found that the trained twins equalled and excelled the formerly superior twins. The three sorts of psychomotor development developed at different rates. The most elementary developed very rapidly, and were relatively independent of training, though training increased the rate. The more complex psychomotor functions appeared to depend much less on maturation, but were changed strikingly by training. The measure of resemblance between the members of the pairs became several times less than it had been before training.

Marked alterations occurred in the whole behaviour and in the general development of the trained twins. They became more active, more independent and more disciplined. The intellectual level of the trained twins also rose in comparison with the untrained. Some characters appeared to develop due to the direct influence of training, while others probably developed through the organization of the processes of training.

A. N. Mirenova and V. N. Kolbanovsky have made a Comparative Evaluation of Methods for the Development of Combinative Functions in Children of Pre-school Age. Five pairs of identical twins aged 5 to $5\frac{1}{2}$ years were subjected to two months of training. In one method of training, named the Elementary Figure method, the child has to reproduce with toy bricks or wooden blocks certain given figures in which all the component elements and combinations are visible to him.

In another method, named the method of Models, the same figures are presented, but in the form of paper-covered models, in which the construction of the parts was concealed from the child. In the first case, the child copied the model passively; in the second he constructed it actively.

After two months of such training, a control task was

presented to the children. A new and more complex figure was given to both partners. Each of them had to build it in two ways; by the method which was customary for him, and by the converse method in which his partner was trained.

It was observed that the process of combination was much slower and more difficult for the children trained by the Model method than for those by the Elementary Figure method. But the children trained by the Model method developed a great abundance and diversity of manipulatory skills, while among the children trained by the Elementary Figure method such development appeared to be absent. At the end of the training period all of the Model method students surpassed the Elementary Figure method students in the execution of the control figure.

Besides these tests, other tests for creative power, before and after training, were given, in order to see whether training had an influence on the general creative faculties of the children.

It was found that the free constructions by the Model method students were more complicated in intention and more complex in execution than those made by the Elementary Figure students.

The authors conclude that the method of active and independent construction develops the combinative functions much more effectively than the method of passive copying and imitation, and that for pedagogical practice the method of active stimulation is the most desirable method of teaching.

This remarkable investigation appears to be of first-class scientific and educational importance. Owing to the use of identical twins as experimental subjects, its results have an exceptionally high degree of scientific certainty; much more than in most, and perhaps all, previous researches on the value of free, experimental methods of education. It is obvious, of course, that the technique of this free method, as exemplified by Mirenova and V. N. Kolbanovsky, is of a highly developed character, and is a product of the investigators' intelligence and application. This free method of training is the reverse of haphazard, as the trainer has evolved it through much disciplined thought. The child is free to act within a carefully constructed situation. In this sense, the child educated by the free technique is presented with a given situation as definitely as the child set to learn by copying and learning by rote.

L. J. Bossik, E. I. Passynkov and J. B. Gurevich have studied the effects of therapeutic treatments on identical twins in which patients suffering from rickets and from tuberculous broncho-adenitis were treated with ultra-violet rays from a quartz lamp. Five pairs of twins had rickets, and nine pairs suffered from tuberculous broncho-adenitis. One child from each pair was subjected to radiation, and the other not. The treatment was given at intervals of two days, during a period of six weeks. The patient usually had twenty sittings, and the electric current used in the lamp was 6 amperes at 165 volts.

The condition of the five members of the twin pairs suffering from rickets who were irradiated showed considerable improvement, while that of the five non-irradiated members remained the same. The clinical symptoms of bone features, teeth, spleen, blood composition, etc., showed the same division. The mean increase in the weight of the irradiated members was 540 grams, and the non-irradiated 280 grams. The irradiated members suffering from broncho-adenitis showed improvement, while the non-irradiated did not. The peripheral lymphatic apparatus of four members showed improvement, but the remaining five, and the non-irradiated, did not. The weight of the irradiated members increased by 406 grams, whereas the non-irradiated increased by 168 grams only.

Continued observation showed that the positive effects of the ultra-violet ray treatment were not permanent. After a period of seven to ten months, the members that had not been treated with ultra-violet radiation weighed more than those that had. The non-irradiated members also suffered less from contagious diseases throughout this period.

This research is of high interest and importance, and

shows that the effects of the use of ultra-violet rays in the treatment of disease are complex, and require very comprehensive investigation.

A. E. Levin and B. A. Kuchur have investigated the rôle of hereditary factors in ulcerous disease. They have examined the pedigrees of 310 ulcerous patients.

Relatives suffering from ulcers, and suspected of suffering from ulcers, were noted in 41·9 per cent of the pedigrees. Out of 1669 people, consisting of parents, brothers and sisters of the patients, 179 were affected by the disease. 13·6 per cent of the 1669 were men, and 7·6 were women, the average together being 10·7 per cent. For comparison 500 ordinary patients of the Dental Polyclinic were examined for the same disease, and 3·2 per cent were found to be suffering from it. The considerably greater incidence of the disease among the relatives compared with the incidence among the general population suggests that ulcerous diseases are connected with a hereditary factor. The parents of the patients are affected more frequently than their brothers and sisters, and there is a relatively small degree of inbreeding among the families of the patients. This is evidence that the hereditary factor is of a genetically dominant type.

G. V. Soboleva has investigated the relation between liability to ulcerous diseases and type of human physique. The morphological or physical types of 180 ulcerous patients were compared with those of a normal population. Of the 180, 148 were between the ages of twenty-one and fifty, and all were Russians. The morphological types were determined according to the classifications of Sigaud, Kretchmer and Bunak, and the data were compared with those complied by Soboleva, Bazarov, and Bunak for a group of the population inhabiting the central part of western Soviet Russia. The comparisons indicated that the ulcerous patients weighed less than the normal, but there was no difference in the measurement of the chest, and of the height. The relative length of the trunk and the relative breadth of shoulders and pelvis did not depart from the normal. Thus the general assumption that ulcerous

patients tend to be of the asthenic, or thin type, is not confirmed.　There was no evidence that the distribution of
types among ulcerous patients is significantly different from
that among the normal population.　But in ulcerous
patients, there was a noticeable decrease in the size of fatty
deposits and muscles.　The decrease in weight was
associated with the decrease in fat and muscle.　Thus the
thinness of ulcerous patients appears to be due to the
secondary effects of the disease, and is not connected with
any particular physique, such as the asthenic.

V. V. Bunak has made interesting contributions to the
problem of the determination of the true sex-ratio in human
beings.　It is well known that in most white races the
number of males born is slightly greater than the number
of females, the ratio in some white populations being as
high as 108 to 100.　This, and other facts concerning the
inequality in the numbers of births of the different sexes,
is of interest in relation to the facts of reproduction.　The
modern knowledge of the mechanism of heredity indicates
that the number of male and female cells should be equal.
This explains the rough equality of the numbers of the
sexes, but directs attention to the problem of the explanation
of the differences.　While more males are born, more
females survive.　The greater hardihood of females is
evident even before birth, as in the United Kingdom the
number of males that die before birth to the number of
females that die before birth is about 150 to 100.　The
proportions of still births is about 135 to 100, and in the
first year of life it is about 120 to 100.　Similar tendencies
occur among the offspring of cattle.　In their discussion
of these phenomena Wells, Huxley and Wells remark on
the fact that as the age and number of pregnancies of a
mother increase, the tendency to bear females increases.
This confirms the suggestion that the worsening of the
condition of the womb causes the males to die more easily
than the females.　The influence of the condition of the
womb is suggested by various social facts.　For instance,
legitimate children show a higher proportion of females
than illegitimate children.　This suggests that care of the

mother during pregnancy enables more males to survive. During wars, such as the Great War, the proportion of males born increases slightly. This is perhaps due to the absence of fathers on military duty, so that their pregnant wives are able to lead an easier life, and are free from the sexual demands of their husbands, and also have not to keep house for them, even when feeling unwell. The connection of the phenomenon with the absence of the fathers seems confirmed by the fact that it occurred only in the fighting and not in the neutral populations.

Another indication of the influence of care before birth is shown by the exceptionally high proportion of male Jewish children. This is perhaps due to the superior hygienic traditions of Jewish women over those of Christian women. In America, the proportion of males among the new-born children of Christian women is higher than that among negro new-born children. These data seem to show that the female egg is more resistant than the male egg, and yet the number of males born is the greater. Apparently the number of males conceived must be much greater than the number of females. Hence the father's male-producing sperms are much more effective in producing a fertile egg, though that egg will be more delicate than one which has been fertilized into a female egg.

Bunak has examined the data on which the relation of sex to prematurity of birth has been based, and finds that some of the statistics which have been used in deriving the above views have been collected by methods that are not entirely clear. He has investigated the sex ratio in the prematurely born, for those still-born, and those born alive, by analysing each case individually. The records of two large Moscow lying-in hospitals for the last ten years have been analysed. It was found that the ratio of prematurely born infants born alive was 108 males to 100 females. In the different months of pregnancy the ratio varies from 100 to 119, without showing any regularity. In 1119 still-born premature births the proportion of males was found to be 145 to 100. The proportion in the ninth, eighth and seventh months of pregnancy was lower, and

not higher, than that in the still-born in the tenth month.
In the sixth and fifth month a sharp increase was observed.
As the percentage of five-month and nine-month infants
still-born is less than 4 per cent, the proportion of males
in four-month fœtuses still-born and born alive exceeds
the standard proportion of 106 to 100 for normal birth
only slightly.

There was not enough data to determine the proportion
of the sexes in three- and four-month fœtuses not capable of
supporting life, as such fœtuses are obtainable from in-
voluntary abortions only, and rarely come under the observation of a gynæcologist.   Owing to the legal recognition
of voluntary abortion by the Soviet State, Bunak was able
to collect important data concerning fœtuses of voluntary
abortions.   These fœtuses, surrendered for social reasons
by women usually healthy, are viable, or capable of supporting life.   Bunak collected 54 three- and four-month
fœtuses, and found the proportion of the sexes to be 158
to 100.   But the methods of determining the sex at this
stage of growth are not easy, and he does not give too much
weight to this figure.

He estimates the true proportion of the sexes at the
moment of impregnation to be 115 males to 100 females,
but he considers that the close connection between the
larger number of males and the rate of pre-natal mortality
has not received sufficient attention.   It is possible that the
inequality between the numbers of the conception of males
and females may be apparent and imaginary only.   He
gives evidence that some of the female embryos develop
male characters and then become incapable of supporting
life and die.   If the proportion of the sexes at conception
is 115 to 100, then 7 per cent of the embryos must make
the anomalous development; if the proportion is 150 to 100,
then the percentage must be 20.

He states that an anomalous development of females into
males is not contrary to known biological facts, and suggests
that this hypothesis should provide a fruitful line for further
research on the differential mortality of the sexes.

According to the modern theory of heredity the units

which transmit hereditary characters are carried in the particles named chromosomes, found in all of the cells of a living organism. Every cell in the human body has a nucleus containing forty-eight of these chromosomes, and each set of forty-eight is similar to every other set of forty-eight in the same body. This is due to the repeated subdivision of the single nucleus of the fertilized egg from which the organism developed. The correlation of hereditary characters in man with the special features of the chromosomes in the cells of his body is a fundamental part of the investigation of human genetics. Unfortunately, human cells are not easily obtained, for obvious reasons. It is not easy to keep a piece of human tissue alive for a long period, so that continued observations on the same material may be made.

G. K. Chroustchov has developed a technique for preparing cultures of human leucocytes that can be kept alive for a long time. The leucocytes are the white corpuscles found in the blood, which have an important rôle in healing wounds, and removing bacteria and foreign bodies from the blood.

About 8 to 10 cubic centimetres of blood are taken from a vein, and by suitable treatment the leucocytes are extracted in a mass. This is washed in Ringer solution and cut into small pieces, which are submitted to various tissue-culture manipulations. In the cultures prepared by this method an extensive migration of leucocytes from the transplanted piece may be observed during the first twenty-four hours. In the second twenty-four hours a variety of other cells come into the zone of migration. On the fourth day the polyblasts combine into groups, forming complexes of tissues within the zone of migration. At this stage the fluid medium of the culture has to be changed, and for the next forty-eight hours the general shape of the cultures changes little, though very large numbers of cell-divisions are observed in all sorts of cells. Large polyblasts may be flattened against the surface of a cover-glass, and the arrangement of chromosomes in their nuclei can easily be sketched and counted. The results show that the method increases the possibility of the continuous study of the chromosomes in man, and allows the organization of the study of the chromosomes of one particular man.

B. D. Morozov and A. R. Striganova have published a paper on the Stimulating Effect of Embryonic Extracts on the Healing of Wounds in Mammals. As embryos are in a very rapid state of growth, it is reasonable to assume that they contain substances that stimulate growth. Extracts from embryos might contain substances which, when put into wounds, would stimulate the rate of healing.

The experiments were made on white and piebald rats weighing 100–180 grams. The embryonic extract was prepared from human embryos of age six weeks to two months. The rats were given two wounds on the back, about 2 to 3 square centimetres in size. One wound was treated with the embryonic extract, and the other with Ringer solution serving as a control.

The wound treated with the extract showed an intense development of the granulation and acceleration of epithelial or lining cells, and an improvement of the general condition of the wound, and in many cases an acceleration of the healing period.

In all cases the application of the extracts produced an acceleration of the rate of diminution of the area of the wound, as compared with that of the control wound.

The best method of applying the extract is by repeatedly moistening the wound while covered with an ordinary gauze bandage.

Eighty-eight per cent of the wounds treated with embryonic extract showed a positive improvement relative to the control wounds treated with Ringer solution.

The authors conclude that embryonic extracts must have therapeutic importance. They are not specific to any species of mammal, so they may be prepared from the embryos of any mammals.

CHAPTER 24

THE INSTITUTE OF EXPERIMENTAL BIOLOGY, MOSCOW

THIS well-known institute was founded during the period between the two revolutions in 1917, and now belongs to the Commissariat of Public Health. It is directed by N. K. Koltzov, and is housed in a former mansion near the centre of the city.

The peculiar gift of its distinguished director is a complete modernity of outlook. Few of the elder biologists in the world possess the gift, and this has led to a conflict between the elder and the younger biologists in many countries. The elder biologists matured under the exceptionally powerful influence of the early Darwinians, who based their natural philosophy on the study of the shapes of animals. The conclusions they drew from their morphological studies were of prodigious importance, and nearly all biologists who were young during the period when Darwinian biology was in its brilliant youth never lost the conviction that the biological methods and principles of that time were profounder than any that came afterwards. About twenty years ago it became clear to some of the biologists with deeper insight that new methods must be added to those of Darwin if biology were to advance in new directions. The study and comparison of the shapes of animals could no longer be expected to give returns of new knowledge adequate to the expense of labour. The old methods of morphological study were no longer efficient ways of discovering new knowledge.

It is interesting to note that the contemporary conflict between the elder and the younger biologists is not paralleled by a similar conflict among physicists. Why are there two camps in biology, and not in physics? One of the explanations is due to the respective proximities of Newton and of Darwin. The tremendous impression made by Newton led to a similar conflict of schools at the beginning of the nineteenth century. The younger English mathematicians called for the introduction of new mathematical methods and conceptions, in opposition to the elder mathematicians of that time, who had matured under the fresh glory of Newtonian methods. They succeeded in introducing the new methods during the nineteenth century, so there is no profound difference of philosophy between the elder and the younger physicists today. The younger biologists having to contend with elders that matured during the first glories of Darwinism, have not yet succeeded in capturing the helm.

For these reasons, elder biologists who have seen that new methods must now be added to those of Darwin, and whose seniority has put them in places of directive influence, are of peculiar importance. They are able to help the birth of the new movement in biology, and to rear it during a harassed infancy, and to prevent it from being distorted by obtuse elders as it grows up.

The existence of such inspired biologists in Russia during the period of the Revolution was of quite exceptional importance, because the creative forces released by the social change provided a powerful stimulus to biological studies. It was very important that the new energy should be put into the new methods, and not be wasted on creating an imposing repetition of old morphological studies.

Koltzov made a large contribution towards the task of setting the new Soviet biological studies along the correct modern lines. Like other members of the world's small band of progressive elders in biological research, he saw that the new biologists should be trained to have an experimental approach to biological research. He has shown remarkable prescience in perceiving the possibilities in many branches of experimental biology, and still preserves an admirable flexibility in appreciating the most original of the newest techniques.

Many of the well-known Soviet biologists, such as M. M. Zavadovsky, have been his pupils.

Koltzov has organized his own researches and those of his colleagues according to the theory that the proper object of modern biological research is to discover the mechanism of evolution. The researches of the Darwinians proved the fact of evolution, and the task of their successors is to elucidate how it occurred. This may be done only through an understanding of how the structure and behaviour of organisms is changed, and the answer to this problem may be given only by controlled experiments which analyse each detail of the mechanism of living matter, and its interaction with the environment.

The structure and behaviour of organisms depends partly on their hereditary constitution and partly on their interactions with the environment. The study of hereditary constitution, the science of genetics, is therefore one of the institute's chief activities.

The director of the genetics department is N. P. Dubinin. He has made extensive researches on the genetics of the fruit fly, *Drosophila*. It is well known that the hereditary constitution of organisms depends on the little bodies named chromosomes, similar groups of which are found in nearly all of the cells in any particular living organism. For instance, nearly every cell in a man contains a group of forty-eight chromosomes. One of the reasons why all men are structurally so similar is that they all have cells with forty-eight chromosomes. If a being were produced from human tissue with ninety-six chromosomes in each of his cells, he would probably be markedly different from a man. When the number of chromosomes in the cells of a plant, such as a cabbage, is doubled, the new plant frequently proves to be a giant.

It is clear that a thorough knowledge of the chromosomes of any species of animal might enable a geneticist to forecast the possibility of producing a new line or race with a particular collection of characteristics, by creating a new constellation of chromosomes.

Dubinin has accomplished this. He has created during

the last two years three complexes of chromosomes in *Drosophila* that have not been previously known. One of these lines of *Drosophila* had three pairs of chromosomes in its cells, instead of the usual four pairs. Sokolov wanted to create a line which had a chromosome in the form of a ring. Mrs. T. H. Morgan found one fly with such a ring chromosome after examining a hundred thousand flies, and now a line of flies with ring chromosomes has been bred and established. Both of these mutations are stable. They give normal offspring when crossed with normal flies.

They have succeeded in crossing some markedly different lines that had not hitherto been crossed.

In their cytological work they have found evidence for the existence of a nucleus in bacteria.

They have studied the evolution of chromosome complexes in different groups of animals, and have found different groups may have sex chromosomes of similar shape. This work has involved the comparison of the chromosome complexes of the hen, pheasant, and turkey, for example, and has led to certain conclusions regarding their evolutionary relationship.

Twenty-eight species have been determined by the nature of their chromosome complexes.

V. Schröder has investigated the separation of the sexes of the sperms in rabbit semen by electrolysis. Ostroumov is making similar experiments with sheep, but they take more time. The semen is put into water and the electrolysis accomplished by the introduction of two electrodes. The male-producing sperm proceed towards one electrode, and the female-producing towards the other.

Three or four hundred female rabbits were impregnated with sperm that had been electrolytically separated into the male and female sorts. When impregnated with one sort 83 per cent of the offspring were of one sex.

Koltzov believes that the 17 per cent of failures were probably due to experimental defects in the separation, rather than to a mistake in principle.

They have been investigating the effect of injections of

urine from pregnant women on the thyroid gland of pigeons
and mice.

The condition of arterio-sclerosis may be produced artificially in rabbits. This enables the relation of this disease,
so common among stockbrokers, which produces hardening
of the arteries and high blood-pressure, to be thoroughly
studied. They are investigating the relation of the condition to the composition of the blood.

The inheritance of the catalase (the substance whose
presence is necessary to promote the combination of the
oxygen in the blood with the tissues) in the blood of guinea-
pigs has been investigated. Nineteen hundred and eighty-
two animals have been examined. Two groups are without
it, and it is inherited as a Mendelian character. Two other
groups possess it in different orders of quantity. The
catalase in the blood of fowls is also investigated.

Sakarov has shown that artificial mutations may be
produced by other radiations besides X-rays.

Astaurov at Tashkent has shown that silkworms can be
bred by artificial parthenogenesis (reproduction without
sexual union) and has obtained a second generation of
offspring.

Mrs. Koltzov has conducted a lengthy research on the
temperament of rats. They are kept inside a cage in the
form of a large hollow wheel which revolves in a vertical
plane. This is known as a Greenman wheel. When the
rat moves, the wheel moves, so that the distance travelled
by the rats may be measured by registering the amount of
rotation of the wheel.

The difference in the activity of rats is remarkable. Some
run only a few metres in an hour, while others run several
hundred metres in an hour.

The inheritance of activity in rats has been investigated.
Some families of rats run from 30 to 300 metres per
hour.

In two families the rats ran 300 metres per hour during
their first month, but in the second month much more.
This coincided with the season of migration.

During pregnancy the activity goes down, and after the

birth of the offspring it goes up again. This coincides with the mother's fresh search for a mate.

Mrs. Koltzov has studied the behaviour of birds and rats in a maze of the form like that at Hampton Court.

Her most capable rats were distinguished by their seeking instinct. Having been drawn for the first time into the maze, they seek with determination, smelling all over and testing each turn by means of their vibrissæ (feeling hairs). It seems that having learned a blind way to the end, the rat keeps it in its memory, and having gone out of it, seeks its way farther, without foreknowledge of the food. Probably this seeking instinct is also determined by some chemical peculiarities of the blood and possibly is correlated with a particular gene of seeking. These seeking rats always make one think of ants, going out of their nest in search of food. As we know, in some species of ants there exists a particular caste of seeking workers, which, contrary to other workers, instead of staying at home, are constantly going out in search of food. Some myrmecologists regard the peculiarities of this caste as being of an innate character. At any rate, the tendency to seeking or the investigatory instinct has proved to be an innate ability in mammals as also in men, and may depend on an endocrine secretion, possibly from the sexual gland, as suggested by N. K. Koltzov.

Mrs. Koltzov's studies of the behaviours of 123 rats in the maze led her to conclude that her observations showed that rats are very various in ability, but that there is no real difference of ability between males and females. There is a correlation between the abilities of parents and children, and the teaching of parents does not influence the abilities of the offspring.

CHAPTER 25

TWO MEDICAL RESEARCH INSTITUTES AT KHARKOV

I

THE Röntgen Institute is the chief centre for X-ray medical research in the Ukraine. Other institutes and hospitals in the Ukraine who use X-ray treatment work under the technical supervision of this chief institute.

Its departments include the general clinic, the X-ray clinic, the laboratory for research on the physics of X-rays, the alternating current laboratory, the biological laboratory, the onchological department, and the museum.

The institute has a staff of 300 persons, including 70 scientific workers. It includes 15 professors and 23 lecturers. It has a technical school, or technicum, for training in technique, attended by 100 students.

The plan of the medical X-ray research and treatment for the whole of the Ukraine is controlled from this institute. There are affiliated institutes at Odessa, Dniepropetrovsk, and Stalingrad. The planning ensures that the newest methods of treatment are immediately adopted by doctors throughout the country, and that those at distant places do not fail to learn of the most recent work.

The institute has treated 50,000 patients, and the clinic has 3,000 patients.

The radiological department has a stock of 600-700 milligrams of radium.

In the physics laboratory researches bearing on the treatment of disease by electric fields are in progress. The dielectric constants for short radio waves for wax, water, flesh, muscle, etc., are being measured. Much research on the influence of high-frequency electric fields on living tissue is in progress in different parts of the world, and Kharkov is making its contribution also. The apparatus used in these researches was made in the institute.

The effects of ultra-sonic waves on blood are being investigated. The waves are produced by a piezo-quartz oscillator.

Methods of measuring irradiation doses with photo-electric cells are being studied.

They have constructed 250,000-volt electron tubes, with a current of 10 milliamperes, for researches on the effect of electron-bombardment on living cells.

They are working on the same lines as Wyckoff in their studies of the effect of irradiation.

The institute has a collection of information concerning patients suffering from cancer in the Ukraine. This has been analysed statistically.

Several biologists are studying the relations between mitogenetic rays and cancer. These rays have been the subject of much controversy. The Kharkov workers seem to be confident of their existence and importance.

They state there are differences between the mitogenetic rays emitted by healthy living cells and cancerous cells.

The mitogenetic rays are said to be emitted by living cells, and to be able to stimulate growth, or mitosis, in other cells. Their existence has been claimed by Gurvitch and his colleagues, who state they are ultra-violet rays of a certain band of wave-lengths. Gurvitch based his first evidence of their existence on the behaviour of the growing-tip of the root of onions. He said that the rays from the cells in the growing-tip, which subdivided (mitosis) during the process of growth, were able to increase the rate of sub-division (mitosis) and hence growth in the root-tip of an adjacent onion. The exact significance of his results has been widely debated, and his interpretation has not received much support outside the Soviet Union. But there is enthusiastic confidence in it in the U.S.S.R. Gurvitch has made other distinguished and universally accepted contributions to biology. He is personally very enthusiastic and convincing, and many highly qualified Soviet scientists are convinced he has discovered something of fundamental importance.

The Kharkov workers have made extensive experiments on the use of mitogenetic rays for diagnosing cancer. They claim cancerous cells can be easily identified by the strength of the mitogenetic rays emitted.

They claim that mitogenetic rays affect the cells in a cancer, and that if the cancer is treated with ultra-violet radiations, it loses its sensitivity to mitogenetic rays.

The first researches on mitogenetic rays at Kharkov were unsuccessful. It is stated that this was due to the proximity of a high-frequency laboratory, whose radiations were interfering with their biological material.

The intensity of the mitogenetic rays is measured by counting the increase in the number of cells that subdivide when the living material is exposed to the rays.

The counting of the increase in the number of sub-divisions, leading to new cells, is said to be not difficult, but the irregularity of the mitosis presents difficulties.

Research on tissue culture is conducted according to the methods of Carrel. Cultures of human cancers are studied.

Pulsating hearts from chick embryos are kept in cultures. After a few days the pulsations slow down, but increase again if the fluid culture medium is renewed.

In the surgical department London's method of taking blood from the vena porta of a dog was demonstrated. Blood may be taken from the liver of cancerous animals.

The biological researches are conducted by a staff of forty-five workers.

The staff of the X-ray clinic have worked out a good method of giving quicker treatment for arthritis and erysipelas. The time of the treatment has been reduced from four weeks to a few days.

They have obtained good results in the treatment of bone tuberculosis.

The assistant director of this fine institute is B. Varshavsky, who courteously showed the equipment, and explained the objects of the institute's researches.

II

The Institute for Industrial Biology was erected in 1930 by the Commissariat of Public Health. It has a staff of 250 persons, including 100 with scientific qualifications. There are 14 professors, 17 medical doctors, and a number of chemists, engineers, biologists, etc. The annual budget amounts to 1,100,000 roubles. The three chief departments are for physiology, pathology, and experimental biology.

They are studying the effects of benzol, phenol, and other vapours on men and animals. The animal experimentation is done in the laboratory, while experiments on human subjects are done in the mining population in the Donbas.

Carbon monoxide poisoning, the influence of dust inhalation, mercury poisoning, and the effects of nitro-benzol are among the industrial poisons whose effects are investigated. The institute designs suitable masks and protective gear for workers who come in contact with these poisons.

The testing of motor-drivers is done in the optical department, under the direction of Rubinstein. Their psychological qualities are analysed by testing with complex operations. They have to perform various operations depending on a combination of sight and movement.

They have found that the capacity for concentrating the focal field is important. The candidate's power of controlling his motor impulses is measured, and his power of changing from one operation to another.

The effects of poisons on the cells of living tissues are studied in the department of pathology.

The laboratories for the study of the effects of dust inhalation are well-equipped. They have studied the electric charges on the particles of various sorts of dust and inorganic smokes. The size of the particles and their electric charges are deduced by putting them into a state of vibration.

The coagulation of dust has been investigated, and the effect of coagulated dust on human physiology.

The physiologists have been investigating the influence

of electricity on nerves and muscles, and electrical phenomena connected with fatigue.

A man pedals on a Krogh ergometer for several hours,
and the development and characteristics of his fatigue are
studied. The galvanic reflexes are recorded regularly, and
during the restitution period.

Vasilievsky has studied the influence of the hypnotic
state on the central nervous system, the motor system, and
oxidation in connection with respiration.

He thinks the nervous system acts on the motor system
and produces a change in the organism's need for oxygen.
The organism's capacity for work may be influenced. The
subject's capacity for physical work can be altered by
hypnotic suggestion. They say to the hypnotized man:
"You are not tired." Then he begins to work harder,
and keeps it up for a considerable time. If told that he is
tired, the respiratory system of the hypnotized subject
changes its mode of operation, though the patient is lying
down and does not move his limbs. This change in mode
does not involve any change in the size of the oxygen
consumption.

If the man is told he has done some work, the rate of his
pulse increases.

The biological effects of rays, gases, vapours, etc.,
emitted during industrial processes, such as metallic
welding, are studied.

On the basis of their results they have advised changes
in the arrangement of various industrial processes.

The institute has a large museum for illustrating the
various dangers of industrial work, and the proper methods
of protection against them. Prominence is given to full-
size models comparing the conditions in pre-revolutionary
workshops with those now introduced in the Soviet factories.
There are graphic models of the homes of workers who
drink excessively, and of the accidents that happen in
factories to workers that enfeeble themselves with drinking.
There are full-scale models of the working place in a coal-
mine, and the best methods of mining, and of the best
set-ups for numerous industrial processes such as welding.

Methods of protecting running machinery are demonstrated by working models.

Parties of workers and students are regularly sent to the museum for practical instruction on the latest methods of industrial hygiene.

CHAPTER 26

TWO BIOLOGICAL INSTITUTES
AT KIEV

I

THE Institute of Experimental Biology is directed by I. Schmalhausen. There are two main lines of research: that of Schmalhausen on the laws of the growth of embryos and mature organisms; and that of B. I. Balinsky on the control of growth by Spemann organizers.

Schmalhausen has given a brief summary of his theory which will be repeated here. He explains that there is a close dependence between the form of the growth of an organism and the course of its differentiation. If a decrease in the speed of the growth of an organism is observed during its individual development, it is connected with the progressive differentiation of the various parts of the organism out of their earlier, simpler form. During the progressive differentiation the process of growth is gradually limited by the ever-decreasing mass of indifferent protoplasm. If the speed of the growth of an organism is constant, there is no progressive differentiation, and the relative quantity of indifferent protoplasm in the organism remains constant.

Schmalhausen contends that the connection may be explained if it is assumed that the undifferentiated protoplasm grows, under constant conditions, with a constant velocity, and the products of differentiation do not assimilate by themselves: that they accumulate only through the transformation of the indifferent protoplasm.

He considers there are two fundamental forms of growth. One is purely exponential, in which the amount of growth at any instant is proportional to the amount of growing material in existence at that moment. The growth of bacteria, yeast, larvæ of flies and butterflies, and, possibly, some other larvæ, belongs to this type. The other is parabolic and connected with the progressive differentiation of an organism. The growth of vertebrates, and probably molluscs and many other invertebrates, are examples of this type.

The course of the process of differentiation in the growth of the embryos of vertebrates, which is parabolic, should be strictly determined. If the degree of differentiation is defined as the inverse of the relative quantity of indifferent masses, then it increases proportionally with time, and the speed of differentiation is constant. The latter can be measured by the relation of the speed of growth of the indifferent masses to the constant of growth.

The differentiated cells can grow and multiply with a constant speed, as well as the indifferent cells, in the case when their differentiation makes no progress. But if the degree of cellular differentiation increases proportionally with time, then the growth of cells decreases according to the law of parabolic growth. If such cells retain a constant size and capacity for subdivision, the duration of the interkinetic periods must increase in geometrical progression.

The constant of parabolic growth is the relation of the velocity of growth of indifferent masses to the speed of differentiation. Because of this the constant of the growth has a constant value only so far as it expresses the relation between two other constants.

On the basis of his two assumptions Schmalhausen deduces that the determinate course of the progressive differentiation may be expressed in the following way. The speed of the formation of the products of differentiation in a unit volume of the indifferent protoplasm approaches indefinitely near to a quantity that is equal to the speed of the synthesis of the protoplasm itself. In other words, in each differentiated cell the mass of the indifferent protoplasm is limited by a maximum. If after reaching this maximum the synthesis continues, then all the superfluous indifferent material is transformed into the products of differentiation.

PLATE 16

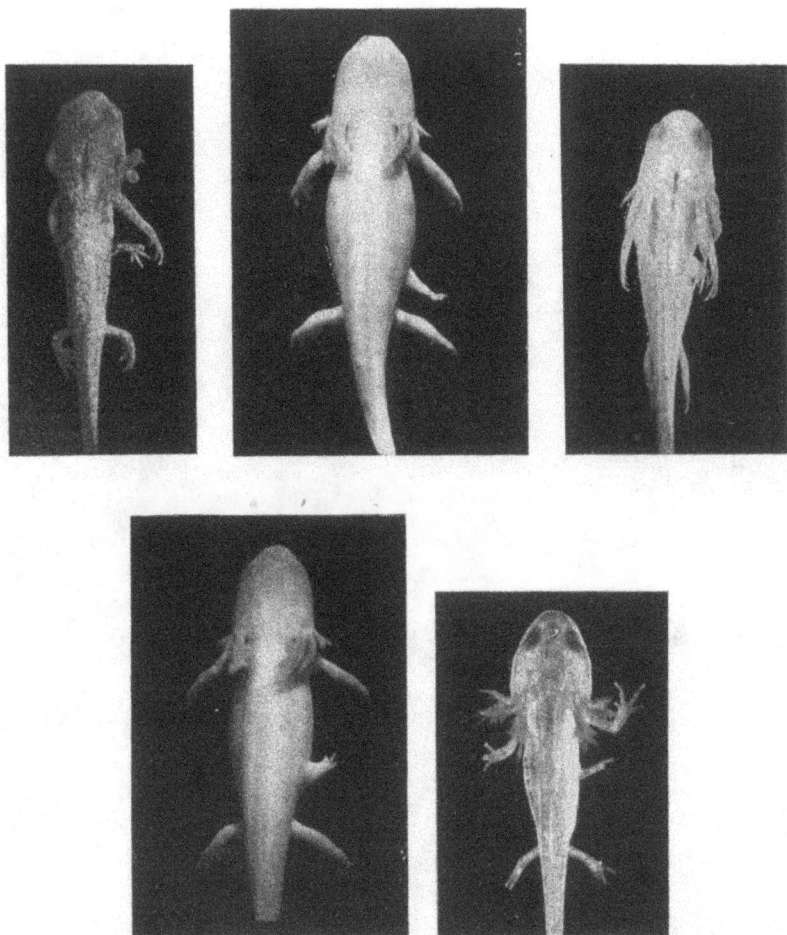

Induction of limbs in newts. Experiments by B. I. Balinsky of the Institute of Experimental Biology, Kiev

Schmalhausen has recently studied the peculiarities that appear in the development of poultry with hereditary abnormal characters, such as leg-feathers, and abnormal numbers of claws. These characters are due to mutations. The leg-feathering begins to appear in the early stages of growth, little later than the wing-feathering, and is due to the mutation of a hereditary factor.

The abnormal formation of the feet that accompanies the peculiar feathering appears to be a secondary effect produced by the disordering of the normal process of development by the mutated gene. Thus the connection between leg-feathering and feet abnormalities is determined by dynamical correlations varying in space and time. The decisive factors that determine the result of the interaction are the relative activity of the growth of the rudiments, the distance between them, and the time when the interaction begins. The latter, in turn, depends on the time when the rudiments are formed.

Schmalhausen's ideas resemble those of Minot, and of Julian Huxley.

Balinsky and Drugomirov devote special attention to the development of limbs. Balinsky has discovered a method of inducing a supernumerary limb. The olfactory rudiment is non-specific, and has been made to produce a limb. He believes the whole lateral region of the embryo has the power to produce limbs, and that Balfour's theory is partly right. When the induced limb is near the front limb it resembles a front limb, and when it is near the hind limb it resembles a hind limb. For example, it has the appropriate number of digits.

It is much easier to produce inductions on the front than on the hind part.

Drugomirov works especially on the development of the eye-lens. He has discovered the embryonic lens is a product of induction from the retinal part of the eye. He found that the regulatory power of the eye is very high. The pigmentary part of the eye can induce a whole eye.

This is not the first example of the induction of a whole organ by the part of an organ, but it is a very interesting one, because the inducing part is very small and highly differentiated.

Drugomirov's technique is very complicated, and his transplantations containing only a few cells are excellent.

Balinsky's researches on the induction of extra limbs in newts and lizards arose out of a repetition of an experiment made by Filatov in 1916. Schmalhausen proposed that he should repeat Filatov's discovery that the ear vesicle has the power of inducing the development of the ear capsule. Balinsky confirmed Filatov's result by experiments made in 1924 and 1925, and also found a new phenomenon.

In two cases an almost normal fifth limb grew on the side of the larva where the ear vesicle had been planted, and in other cases there were vestiges of limbs. There was the possibility that these limbs developed from the material of the normal limb rudiment. A part of this material might have been transplanted with the ear vesicle, or the limb rudiment of the larva into which the vesicle was grafted might have been split.

He proved by additional experiments that the induction was not due to a development of limb-material. It was started by the transplanted ear vesicle. But the additional experiments showed that the ear vesicle did not determine the quality of the induction. It only activates the potentialities that belong to the material of the host. Thus all the points along the whole length of the lateral plate of the embryo, at a certain stage of its development, are able to form a limb when suitably irritated. In 1926 Balinsky showed that purely mechanical irritation could be an effective stimulus to the growth of extra limbs on the side of the body of the newt. He has since extended his researches in much detail.

II

The Biological and Geological Museum at Kiev has admirable collections. It was opened in 1928, in a building that had formerly been a large girls' secondary school, and had latterly been extended and repaired.

The active organization of the museum was due to the

stimulus of industrialization and collectivization. The Ukrainian Academy formed a Council for Productive Forces under Zwietalsky, and drew up plans for surveys of the resources and structure of the Ukraine. These were to serve as a basis for the State planning, For example, they have contributed data for the Big Dnieper Plan. The realization of this plan will provide a continuous waterway from Leningrad to the Crimea, and will transform the intervening regions through the establishment of new trade and industry.

Expeditions are sent to survey the provinces and districts. For instance, the polymetallic ores of the Donbas have been specially surveyed and studied, and the red iron ores of Kryvoykok. In the laboratories, for example, the palæobotany of Ukrainian brown coal is being studied.

The Plan for Productive Forces is organized in collaboration with the Department of Heavy Industry and the Commissariat of Education. The pursuit of the plan has led to the provision of large sums of money for research, and this has greatly stimulated scientific activity.

Geological work is done under the direction of a group of geological advisers. The department contains sections for mineralogy, petrology, palæontology, applied geology, botany, quaternary geology, dynamic geology, hydrology and some other related subjects. It has a staff of seventy qualified scientists, with forty technical assistants. The geological museum has an excellent collection of specimens.

The biological museum contains 12,000 specimens of birds and mammals; it has a unique non-hairy southern mammoth.

There is a large palæontological preparation room, with five palæontologists and four laboratory assistants.

Paramonov has a magnificent collection of diptera, containing 5000 specimens, and Karaviev has many unique specimens in his collection of ants, especially from the Dutch Indies. Both have written standard monographs on their respective specialities.

PART VI

THE HISTORY OF SCIENCE

CHAPTER 27

THE HISTORY OF SCIENCE

THERE is a keen interest in the Soviet Union in the problems of the relation of science and literature, and of the history of science. According to the philosophy of Marxism the nature of the culture of any period is based on the nature of the contemporary system of social production. The Marxist expects to find relations between the science and the system of production at any period. He is naturally impelled to seek relations between the aspects of the various sciences and the social environment of the time. This principle has given research in the history of science an original feature, and the possession of a new point of view has in turn invigorated historical research. The Academy of Sciences has a department devoted to the study of the history of science. Its secretary is Professor Goukovsky, who is engaged in the preparation of a critique of the scientific researches of Leonardo da Vinci. The Moscow University also has a cabinet for research in the history of science. It is directed by Professor Max Levin. Another leader in the study of the history of science is Professor B. Hessen, the director of the Physical Institute of the Moscow University. His remarkable essay on *The Social and Economic Roots of Newton's "Principia"* has appeared in English, and has already begun to influence British studies

in the history of science.   In his essay, Professor Hessen
has described the importance of transport for developing
trade beyond the degree reached in the Middle Ages.
The roads of that period were extremely bad.   "The ideal
road was one on which three horses could travel side by side,
where, in the expression of the time (fourteenth century),
'A bride could ride by without touching the funeral cart.' "
In that century the journey from Constantinople to Venice
was three times as quick by sea as by land.   Further, land
freight had to be carried in small packs on horses or in
carts drawn by oxen which could not carry more than two
tons of goods.   Ships could carry freights upwards of 600
tons.   The feudal village was more or less self-contained.
The change into a more advanced economy of exchange
between the villages and towns by trade was dependent on
the development of transport, and especially water transport.
The traders, the leaders of the new and higher form of
social production, were therefore deeply interested in the
development of water transport.   They wanted bigger and
faster ships.   They wanted safer ships, which were stable
in rough seas and could easily be manœuvred.   Reliable
and exact methods of navigation were required to reduce
risks and time of passage, and inland waterways were
required to mitigate the inefficiency of road transport.   It
will be seen at once that the solution of the problems raised
by these wants depends on a knowledge of the sciences of
hydrostatics, hydrodynamics, of mathematical astronomy
and the optics of exact instruments of observation.

Ocean navigation depended on the determination of
longitude.   This cannot easily be done without accurate
clocks, so there was an intense search for an accurate form
of clock, and Huygens was inspired to invent the pendulum
clock.   He became interested in the theory of oscillations
and then proceeded to the invention of the wave-theory of
light.

The method of determining longtitude, before adequate
clocks had been evolved, was worked out by Amerigo
Vespucci, and depended on the observation of the anomalies
of the moon's motion.   The continents of America, and

everything that they imply, take their name from a distinguished scientist.

Hessen remarks that Stevin in 1590 constructed tables on the relation between the tides and the position of the moon, long before Newton published his general theory of tides.

The construction of canals and locks involved a knowledge of the pressure of liquids. In 1598 Stevin saw that water could exert a pressure on the bottom of a vessel greater than its weight. In 1642 Castelli published a treatise on the movement of water in canals of various cross-sections and in 1646 Torricelli was studying jets of liquids.

While the development of transport set one set of problems, that of mining and military science set another. The growth of trade stimulated the demand for metals, as a medium of exchange. The discovery of America was chiefly due to the hunger for gold for currency. The development of cannons increased the demand for iron and copper. The expansion of mining to satisfy the new demands for gold, silver, copper and iron involving the raising of ores from considerable depths, ventilation, water-pumping and metal-working machinery. The development of these technical processes depended on further knowledge of simple mechanical machines, the properties of gases, pumps and fluid pressures.

The invention of gunpowder and the cannon stimulated the study of the motions of projectiles. The theory of the parabolic path of a cannon-ball was first given by Galileo, who was also the first scientist with a thoroughly modern point of view.

With many more illustrations of this sort, Hessen has described the vast collection of data of physics that had been made by Newton's predecessors. He then explains why his most important work was named the *Principia*. Newton sought, and found, a synthetic theory of this accumulation of data. His achievement was immense, but his opportunity was also immense.

This account of Hessen's analysis of the origins of Newton's physics may help to show the brilliant possibilities of the Soviet school of historians of science. In the spirit of his essay, he is supervising a collected edition of Newton's works.

Professor Levin is supervising a similar collected edition of Darwin's works. It is noticeable that no critical editions of the collective works of Newton and Darwin have been prepared by British scholars.

The relations between a mathematician and his environment have been discussed in interesting essays by V. Kaverin. The inventor of non-Euclidean geometry was N. I. Lobachevsky. Through this achievement Lobachevsky freed humanity from the opinion, which during two thousand years had hardened into belief, that Euclid's geometry and logic were examples of absolute truth. His intellectual achievement was of the finest quality, and the greatest contribution yet made by a Russian to the progress of science. His contemporaries failed to recognize his genius. He had studied in the University of Kazan and presently became professor of mathematics, and afterwards was appointed principal of the University, and patron of the Kazan school district. During the whole of his life he left Kazan twice only, on short visits.

He was an admirable principal, and his memory received many compliments at his burial in 1856. He had been like a father to his students, he had been scrupulous with the funds of the University, had been an admirable patron to the schools of the province, and he had been a model husband. But no one referred to his great discovery. They did not know of its existence, or believed it to be nonsensical.

Lobachevsky had striven for thirty years to secure notice for his discovery. He published four accounts of it in Russian, two in German and one in French. He had gifted mathematical pupils, but even these failed to understand him. His non-Euclidean geometry, or Pan-geometry as he named it, was regarded as a product of harmless eccentricity, and the reviewers treated it with scepticism or ridicule.

At the time when Lobachevsky was engaged in the mathematical researches that were to make the University of Kazan famous for the remainder of human history, his colleague Professor Nikolsky used to prove theorems by saying: "With the help of God, these two triangles may be taken to be congruent."

Though Lobachevsky appears to have invented non-Euclidean geometry without the help of the Almighty, he built a church on the instructions of the University council. It is said that he was an atheist.

Kaverin inquires how it happened that this bold genius, who successfully questioned the finality of conceptions that had been accepted for two thousand years, should have arisen in the Kazan backwater. The Soviet school of historians of science are attacking problems of this sort. A particular interest of Lobachevsky's case is provided by the contrast of the success of his ordinary life with the difficulties of his intellectual life. There are at least two sorts of genius. One sort includes the lopsided, who have an abnormal amount of intellectual ability in one direction and an insufficient amount in others. This is the sort which shows symptoms of madness or idiocy. The other sort of genius is the super-man, the person who is rather abler than the ordinary man in every direction. Lobachevsky was of the second sort, which is frequently the happier, because it is able enough in general affairs to secure notice for its particular contributions. In spite of his success as a man of affairs, however, Lobachevsky was unable to use his position to enforce the acceptance of his discovery. Though belonging to the super-man type, he suffered the experience more common to genius of the lop-sided type. This is a measure of the intellectual darkness of the mathematical atmosphere of Kazan University, of the provincialism of Western European culture, and of the originality of his discovery.

Lobachevsky's life has features parallel with some of the life of Mendel, the discoverer of the laws of inheritance. Both made discoveries not recognized while they lived, and both were sufficient men of affairs to become the principals of their respective institutions.

Interesting historical studies are being made on the work of the Russian chemist Lomonossov, who foreshadowed Lavoisier and other famous chemists in the development of ideas, but whose researches remained unknown or unappreciated.

Professor Vassiliev has published an interesting study on the influence of the ideas of Descartes, and has pointed out that Faraday's notion of the continuous field of force, as opposed to the Newtonian idea of action at a distance, was derived from Euler, who in turn derived it from Descartes. Thus the idea of field physics, as established by Faraday and Clerk Maxwell, owes much to Descartes. Indeed, in Descartes' writings on mechanics, among many errors, propositions may be found which resemble some of those in the theory of relativity.

The Academy of Science's department for the history of science and technology, is organized in four sections, and has twenty-four research workers. The sections are for technology, physics and mathematics, agricultural science, and the history of the Academy itself. A fifth section for biology is to be added later. The secretary of the department, Professor Goukovsky, in his studies of the work of Leonardo da Vinci, has collected interesting material on the influence of the development of textile technology on Leonardo's development. It appears that some of Leonardo's earliest drawings consisted of designs for textile machinery. The wealth of Florence in her greatest period owed much to her textile manufactures. At the end of the fifteenth century she began to suffer from competition in textiles from England, Holland and Spain. She attempted to meet this competition by improving her machinery, and Leonardo's early sketches were of improvements in textile machines.

Leonardo was also engaged in building fortifications and cannon for the protection of Milan. In a letter he writes that architects can do little without the knowledge of science. Leonardo came to science through technology, whereas the Greeks came to technology through science. The Greek philosophers, who had the time and money of free men in a slave state, wanted to know how the world is built, rather than withstand industrial competition.

Professor Vassiliev is collecting material for a history of electricity, and he will lead the physics section of the history of science department. It is proposed that a history of atomism in science and sociology shall be prepared.

Professor Vassiliev is interested in the explanations of the origin of Greek science. He emphasizes the poverty of data for consideration, but suggests that the Greek secular tendency was an important influence. The Greeks had no priests of the Oriental type. They secularized Oriental science. It is possible that Thales liberated science from religion. Priests have less influence in island societies. The absence of deep religious feeling in the Greeks is illustrated by their erection of a temple to the Unknown Gods. A people with a robust belief in the effectiveness of the processes of revelation would not have acted with such nice definition.

As already mentioned, Vassiliev has commented on the debt of Faraday, through Euler, to Descartes. He considers that Descartes founded the modern ideas of cosmogony. The notions of Euler, Faraday, J. J. Thomson and Kelvin concerning the ether were derived from Descartes. Meyerson has commented on the modernity of many of Descartes' conceptions, and has pointed out that they were anachronisms in the seventeenth century. The cosmogonies of Leibnitz and of Kant owed much to Descartes. The Jesuits tried to reintroduce Aristotelian conceptions. As Cotes and Bentley adapted the conceptions of Newton to conventional British philosophy, the Jesuits tried to adapt the new cosmogonical conceptions of Descartes to the conventional ideas of the continental philosophers. The Jesuit Cabeo in his *Philosophia Magnetica* tried to adapt the ideas of Gilbert on magnetism to those of Aristotle.

The Jesuit Grimaldi discovered the phenomenon of the diffraction of light. Scheiner preceded Galileo in the discovery of the dark bands on the sun, but his Jesuit superiors would not permit the publication of his discovery.

The department has already published four volumes of papers on the history of science.

A. G. Grumm-Grzimailo has contributed an interesting paper on the history of the introduction of cotton-growing into China. He writes that the cotton grown in China is not of local origin. The first references to the cotton plant and cotton goods occur at a date several centuries before the beginning of our era, but cotton-growing by Chinese farmers was not common until the thirteenth and fourteenth centuries. The cotton plant was widely established in Eastern Turkestan in the fourth century, and it passed into West China from that region, besides from Indo-China, which is one of the principal centres of origin of Asiatic cottons. The cottons from the W st belonged to the African group, *Gossypium herbaceum* L., while those from Indo-China belonged to the *G. Nanking* Meyen.

These routes have been established by botanical and linguistic data. The north Chinese name for the cotton plant is of Turkish origin, while an old south Chinese name is of Malayan origin. The modern Chinese names for the cotton plant and lint cotton were introduced not earlier than the fourteenth century, during the Ming Dynasty. Before the cultivation of the cotton plant became established it had to withstand competition from the pre-established cultivation of silk and hemp.

The slow introduction of the cotton plant by the northern Chinese farmers into their rotation of crops was due to their belief that the plant, which was grown as a perennial in south China, could not flourish in the northern climate. The change from perennial to annual crop cultivation occupied centuries, and became successful only when the Chinese began to cultivate forms in which a considerable number of fruits ripen in the first year. The first cotton-growing regions were Yunnan, Kwangtung, Fukien, Shensi and Shansi. Kwangtung and Fukien received strong foreign influences after the second century A.D., and in the third century they contained many Arab settlements. Shensi and Shansi were colonized by the Mongols with Iranians, whose descendants were the modern Dungans.

These were the first to cultivate cotton in this country. The Chinese populace and governing classes of these regions long held the erroneous opinion that cotton could not flourish in their climate and soil, in spite of the advice of the Chinese scientists of the Sung and Yuan periods. The development of large-scale cotton cultivation occurred after 1368, and was due to the Ming dynasty. After that date cotton was forcibly introduced by Imperial edict into the rotation of crops. Its valuable qualities were explained in the edicts, and part of the poll-tax was required to be paid in cotton. Owing to the activities of the Ming Dynasty, China became one of the world's cotton-growing countries by the beginning of the fifteenth century.

D. O. Sviatsky has examined the references to the *Aurora borealis* in Russian literature and science between the tenth and the eighteenth century. In Russian folk-lore and early literature the *Aurora* were interpreted as celestial armies coming to the help of terrestrial combatants. This conception resembled those current in western Europe during the Middle Ages. After the fourteenth century the clergy began to interpret them as divine commands to build churches. The *Aurora* appeared in the northern sky, and at that time the attention of the Russian rulers was also directed to the North, in their colonizing activity. There was a connection between the change in the interpretation of the *Aurora* and the change of political interest towards northern colonization.

The chronicle of the city of Novgorod shows that a natural interpretation of the *Aurora* developed in the sixteenth century. In a sixteenth-century manuscript of the city of Pskov a Russian scientist gives an optical hypothesis of the *Aurora*. He attributed it to the reflection of the sun's light by the Arctic Ocean on to the sky, so that it appeared to observers as an image of the Arctic Ocean. This idea was expressed before Descartes had published his optical theory of the *Aurora*. After the foundation of the Academy of Sciences in St. Petersburg, the *Aurora* was observed systematically. The Russian scientific genius Lomonossov, who was a native of the northern Archangel district, observed the *Aurora* from St. Petersburg during the period 1743–63, and left copper engravings of various forms. He proposed an electrical theory of their nature. He suggested the cold and heavy air, descending from above, coming in contact with rising streams of warm air, produced electricity by friction, and the discharge of the accumulation of electricity produced the auroral light.

In the tradition of northern Russia the *Aurora* is not represented as miraculous, owing to the frequency of its appearances.

V. P. Taranovich has described the contents of hitherto unpublished papers of I. I. Lepekhin, who was commissioned by the Academy of Sciences to make voyages in various parts of Russia in 1768–72. He completed his journeys with visits to the White Sea and the Kanin Peninsula. The Academy published four volumes of Lepekhin's reports, but the explorer died before the reports of the latter part of his expeditions were ready for publication. The notes of his visit to the Kanin Peninsula, which describe the natural history, geography, economy, climate, sea-currents, and local trade in silver, mica, amber and pearls, is probably the first description of that region.

An interesting letter on Hints respecting Railways, written by William Vaughan to Admiral Chichagov and dated June 14th, 1804, has been published. It contains an admirable short account, with sketches, of the advantages and methods of construction of horse railways.

Nine interesting letters written by C. F. Gauss to the Academy have been published, with comments by Professor A. N. Krylov. These are dated between 1801 and 1807, when Gauss passed from his twenty-fourth to his thirtieth year. At the earlier date Gauss was living in Brunswick on about 24 marks a month. During the correspondence, mainly about astronomy, he received a handsome offer to become an active member of the Academy in St. Petersburg. He replied in an extremely servile style, and explained how, through loyalty to his fatherland and the reigning Duke of Brunswick he would be unable to accept the already large offer if it were not further increased. In the last letter he is explaining that circumstances have changed, owing to the Napoleonic Wars, and he will now be glad to accept their former offer, and he writes that he has recently sent several letters, to which he has received no reply. The correspondence is amusingly similar to analogous correspondence that has passed in recent years between the Soviet Government and some foreign scientists and technicians.

At the end of 1807 Gauss was appointed professor of astronomy and director of the observatory at Göttingen, and remained there until he died in 1855. The immense achievements of the Göttingen school of mathematics owes much to Gauss's inspiration, and the history of German mathematics might have been much less distinguished if he had followed the example of Euler, the great German-Swiss mathematician, and had accepted a Russian offer and remained in St. Petersburg from 1801 until the end of his life.

M. A. Shatelain has published a paper on the invention of the electric glow-lamp by A. N. Lodygin. He states he was the first to use carbon filament lamps for the illumination of streets and houses in St. Petersburg in 1876. The Academy of Sciences awarded him a prize, and a company was formed for the exploitation of the lamp. Lodygin also invented the use of tungsten and molybdenum as alternative to carbon for filaments. This has been forgotten, and his priority has been recalled only through patent disputes concerning the lamps of Edison and Swan. The history of the first inventor of the incandescent electric lamp has been rescued from oblivion through these disputes.

L. B. Modzalevsky has described the results of a preliminary examination of the collection of material left by the eminent German physicist M. H. Jakobi, who was born in Potsdam in 1801, and later became a member of the Academy of Sciences, and died in St. Petersburg in 1874. The collection contains documents concerning the invention and application of galvano-plastics, that is, the coating of metals by electricity, between 1838 and 1873. There is a correspondence with Faraday during 1839–40, and many

others.   There are accounts of his work on the application
of electricity to mines, and military purposes, and of the
introduction of electric lighting into Russia.   There are
papers on the standardization of weights, measures and
money.   The collection contains a considerable quantity
of material of value to the history of physics and technology.

INDEX

For Product Safety Concerns and Information please contact our EU
representative GPSR@taylorandfrancis.com
Taylor & Francis Verlag GmbH, Kaufingerstraße 24, 80331 München, Germany